W9-AFZ-052

Story Link®
Program

This book belongs to:

physical properties like hardness. X-ray diffraction not only showed the wave nature of X-rays, but also allowed investigation of the internal structure of crystals and of their constituent molecules or ions, in atomic detail. Therefore, for a protein crystallographer the beauty of protein crystals is not in their external faceted shape, but in the periodic arrangement of the molecules in the crystal. Without crystals there is no structure determination (at least not by X-ray crystallography), and the better the quality of the crystals, the more accurately the structure can be determined. Since crystals are the main tool for a crystallographer, familiarity with their properties, with lattice planes, symmetry, space groups and asymmetric units, is a requirement.

Chapter 4
The Theory of X-ray Diffraction by a Crystal

4.1. Introduction

The best way to learn protein X-ray diffraction is by practical work in the laboratory. However, it would be very unsatisfying to perform the experiments without understanding why they have to be done in such and such a way. Moreover, at several stages in the determination of protein structure it is necessary to decide what the next step should be. For instance, after growing suitable crystals and soaking these crystals in solutions of heavy atom reagents, applying the isomorphous replacement method, how do you obtain the positions of the heavy atoms in the unit cell and, if you do have them, how do you proceed? Questions such as these can be answered only if you have some knowledge of the theoretical background of protein X-ray crystallography. This is presented in this chapter. A slow path will be followed, and a student with a minimal background in mathematics, but the desire to understand protein X-ray crystallography should be able to work through the chapter. A working knowledge of differentiation and integration is required. If you further accept that an X-ray beam can be regarded as a wave that travels as a cosine function and if you know what a vector is, you have a good start. Derivations and explanations that are not absolutely necessary to follow the text are set off within rules; these can be skipped, if you want.

Chapter 1 introduced the diffraction of X-rays by a crystal. In analogy with the scattering of visible light by a two-dimensional grid, a crystal diffracts an X-ray beam in a great many directions. From the diffraction experiment with lysozyme it was concluded that diffraction by an X-ray beam can be understood as being derived from the intersection of an imaginary lattice, the reciprocal lattice, and a sphere, called the Ewald sphere. From the direction of the diffracted beams the dimensions of the unit cell can be derived. But we are, of course, more interested in the content of the unit cell, that is, in the structure of the protein molecules. The molecular structure and the arrangement of the molecules in the unit cell determine the intensities of the diffracted beams. Therefore, a relationship must be found between the intensities of the diffracted beams and the crystal structure. In fact, this relation is between the diffraction data and the electron density distribution in the crystal structure, because X-rays are scattered exclusively by the electrons in the atoms and not by the nuclei.

The scattering is an interaction between X-rays as electromagnetic waves and the electrons. If an electromagnetic wave is incident on a system of electrons, the electric and magnetic components of the wave exert a force on the electrons. This causes the electrons to oscillate with the same frequency as the incident wave. The oscillating electrons act as radiation scatterers and they emit radiation of the same frequency as the incident radiation. Energy from the incident wave is absorbed by the electrons and then emitted. Because of the attraction between the electrons and the atomic nucleus, an electrical restoring force exists for the electrons of an atom. However, in X-ray diffraction the electrons in an atom can be regarded, to a good approximation, as free electrons.

The wave scattered by the crystal may be described as a summation of the enormous number of waves, each scattered by one electron in the crystal. This may sound somewhat intimidating because a single unit cell in a protein crystal contains approximately 10,000 or more electrons, and there are a great many unit cells in a crystal. And all these waves must be added! It is clear that we need a convenient way to add waves. This method shall be presented first; familiarity with the technique will reveal how it simplifies the whole process. It is then fairly easy to derive an expression that relates each wave scattered by the crystal to the electron density distribution in the crystal and in its unit cells. The next step is to reverse this expression and derive the electron density distribution as a function of the scattering information.

4.2. Waves and Their Addition

An electromagnetic wave travels as a cosine function (Figure 4.1a). E is the electromagnetic field strength, λ is the wavelength of the radiation, and $v = c/\lambda$ is the frequency, with c the speed of light (and of any other electromagnetic radiation). A is the amplitude of the wave.

Let Figure 4.1a show the wave at time $t = 0$. The electric field strength at time $t = 0$ and position z is

$$E(t = 0; z) = A \cos 2\pi \frac{z}{\lambda}$$

During a time period t the wave travels over a distance $t \times c = t \times \lambda \times v$. Therefore, at time t the field strength at position z is equal to what it was at time $t = 0$ and position $z - t \times \lambda \times v$.

$$E(t; z) = A \cos 2\pi \frac{1}{\lambda}(z - t \times \lambda \times v)$$

$$= A \cos 2\pi \left(\frac{z}{\lambda} - vt\right) = A \cos 2\pi v\left(t - \frac{z}{c}\right)$$

At $z = 0$ the field strength is $E(t; z = 0) = A \cos 2\pi vt$, and substituting for convenience ω for $2\pi v$:

$$E(t; z = 0) = A \cos \omega t$$

Let us now consider a new wave with the same λ and the same amplitude A, but displaced over a distance Z with respect to the original wave (Figure 4.1b). Z corresponds with a phase shift $(Z/\lambda) \times 2\pi = \alpha$.

Original wave at $z = 0$ and time t: $E_{orig}(t; z = 0) = A \cos \omega t$

New wave at $z = 0$ and time t: $E_{new}(t; z = 0) = A \cos(\omega t + \alpha)$

Let us now consider only the new wave as representing any wave with a phase angle difference with respect to a reference wave:

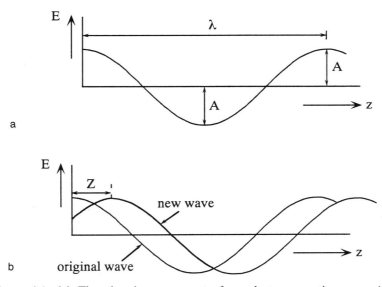

Figure 4.1. (a) The electric component of an electromagnetic wave. A is the amplitude and λ the wavelength. The accompanying magnetic component is perpendicular to the electric one, but we do not need to consider it here. (b) A new wave, displaced over a distance Z, is added.

Figure 4.2. The real component $A \cos \alpha$ and the imaginary component $A \sin \alpha$ of vector **A** in an Argand diagram.

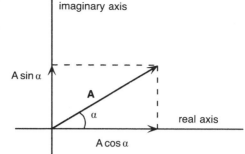

$$A \cos(\omega t + \alpha) = A \cos \alpha \cos \omega t - A \sin \alpha \sin \omega t$$
$$= A \cos \alpha \cos \omega t + A \sin \alpha \cos(\omega t + 90°)$$

Therefore, the wave $A \cos(\omega t + \alpha)$ can be regarded as being composed of two waves: wave 1 of amplitude $A \cos \alpha$ and phase angle 0° and wave 2 of amplitude $A \sin \alpha$ and phase angle 90°. Wave 1 is called the real part and wave 2 the imaginary part of the total wave. To add several waves with different phase angles, their real parts may be added together because they all have phase angle 0. Similarly, their imaginary parts, with phase angle 90°, may be added together. This can be represented conveniently in an axial system called an Argand diagram, in which the real axis is horizontal and the imaginary axis vertical (Figure 4.2). The wave itself is represented by vector **A**, with projections $A \cos \alpha$ on the real axis and $A \sin \alpha$ on the imaginary axis.[1] Addition of all the real parts and of all the imaginary parts of several waves is the same as adding the several wave vectors (like **A**) together.

Conclusion: We have simplified the problem of adding waves with the same frequency (or wavelength) by applying the following procedure:

- Represent each wave as a vector in a two-dimensional axial system. The length of each vector is equal to the amplitude of the wave. The vector makes an angle with the horizontal, or real axis equal to its phase with respect to a reference wave (angle α in Figure 4.2).
- The vector representing the total wave of a system is obtained by adding the vectors of the separate waves together.

Though the representation of waves as vectors in the Argand diagram is extremely convenient, it would still require an enormous amount of work to add thousands of these vectors together manually. This problem is solved by writing the vectors in mathematical form. Consider the wave of

---

[1] A vector will be indicated by boldface type (**A**). The length of this vector is given by $|A|$.

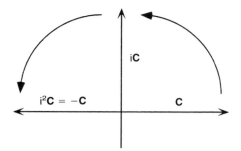

Figure 4.3. Multiplication of a vector **C** in the Argand diagram by i simply means rotating **C** 90° counterclockwise. Therefore, $i^2\mathbf{C} = -\mathbf{C}$.

Figure 4.2 with the two components, $A \cos \alpha$ (horizontal) and $A \sin \alpha$ (vertical). The entire wave is written in mathematical form as $A \cos \alpha + iA \sin \alpha$. i simply means that the $(A \sin \alpha)$ component points vertical, or i means that this component has been rotated 90° counterclockwise with respect to the positive direction of the horizontal axis. It is then clear that $i = \sqrt{-1}$ (Figure 4.3). A further simplification is to write $A \cos \alpha + iA \sin \alpha$ as $A \exp[i\alpha]$.

Properties of Exponential Terms

We shall not prove that $A \cos \alpha + iA \sin \alpha = A \exp[i\alpha]$. You must know, however, the properties of exponential terms:

$$\exp[a] \times \exp[b] = \exp[a + b] \quad ; \quad \frac{\exp[a]}{\exp[b]} = \exp[a - b]$$

$$\exp[k \cdot a] = \{\exp[a]\}^k \quad ; \quad \exp[0] = 1$$

$$\exp[a] \to +\infty \quad \text{for} \quad a \to +\infty$$

$$\exp[a] \to 0 \quad \text{for} \quad a \to -\infty$$

Now we are ready to work with waves and electrons. We shall start with a simple system of only two electrons.

4.3. A System of Two Electrons

The system in Figure 4.4 has only two electrons: e_1 and another electron e_2 at position **r** with respect to e_1. An X-ray beam, indicated by the wave vector $\mathbf{s}_0$ with length $1/\lambda$ hits the system and is diffracted in the direction of wave vector **s**, which also has a length of $1/\lambda$. The beam that passes along electron e_2 follows a longer path than the beam along electron e_1.

The path difference between the two beams $(p + q)$ depends on (1) the position of electron e_2 with respect to e_1 and (2) the direction of

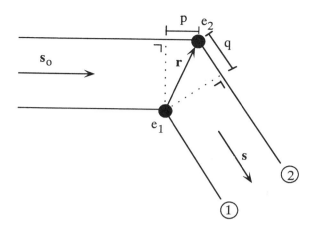

Figure 4.4. A system of two electrons: e_1 and e_2. The path difference between the scattered waves 1 and 2 is $p + q$.

diffraction. Since s_0 and s are wave vectors of magnitude $1/\lambda$ each, $p = \lambda \cdot \mathbf{r} \cdot s_0$ and $q = -\lambda \cdot \mathbf{r} \cdot s$ (the minus sign is due to the fact that the projection of $\mathbf{r}$ on s has a direction opposite to s).[2] The path difference is, therefore, $p + q = \lambda \cdot \mathbf{r} \cdot (s_0 - s)$.

The wave along electron e_2 is lagging behind in phase compared with the wave along e_1. With respect to wave 1, the phase of wave 2 is

$$-\frac{2\pi \mathbf{r} \cdot (s_0 - s) \cdot \lambda}{\lambda} = 2\pi \mathbf{r} \cdot \mathbf{S}$$

where

$$\mathbf{S} = \mathbf{s} - \mathbf{s}_0 \qquad\qquad (4.1)$$

It is interesting to note that the wave can be regarded as being reflected against a plane with θ as the reflecting angle and $|S| = 2 \sin \theta / \lambda$ (Figure

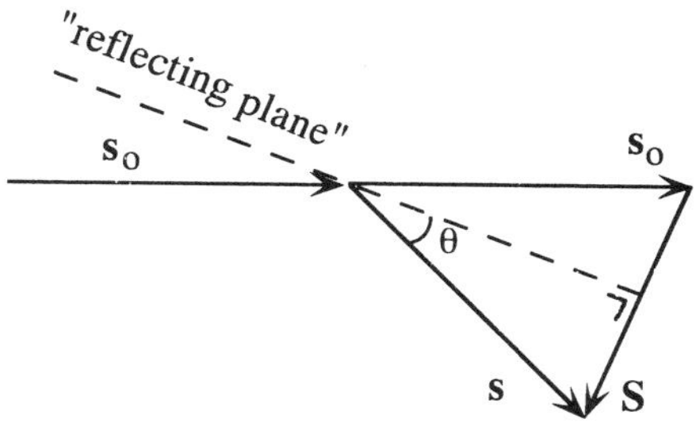

Figure 4.5. The primary wave, represented by s_0, can be regarded as being reflected against a plane. θ is the reflecting angle. Vector $\mathbf{S}$ is perpendicular to this plane.

---

[2] $\mathbf{r} \cdot \mathbf{S}$ is the scalar product of the vector $\mathbf{r}$ and s (see p. 80).

4.5). The physical meaning of vector $\mathbf{S}$ is the following: Since $\mathbf{S} = \mathbf{s} - \mathbf{s}_0$, with $|s| = |s_0| = 1/\lambda$, $\mathbf{S}$ is perpendicular to the imaginary "reflecting plane," which makes equal angles with the incident and reflected beam.

The Product of Two Vectors a and b

Let vectors $\mathbf{a}$ and $\mathbf{b}$, with lengths $|a|$ and $|b|$, be inclined at an angle θ.

Scalar product: Their scalar product is the number $\mathbf{a} \cdot \mathbf{b} = ab \cos \theta$ and $\mathbf{a} \cdot \mathbf{b} = \mathbf{b} \cdot \mathbf{a}$.

Vector product: Let $\mathbf{a}$ and $\mathbf{b}$ again be inclined at an angle θ with $0 \leqslant \theta \leqslant \pi$. Their vector product is a vector $\mathbf{c}$, which has a length $|c| = ab \sin \theta$ and points in a direction perpendicular to both $\mathbf{a}$ and $\mathbf{b}$, such that the vector system $\mathbf{a}$, $\mathbf{b}$, $\mathbf{c}$ is a right-handed triad; $\mathbf{c} = \mathbf{a} \times \mathbf{b} = -\mathbf{b} \times \mathbf{a}$.

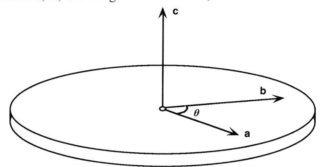

If we add the waves 1 and 2 in Figure 4.4, the Argand diagram shows two vectors $\mathbf{1}$ and $\mathbf{2}$ with equal length (amplitude) and a phase of $2\pi\mathbf{r} \cdot \mathbf{S}$ for wave $\mathbf{2}$ with respect to wave $\mathbf{1}$ (Figure 4.6). Vector $\mathbb{T}$ represents the sum of the two waves. In mathematical form: $\mathbb{T} = \mathbf{1} + \mathbf{2} = \quad 1 + 1$

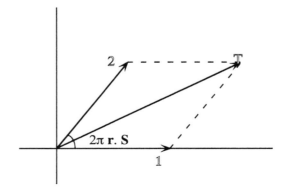

Figure 4.6. The summation of the two scattered waves in Figure 4.4 with the origin in electron e_1.

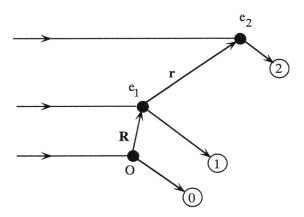

Figure 4.7. The origin, or reference point, for the scattered waves of the two-electron system is now located at O.

$\exp[2\pi i\mathbf{r} \cdot \mathbf{S}]$ if the length of the vectors equals 1. So far we had the origin of this two-electron system in e_1. Suppose we move the origin over $-\mathbf{R}$ from e_1 to point O (Figure 4.7). Then we obtain the following: With respect to a wave $\mathbf{0}$, wave $\mathbf{1}$ has a phase of $2\pi\mathbf{R} \cdot \mathbf{S}$, and wave $\mathbf{2}$ has a phase of $2\pi(\mathbf{r} + \mathbf{R}) \cdot \mathbf{S}$ (Figure 4.8).

$$\mathbb{T} = \mathbf{1} + \mathbf{2} = \exp[2\pi i\mathbf{R} \cdot \mathbf{S}] + \exp[2\pi i(\mathbf{r} + \mathbf{R}) \cdot \mathbf{S}]$$
$$= \exp[2\pi i\mathbf{R} \cdot \mathbf{S}]\{1 + \exp[2\pi i\mathbf{r} \cdot \mathbf{S}]\}$$

Conclusion: A shift of the origin by $-\mathbf{R}$ causes an increase of all phase angles by $2\pi\mathbf{R} \cdot \mathbf{S}$. The amplitude and intensity (which is proportional to the square of the amplitude) of wave $\mathbb{T}$ do not change.

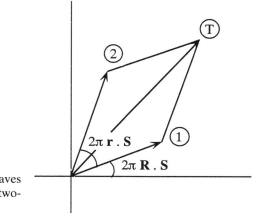

Figure 4.8. The summation of waves ① and ② with the origin of the two-electron system in position O.

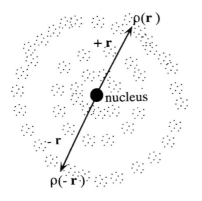

Figure 4.9. The electron cloud of an atom. $\rho(\mathbf{r})$ is the electron density. Because of the centrosymmetry $\rho(\mathbf{r}) = \rho(-\mathbf{r})$.

From the two-electron system we shall now move to more complicated systems: first an atom, then a combination of atoms in a unit cell, and finally a crystal.

4.4. Scattering by an Atom

The electron cloud of an atom scatters an X-ray beam: the scattering is dependent on the number of electrons and their positions in the cloud. We wish to understand the scattering of an atom with the origin of the system in the nucleus because the scattering by an atom located elsewhere will be the same, except for a phase shift, as was shown in the previous section (Figure 4.9). The electron density at position $\mathbf{r}$ is denoted by $\rho(\mathbf{r})$. The cloud is centrosymmetric around the origin, which means that $\rho(\mathbf{r}) = \rho(-\mathbf{r})$. From Figure 4.10 we can easily derive that the scattering by an

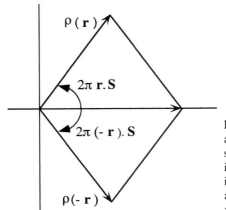

Figure 4.10. The scattering factor f of an atom is always real if we assume centro-symmetry of the electron cloud. The imaginary part of every scattering vector is compensated by the imaginary part of a vector with equal length but a phase angle of opposite sign.

atom is always real; the vector of the scattered wave is directed along the real axis in the Argand diagram.

The atomic scattering factor f is

$$f = \int_r \rho(\mathbf{r}) \exp[2\pi i \mathbf{r} \cdot \mathbf{S}] \, d\mathbf{r} \tag{4.2}$$

where the integration is over the entire space $\mathbf{r}$.

$$f = \int_r \rho(\mathbf{r})\{\exp[2\pi i \mathbf{r} \cdot \mathbf{S}] + \exp[-2\pi i \mathbf{r} \cdot \mathbf{S}]\} \, d\mathbf{r}$$
$$= 2\int_r \rho(\mathbf{r}) \cos[2\pi \mathbf{r} \cdot \mathbf{S}] \, d\mathbf{r}$$

Now the integration is over half of the entire space. Generally in X-ray crystallography it is assumed that the electron cloud of an atom is spherically symmetric. Therefore, it does not make any difference if the orientation of the atom changes with respect to the direction of $\mathbf{S}$. Furthermore, the atomic scattering factor is independent of the direction of $\mathbf{S}$, but does depend on the length of $\mathbf{S}$:

$$|\mathbf{S}| = \frac{2\sin\theta}{\lambda}$$

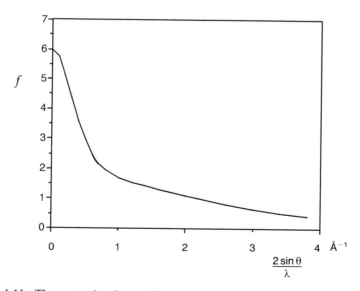

Figure 4.11. The scattering factor f for a carbon atom as a function of $2(\sin\theta/\lambda)$. f is expressed as electron number and for the beam with $\theta = 0$, $f = 6$.

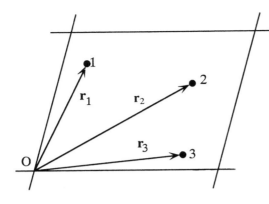

Figure 4.12. A unit cell with three atoms (1, 2, and 3) at positions $\mathbf{r}_1$, $\mathbf{r}_2$, and $\mathbf{r}_3$.

Values for the atomic scattering factor f can be looked up in tables, in which f is expressed as a function of $2\sin\theta/\lambda$ (see Figure 4.11).

4.5. Scattering by a Unit Cell

Suppose a unit cell has n atoms at positions $\mathbf{r}_j$ ($j = 1, 2, 3, \ldots, n$) with respect to the origin of the unit cell (Figure 4.12). With their own nuclei as origins, the atoms diffract according to their atomic scattering factor. If the origin is now transferred to the origin of the unit cell, the phase angles change by $2\pi\mathbf{r}_j \cdot \mathbf{S}$. With respect to the new origin the scattering is given by

$$\mathbf{f}_j = f_j \exp[2\pi i \mathbf{r}_j \cdot \mathbf{S}]$$

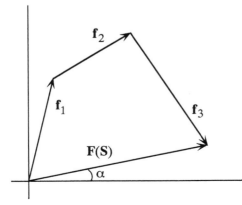

Figure 4.13. The structure factor $\mathbf{F(S)}$ is the sum of the scattering by the separate atoms in the unit cell.

where the $\mathbf{f}_j$s are the vectors in the Argand diagram. The total scattering from the unit cell is

$$\mathbf{F(S)} = \sum_{j=1}^{n} f_j \exp[2\pi i \mathbf{r}_j \cdot \mathbf{S}] \qquad (4.3)$$

$\mathbf{F(S)}$ is called the *structure factor* because it depends on the arrangement (structure) of the atoms in the unit cell (Figure 4.13).

4.6. Scattering by a Crystal

Suppose the crystal has translation vectors $\mathbf{a}$, $\mathbf{b}$, and $\mathbf{c}$ and contains a large number of unit cells: n_1 in the $\mathbf{a}$ direction, n_2 in the $\mathbf{b}$ direction, and n_3 in the $\mathbf{c}$ direction (Figure 4.14). To obtain the scattering by the crystal we must add the scattering by all unit cells with respect to a single origin. We choose the origin O in Figure 4.14. For a unit cell with its own origin at position $t \cdot \mathbf{a} + u \cdot \mathbf{b} + v \cdot \mathbf{c}$, in which t, u, and v are whole numbers, the scattering is

$$\mathbf{F(S)} \times \exp[2\pi i t \mathbf{a} \cdot \mathbf{S}] \times \exp[2\pi i u \mathbf{b} \cdot \mathbf{S}] \times \exp[2\pi i v \mathbf{c} \cdot \mathbf{S}]$$

The total wave $\mathbf{K(S)}$ scattered by the crystal is obtained by a summation over all unit cells:

$$\mathbf{K(S)} = \mathbf{F(S)} \times \sum_{t=0}^{n_1} \exp[2\pi i t \mathbf{a} \cdot \mathbf{S}] \times \sum_{u=0}^{n_2} \exp[2\pi i u \mathbf{b} \cdot \mathbf{S}]$$

$$\times \sum_{v=0}^{n_3} \exp[2\pi i v \mathbf{c} \cdot \mathbf{S}]$$

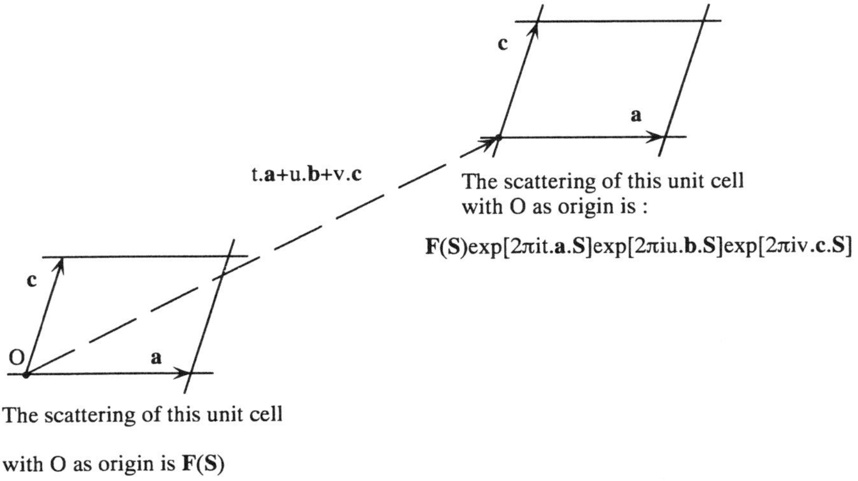

t.a+u.b+v.c

The scattering of this unit cell with O as origin is :

$\mathbf{F(S)}\exp[2\pi i t.\mathbf{a}.\mathbf{S}]\exp[2\pi i u.\mathbf{b}.\mathbf{S}]\exp[2\pi i v.\mathbf{c}.\mathbf{S}]$

The scattering of this unit cell

with O as origin is $\mathbf{F(S)}$

Figure 4.14. A crystal contains a large number of identical unit cells. Only two of them are drawn in this figure.

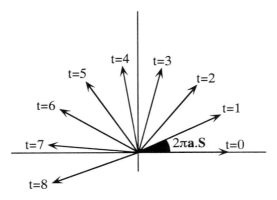

Figure 4.15. Each arrow represents the scattering by one unit cell in the crystal. Because of the huge number of unit cells and because their scattering vectors are pointing in different directions, the scattering by a crystal is in general zero. However in the special case that $\mathbf{a} \cdot \mathbf{S}$ is an integer h, all vectors point to the right and the scattering by the crystal can be of appreciable intensity.

Since n_1, n_2, and n_3 are very large, the summation $\sum_{t=0}^{n_1} \exp[2\pi i t \mathbf{a} \cdot \mathbf{S}]$ and the other two over u and v are almost always equal to zero unless $\mathbf{a} \cdot \mathbf{S}$ is an integer h, $\mathbf{b} \cdot \mathbf{S}$ is an integer k, and $\mathbf{c} \cdot \mathbf{S}$ is an integer l. This is easy to understand if we regard $\exp[2\pi i t \mathbf{a} \cdot \mathbf{S}]$ as a vector in the Argand diagram with a length of 1 and a phase angle $2\pi t \mathbf{a} \cdot \mathbf{S}$ (see Figure 4.15).

Conclusion: A crystal does not scatter X-rays, unless

$$\mathbf{a} \cdot \mathbf{S} = h$$
$$\mathbf{b} \cdot \mathbf{S} = k \qquad\qquad (4.4)$$
$$\mathbf{c} \cdot \mathbf{S} = l$$

These are known as the Laue conditions. h, k, and l are whole numbers, either positive, negative or zero. The amplitude of the total scattered wave is proportional to the structure factor $\mathbf{F}(\mathbf{S})$ and the number of unit cells in the crystal.

4.7. Diffraction Conditions

4.7.1. Laue Conditions

For the formulation of the diffraction conditions we consider an infinitely large crystal. As we have just seen, the scattered wave has zero amplitude $[\mathbf{K}(\mathbf{S}) = 0]$ unless the Laue conditions are fulfilled ($\mathbf{a} \cdot \mathbf{S} = h$, etc.), in which case all unit cells scatter in phase and $\mathbf{K}(\mathbf{S})$ is proportional to $\mathbf{F}(\mathbf{S})$.

4.7.2. Bragg's Law

The numbers h, k, and l in the Laue conditions are called the indices of the reflections from the crystal. Why are the scattered or diffracted beams called "reflections"? The answer is that they can be regarded as reflections against an imaginary series of planes in the crystal. This can be understood in the following way: Starting from the Laue conditions we write

$$\frac{\mathbf{a}}{h} \cdot \mathbf{S} = 1; \quad \frac{\mathbf{b}}{k} \cdot \mathbf{S} = 1; \quad \frac{\mathbf{c}}{l} \cdot \mathbf{S} = 1$$

The scalar product of the two vectors $\mathbf{a}/h$ and $\mathbf{S}$ is equal to 1. In other words, the vector $\mathbf{a}/h$ projected on the vector $\mathbf{S}$ and multiplied with $|S|$ gives unity. Since this is also true for $\mathbf{b}/k$ and $\mathbf{c}/l$, the endpoints of the vectors $\mathbf{a}/h$, $\mathbf{b}/k$, and $\mathbf{c}/l$ form a plane perpendicular to vector $\mathbf{S}$ (Figure 4.16).

In Section 4.3 we noted that $\mathbf{S}$ is perpendicular to a "reflecting" plane, and comparison with Figure 4.16 shows that the plane considered here is the lattice plane ($h\ k\ l$). According to Figure 4.17, both the incident and the reflected beam make an angle θ with this plane. The diffracted beam can thus be considered as being reflected by the plane ($h\ k\ l$). The phase difference $2d \sin\theta/\lambda$ between successive planes can now easily be calculated as follows: consider the projection of $\mathbf{a}/h$ on the diffraction vector $\mathbf{S}$. The projection has a length of $1/|S|$ (Laue condition) and is also equal to d (Figure 4.16). From $|S| = d^{-1}$ and $|S| = 2(\sin\theta)/\lambda$ (Section 4.3), the well-known Bragg law emerges:

$$\frac{2d \sin\theta}{\lambda} = 1 \tag{4.5}$$

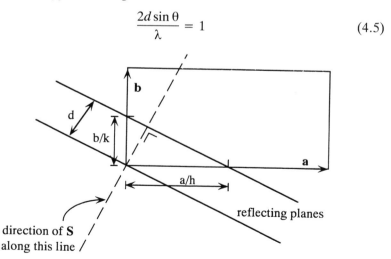

Figure 4.16. For simplicity a two-dimensional unit cell is drawn. The endpoints of the vectors $\mathbf{a}/h$, $\mathbf{b}/k$, and $\mathbf{c}/l$ form a lattice plane perpendicular to vector $\mathbf{S}$ (see the text). d is the distance between these lattice planes.

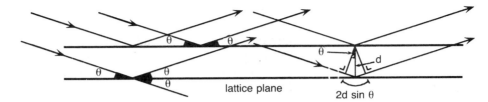

Figure 4.17. Two lattice planes are drawn separated by a distance d. The incident and the reflected beams make an angle θ with the lattice planes.

The path difference between beams from successive planes is $2d \sin \theta$. Therefore, the phase difference between beams scattered from successive planes is one full period (360°), implying that the points in successive planes scatter in phase.

4.8. Reciprocal Lattice and Ewald Construction

In Chapter 1 we noted the reciprocity between the crystal lattice and the diffraction pattern. The Ewald sphere was also introduced, as a convenient tool to construct the diffraction pattern. This will now be formulated in a more quantitative way. There is a crystal lattice and a reciprocal lattice. The crystal lattice is real, but the reciprocal lattice is an imaginary lattice.

Question: What is the advantage of the reciprocal lattice?
Answer: With the reciprocal lattice the directions of scattering can easily be constructed.

4.8.1. Construction of the Reciprocal Lattice

In Section 4.3 we noticed that vector $\mathbf{S}$ is related to the direction and angle of the reflected beam. Properties of $\mathbf{S}$:

$\mathbf{S} \perp$ reflecting plane

$$|S| = \frac{2 \sin \theta}{\lambda} \text{ because } \mathbf{S}' = \mathbf{s} - \mathbf{s_0} \text{ and } |s_0| = |s| = \frac{1}{\lambda}$$

We also noted (Section 4.7) that the reflecting planes are in fact the lattice planes and that these lattice planes divide the $\mathbf{a}$, $\mathbf{b}$, and $\mathbf{c}$ axes into an integral number (h, k, and l) of equal pieces. Moreover, we found that $|S| = 1/d$, where d is the distance between the lattice planes in one set of planes.

We now pay attention to the special planes (100), (010), and (001). For (100), the indices are $h = 1$, $k = 0$, and $l = 0$. If this plane is in reflection orientation, $S(100)$ is perpendicular to this plane and has a length of $1/d(100)$; we call this vector $\mathbf{a}^*$. In the same way $S(010) \perp$ plane (010) with length $1/d(010)$; we call this vector $\mathbf{b}^*$. And $S(001) \perp$ plane (001) with length $1/d(001)$; we call this vector $\mathbf{c}^*$. Because $\mathbf{a}^* \perp$ plane (100), it is perpendicular to the b- and the c-axis, and, therefore, $\mathbf{a}^* \cdot \mathbf{b} = \mathbf{a}^* \cdot \mathbf{c} = 0$, but $\mathbf{a} \cdot \mathbf{a}^* = \mathbf{a} \cdot S(100) = h = 1$. In the same way it can be shown that $\mathbf{b} \cdot \mathbf{b}^* = \mathbf{b} \cdot S(010) = k = 1$ and $\mathbf{c} \cdot \mathbf{c}^* = \mathbf{c} \cdot S(001) = l = 1$.

Why did we introduce the vectors $\mathbf{a}^*$, $\mathbf{b}^*$, and $\mathbf{c}^*$? The answer is that the endpoints of the vectors $S(h\,k\,l)$ are located in the lattice points of a lattice constructed with the unit vectors $\mathbf{a}^*$, $\mathbf{b}^*$, and $\mathbf{c}^*$.

Proof: S can always be written as $\mathbf{S} = X \cdot \mathbf{a}^* + Y \cdot \mathbf{b}^* + Z \cdot \mathbf{c}^*$. Multiply by $\mathbf{a}$:

$$\mathbf{a} \cdot \mathbf{S} = X \cdot \mathbf{a} \cdot \mathbf{a}^* + Y \cdot \mathbf{a} \cdot \mathbf{b}^* + Z \cdot \mathbf{a} \cdot \mathbf{c}^*$$

$$= h \quad\quad = X \cdot 1 \quad\quad = 0 \quad\quad = 0$$

It follows that $X = h$, and by the same token $Y = k$ and $Z = l$. Therefore, $\mathbf{S} = h \cdot \mathbf{a}^* + k \cdot \mathbf{b}^* + l \cdot \mathbf{c}^*$. The crystal lattice based on $\mathbf{a}$, $\mathbf{b}$, $\mathbf{c}$ is called the *direct* lattice and that based on $\mathbf{a}^*$, $\mathbf{b}^*$, $\mathbf{c}^*$ is called the *reciprocal* lattice. Each reflection $(h\,k\,l)$ is denoted by a point $(h\,k\,l)$ in the reciprocal lattice. The relation between direct and reciprocal unit cells is drawn schematically in Figure 4.18.

The relationship between the axes and the angles of the unit cell in both lattices is given in Table 4.1 for a triclinic lattice. Note that the

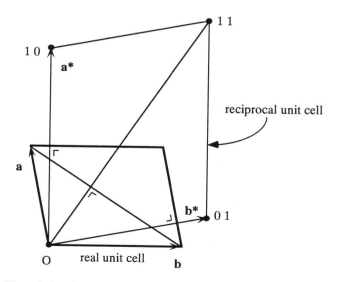

Figure 4.18. The relation between a real unit cell and the corresponding reciprocal unit cell. For simplicity a two-dimensional cell is chosen.

Table 4.1. The Relationship between the Axes and Angles in the Direct and the Reciprocal Lattice in a Triclinic Space Group

$$a^* = \frac{bc \sin \alpha}{V} \qquad\qquad\qquad\qquad a = \frac{b^*c^* \sin \alpha^*}{V^*}$$

$$b^* = \frac{ac \sin \beta}{V} \qquad\qquad\qquad\qquad b = \frac{a^*c^* \sin \beta^*}{V^*}$$

$$c^* = \frac{ab \sin \gamma}{V} \qquad\qquad\qquad\qquad c = \frac{a^*b^* \sin \gamma^*}{V^*}$$

$$V = \frac{1}{V^*} = abc\sqrt{1 - \cos^2\alpha - \cos^2\beta - \cos^2\gamma + 2 \cos\alpha \cos\beta \cos\gamma}$$

$$V^* = \frac{1}{V} = a^*b^*c^*\sqrt{1 - \cos^2\alpha^* - \cos^2\beta^* - \cos^2\gamma^* + 2 \cos\alpha^*\cos\beta^*\cos\gamma^*}$$

$$\cos\alpha^* = \frac{\cos\beta \cos\gamma - \cos\alpha}{\sin\beta \sin\gamma} \qquad\qquad \cos\alpha = \frac{\cos\beta^*\cos\gamma^* - \cos\alpha^*}{\sin\beta^* \sin\gamma^*}$$

$$\cos\beta^* = \frac{\cos\alpha \cos\gamma - \cos\beta}{\sin\alpha \sin\gamma} \qquad\qquad \cos\beta = \frac{\cos\alpha^*\cos\gamma^* - \cos\beta^*}{\sin\alpha^* \sin\gamma^*}$$

$$\cos\gamma^* = \frac{\cos\alpha \cos\beta - \cos\gamma}{\sin\alpha \sin\beta} \qquad\qquad \cos\gamma = \frac{\cos\alpha^*\cos\beta^* - \cos\gamma^*}{\sin\alpha^* \sin\beta^*}$$

volume V of the unit cell in the direct lattice is the reciprocal of the unit cell volume V^* in the reciprocal lattice: $V = 1/V^*$.

If the magnitude of scattering $\mathbf{G(S)}$, corresponding to each vector $\mathbf{S}$, is plotted at the tip of $\mathbf{S}$ in reciprocal space, a so-called *weighted reciprocal lattice* is obtained. For crystals, $\mathbf{G(S)}$ has nonzero values only at the lattice points and then $\mathbf{G(S)} = \mathbf{F(S)}$. However, for nonperiodic objects $\mathbf{G(S)}$ can have a nonzero value anywhere in reciprocal space.

With the reciprocal lattice the diffraction directions can easily be constructed. The following procedure is applied:

Step 1: Direct the incoming (primary) X-ray beam ($\mathbf{s_0}$) toward the origin O of reciprocal space. Take the length of $\mathbf{s_0}$ equal to $1/\lambda$ (Figure 4.19).

Step 2: Construct a sphere with the origin O of reciprocal space on its surface, with center M on the line $\mathbf{s_0}$, and radius $MO = 1/\lambda$. This sphere is called the Ewald sphere.

Step 3: If a wave vector S has its endpoint on the Ewald sphere, e.g., at point P, then MP is the scattered beam s. This is true because as shown in Figure 4.3, $s_0 + S = s$, or $S = s - s_0$.

4.8.2. Conclusions Concerning the Reciprocal Lattice

The reciprocal lattice is a convenient concept useful for constructing the directions of diffraction by a crystal. But remember that it exists only theoretically and not in reality.

Scattering occurs for all scattering vectors S having their endpoint P on the sphere and $G(S) \neq 0$. For crystals, $G(S) \neq 0$ implies that P must be a reciprocal lattice point. Crystal lattice planes for which the reciprocal lattice points $(h\ k\ l)$ do not lie on the sphere and thus are not in reflecting position can be brought to reflection by rotating the reciprocal lattice around O. From this construction with the imaginary reciprocal lattice we now return to the reality of the crystal lattice and note the following:

- The reciprocal lattice rotates exactly as the crystal does.
- The direction of the beam diffracted from the crystal is parallel to MP for the orientation of the crystal, which corresponds to the orientation of the reciprocal lattice.

From Figure 4.19 two properties of $S(h\ k\ l)$ can easily be derived:

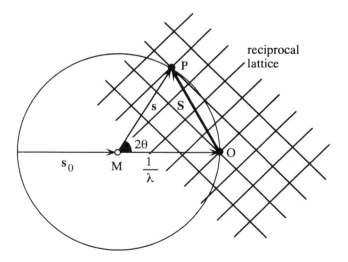

Figure 4.19. The Ewald sphere as a tool to construct the direction of the scattered beam. The sphere has radius $1/\lambda$. The center of the reciprocal lattice is at O. s_0 indicates the direction of the incident beam; s indicates the direction of the scattered beam.

1. $S(h\ k\ l)$ is perpendicular to the plane $(h\ k\ l)$ because the reciprocal space vector $S(h\ k\ l) = OP(h\ k\ l)$ is perpendicular to the reflecting plane $h\ k\ l$.
2. $|S(h\ k\ l)| = 2(\sin\theta)/\lambda = 1/d$ and Bragg's law is fulfilled.

One more comment on lattice planes: If the beam $h\ k\ l$ corresponds to reflection against one face (let us say the front) of a lattice plane, then

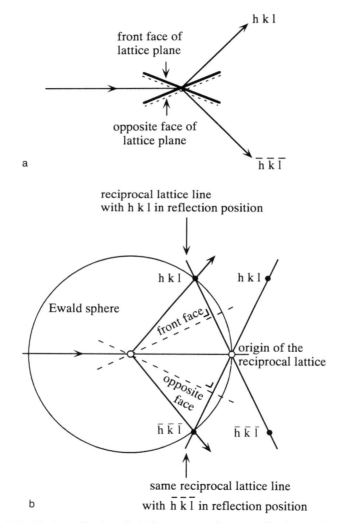

Figure 4.20. If the reflection $(h\ k\ l)$ corresponds to a reflection against the front face of a lattice plane, then $(\bar{h}\ \bar{k}\ \bar{l})$ corresponds to reflection against the opposite face of the plane. (a) Simple presentation of the reflections. (b) An explanation by means of the reciprocal lattice.

$(\bar{h}\ \bar{k}\ \bar{l})$ [or $(-h,\ -k,\ -l)$ corresponds to the reflection against the opposite face (the back) of the plane (Figure 4.20).

4.9. The Temperature Factor

The size of the electron density cloud around an atomic nucleus is independent of the temperature, at least under normal conditions. This would
suggest that X-ray scattering by a crystal would also be independent of
the temperature. However, this is not true because the atoms vibrate
around an equilibrium position. The X-rays do not meet identical atoms
on exactly the same position in successive unit cells. This is similar to an
X-ray beam meeting a smeared atom on a fixed position, the size of the
atom being larger if the thermal vibration is stronger. This diminishes
the scattered X-ray intensity, especially at high scattering angles. Therefore, the atomic scattering factor of the atoms must be multiplied by a
temperature-dependent factor (Figure 4.21).

The vibration of an atom in a reflecting plane $h\,k\,l$ has no effect on the
intensity of the reflection $(h\ k\ l)$. Atoms in a plane diffract in phase and
therefore a displacement in that plane has no effect on the scattered
intensity. The component of the vibration perpendicular to the reflecting
plane does have an effect. In the simple case in which the components of
vibration are the same in all directions, the vibration is called *isotropic*.

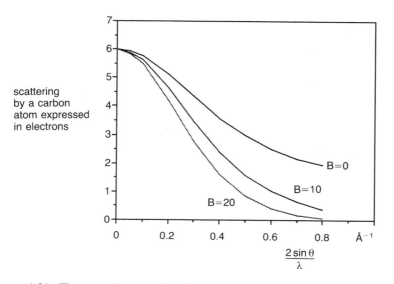

Figure 4.21. The atomic scattering factor of a carbon atom multiplied by the
appropriate temperature factor.

Then the component perpendicular to the reflecting plane and thus along **S** is equal for each $(h\,k\,l)$ and the correction factor for the atomic scattering factor is

$$T(\text{iso}) = \exp\left[-B\frac{\sin^2\theta}{\lambda^2}\right] = \exp\left[-\frac{B}{4}\left(\frac{2\sin\theta}{\lambda}\right)^2\right]$$

$$= \exp\left[-\frac{B}{4}\left(\frac{1}{d}\right)^2\right] \qquad (4.6)$$

It can be shown that the thermal parameter B is related to the mean square displacement $\overline{u^2}$ of the atomic vibration:

$$B = 8\pi^2 \times \overline{u^2} \qquad (4.7)$$

For anisotropic vibration the temperature factor is much more complicated. In this case $\overline{u^2}$ depends on the direction of **S**. It can be shown that the temperature factor is given by

$$T(\text{aniso}; h\,k\,l) = \exp\left[-2\pi^2\left(\begin{array}{l}U_{11}h^2a^{*2} + U_{22}k^2b^{*2} + U_{33}l^2c^{*2} +\\ 2U_{12}hka^*b^* + 2U_{13}hla^*c^* + 2U_{23}klb^*c^*\end{array}\right)\right]$$

with U_{11} the $\overline{u^2}$ value along $\mathbf{a}^*$, U_{22} along $\mathbf{b}^*$, and U_{33} along $\mathbf{c}^*$. In general $\overline{u^2}(\mathbf{e})$ along a unit vector **e** is given by

$$\overline{u^2}(\mathbf{e}) = U_{11} \cdot e_1^2 + U_{22} \cdot e_2^2 + U_{33} \cdot e_3^2 + 2U_{12} \cdot e_1 e_2$$
$$+ 2U_{13} \cdot e_1 e_3 + 2U_{23} \cdot e_2 e_3$$

with e_1, e_2, and e_3 the components of **e** along unit axes $\mathbf{a}^*$, $\mathbf{b}^*$, and $\mathbf{c}^*$. The points for which $\overline{u^2}(\mathbf{e})$ is constant form an ellipsoid: *the ellipsoid of vibration*. For display purposes the constant can be chosen such that the vibrating atom has a chance of, e.g., 50% of being within the ellipsoid (Figure 4.22).

In protein structure determinations it is common to work with isotropic temperature factors for the individual atoms. Then there are four unknown parameters per atom: x, y, z, and B. For a protein with 2000 atoms in the asymmetric unit, 8000 unknown parameters must be determined. To obtain a reliable structure the number of measured data (= reflection intensities) should well exceed the number of parameters. In general, because of the restricted number of data, this condition is fulfilled for the determination of isotropic, but not anisotropic, temperature factors. Average values for B in protein structures range from as low as a few Å^2 to $30\,\text{Å}^2$ in well-ordered structures. The highest values are found in more or less flexible surface loops.

The temperature factor is a consequence of the dynamic disorder in the crystal caused by the temperature-dependent vibration of the atoms in

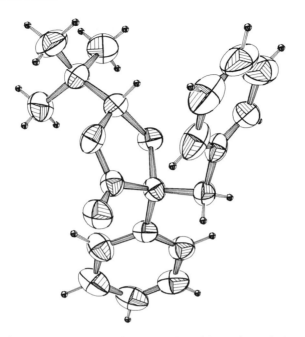

Figure 4.22. The plot of an organic molecule with 50% probability thermal ellipsoids. (Reproduced with permission from Strijtveen and Kellogg of Pergamon Press 1987.)

the structure. In addition to this *dynamic disorder*, protein crystals have *static disorder*: molecules, or parts of molecules, in different unit cells do not occupy exactly the same position or have exactly the same orientation. The effect of this static disorder on the X-ray diffraction pattern is the same as for the dynamic disorder and they cannot be distinguished, unless intensity data at different temperatures are collected. For $B = 30 \,\text{Å}^2$ the root mean square displacement $\sqrt{\overline{u^2}}$ of the atoms from their equilibrium position is $\sqrt{30/8\pi^2} = 0.62 \,\text{Å}$. This gives an impression of the flexibility or disorder in protein structures, which are by no means completely rigid. Because of the disorder in the crystal the diffraction pattern fades away at some diffraction angle θ_{max}. The corresponding lattice distance d_{min} is determined by Bragg's law:

$$d_{min} = \frac{\lambda}{2 \sin \theta_{max}}$$

d_{min} is taken as the resolution of the diffraction pattern and it is said that a structure has been determined to a resolution of, for instance, $2 \,\text{Å}$. It is clear that the accuracy with which a structure can be determined depends strongly on the resolution of the diffraction pattern.

4.10. Calculation of the Electron Density ρ (x y z)

The intensity of the diffracted beam $(h \; k \; l)$ is proportional to the square of the amplitude of the structure factor $F(h \; k \; l)$. The structure factor is a function of the electron density distribution in the unit cell:

$$F(\mathbf{S}) = \sum_j f_j \exp[2\pi i \mathbf{r}_j \cdot \mathbf{S}] \tag{4.3}$$

The summation is over all atoms j in the unit cell. Instead of summing over all separate atoms we can integrate over all electrons in the unit cell:

$$F(\mathbf{S}) = \int_{\text{cell}} \rho(\mathbf{r}) \exp[2\pi i \mathbf{r} \cdot \mathbf{S}] \, dv \tag{4.8}$$

where $\rho(\mathbf{r})$ is the electron density at position $\mathbf{r}$ in the unit cell. If x, y, and z are fractional coordinates in the unit cell ($0 \leqslant x < 1$; the same for y and z) and V is the volume of the unit cell, we have

$$dv = V \cdot dx \, dy \, dz$$

and

$$\mathbf{r} \cdot \mathbf{S} = (\mathbf{a} \cdot x + \mathbf{b} \cdot y + \mathbf{c} \cdot z) \cdot \mathbf{S} = \mathbf{a} \cdot \mathbf{S} \cdot x + \mathbf{b} \cdot \mathbf{S} \cdot y + \mathbf{c} \cdot \mathbf{S} \cdot z$$
$$= hx + ky + lz$$

Therefore, $F(\mathbf{S})$ can also be written as $F(h \; k \; l)$.

$$F(h \; k \; l) = V \int_{x=0}^{1} \int_{y=0}^{1} \int_{z=0}^{1} \rho(x \; y \; z) \quad \exp[2\pi i(hx + ky + lz)] \, dx \, dy \, dz \tag{4.9}$$

However, the goal of protein X-ray crystallography is not to calculate the diffraction pattern but to calculate the electron density ρ at every position x, y, z in the unit cell. How can this be done? The answer is by Fourier transformation (see p. 97).

$F(h \; k \; l)$ is the Fourier transform of $\rho(x \; y \; z)$ but the reverse is also true: $\rho(x \; y \; z)$ is the Fourier transform of $F(h \; k \; l)$ and therefore, $\rho(x \; y \; z)$ can be written as a function of all $F(h \; k \; l)$:

$$\rho(x \; y \; z) = \frac{1}{V}\sum_h \sum_k \sum_l F(h \; k \; l) \exp[-2\pi i(hx + ky + lz)] \tag{4.10}$$

The Laue conditions tell us that diffraction occurs only in discrete directions and therefore, in Eq. (4.10) the integration has been replaced by a summation. Because $\mathbf{F} = |F| \exp[i\alpha]$ we can also write

$$\rho(x \; y \; z) = \frac{1}{V}\sum_h \sum_k \sum_l |F(h \; k \; l)|\exp[-2\pi i(hx + ky + lz) + i\alpha(h \; k \; l)] \tag{4.11}$$

It now seems easy to calculate the electron density $\rho(x\ y\ z)$ at every position $(x\ y\ z)$ in the unit cell. However, there is a problem. Although the $|F(h\ k\ l)|$s can be derived from the intensities $I(h\ k\ l)$, the phase angles $\alpha(h\ k\ l)$ cannot be obtained directly from the diffraction pattern. Fortunately, indirect ways have been developed and will be discussed later.

Fourier Transforms and the Delta Function

We want to know why Eq. (4.10) is true, or why $\rho(x\ y\ z)$ is the Fourier transform of $F(h\ k\ l)$. Take $F(h\ k\ l)$ in the form of Eq. (4.8):

$$\mathbf{F(S)} = \int_{\substack{\mathbf{r}\ \text{over}\\ \text{the cell}}} \rho(\mathbf{r}) \exp[2\pi i \mathbf{r'} \cdot \mathbf{S}]\, dv_r$$

Multiply by $\exp[-2\pi i \mathbf{r'} \cdot \mathbf{S}]$ and integrate over $\mathbf{S}$. dv_r is a small volume in real space ($\mathbf{r}$ space) and dv_S in reciprocal space ($\mathbf{S}$ space).

$$\int_{\mathbf{S}=-\infty}^{+\infty} \mathbf{F(S)} \exp[-2\pi i \mathbf{r'} \cdot \mathbf{S}]\, dv_S$$

$$= \int_{\mathbf{S}=-\infty}^{+\infty} dv_s \int_{\mathbf{r}} \rho(\mathbf{r}) \exp[2\pi i (\mathbf{r} - \mathbf{r'}) \cdot \mathbf{S}]\, dv_r \qquad (4.12)$$

Because $\rho(\mathbf{r})$ is independent of $\mathbf{S}$, Eq. (4.12) is equal to

$$\int_{\mathbf{r}} dv_r \rho(\mathbf{r}) \int_{\mathbf{S}=-\infty}^{+\infty} \exp[2\pi i (\mathbf{r} - \mathbf{r'}) \cdot \mathbf{S}]\, dv_S \qquad (4.13)$$

The integral $\int_{\mathbf{S}=-\infty}^{+\infty} \exp[2\pi i(\mathbf{r} - \mathbf{r'}) \cdot \mathbf{S}]\, dv_S$ can be regarded as a summation of vectors in the Argand diagram. These vectors have a length equal to 1 but point in many different directions, because $\mathbf{S}$ has an infinite number of values in reciprocal space and hence the result of the integration is, in general, zero, except if $\mathbf{r} - \mathbf{r'} = 0$ or $\mathbf{r} = \mathbf{r'}$. In that case all vectors in the Argand diagram point to the right along the horizontal axis. Therefore, $\int_{\mathbf{S}=-\infty}^{+\infty} \exp[2\pi i(\mathbf{r} - \mathbf{r'}) \cdot \mathbf{S}]\, dv_S$ is a strange function: it is zero for $\mathbf{r} \neq \mathbf{r'}$ and infinite for $\mathbf{r} = \mathbf{r'}$. Such a function is called a delta function; here we have a three-dimensional delta function:

$$\int_{\mathbf{S}=-\infty}^{+\infty} \exp[2\pi i(\mathbf{r} - \mathbf{r'}) \cdot \mathbf{S}]\, dv_S = \delta(\mathbf{r} - r')$$

A (one-dimensional) delta function has the property

$$\int_{x=-\infty}^{+\infty} f(x)\delta(x - a)\, dx = f(a) \qquad (4.14)$$

and in our three-dimensional case (4.13) becomes

$$\int_{\mathbf{r}} \rho(\mathbf{r}) \cdot \delta(\mathbf{r} - \mathbf{r}') \, dv_r = \rho(\mathbf{r}')$$

This property will be proven further on. Equation (4.12) can now be written as

$$\rho(\mathbf{r}') = \int_{S=-\infty}^{+\infty} F(S) \exp[-2\pi i \mathbf{r}' \cdot S] \, dv_S$$

or with $\mathbf{r}'$ replaced by $\mathbf{r}$:

$$\rho(\mathbf{r}) = \int_{S=-\infty}^{+\infty} F(S) \exp[-2\pi i \mathbf{r} \cdot S] \, dv_S \qquad (4.15)$$

This proves the Fourier transformation.

Because of the Laue conditions the integration in Eq. (4.15) can be replaced by summations over h, k, and l, giving a weight V^* to each term. V^* is the volume of the unit cell in reciprocal space and is equal to $1/V$, where V is the volume of the crystallographic unit cell (Section 4.8). With $\mathbf{r} \cdot S = hx + ky + lz$, Eq. (4.15) is transformed into Eq. (4.10).

The One-Dimensional Delta Function
Consider the function $\delta_a(x)$, which has a constant value $1/2a$ between $-a$ and $+a$, and is zero outside this region.

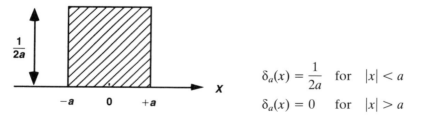

$$\delta_a(x) = \frac{1}{2a} \quad \text{for} \quad |x| < a$$

$$\delta_a(x) = 0 \quad \text{for} \quad |x| > a$$

The surface of the hatched area is $\int_{x=-\infty}^{+\infty} \delta_a(x) \, dx = 1$ and is independent of a.

Now let a tend to zero. Then $\lim_{a \to 0} \delta_a(x)$ is defined as $\delta(x)$. $\delta(x) = 0$ for $x \neq 0$ and $\delta(x) = \infty$ for $x = 0$, but $\int_{x=-\infty}^{+\infty} \delta(x) \, dx = 1$. Although at $x = 0$ the function $\delta(x)$ is ∞, it is also infinitely thin and the surface area under the function is independent of a and remains 1. Of special importance for us is the following property of a delta function:

$$\int_{x=-\infty}^{+\infty} f(x)\delta(x) \, dx = f(0) \qquad (4.16)$$

where $f(x)$ is any normal function. This property can be proven by starting with $\delta_a(x)$:

$$\int_{x=-\infty}^{+\infty} f(x)\delta_a(x)\, dx = \frac{1}{2a} \int_{-a}^{+a} f(x)\, dx \qquad (4.17)$$

If a tends to zero the left part of Eq. (4.17) becomes $\int_{x=-\infty}^{+\infty} f(x)\delta(x)\, dx$, and the right part:

$$\lim_{a \to 0} \frac{1}{2a} \int_{-a}^{+a} f(x)\, dx = f(0) \qquad (4.18)$$

That Eq. (4.18) is true can be understood in the following way: In a very narrow region around $x = 0$, we can assume for $f(x)$ the constant value $f(0)$. The surface area under the function between $-a$ and $+a$ $[\int_{-a}^{+a} f(x)\, dx]$ is then $f(0) \times 2a$ and, therefore, Eq. (4.18) is true. With a change of variables Eq. (4.16) can be written as

$$\int_{x=-\infty}^{+\infty} f(x)\delta(x - a)\, dx = f(a)$$

This proves Eq. (4.14).

We have already met the delta function in deriving the scattering by a crystal (Section 4.6) without mentioning it explicitly. There we had $\Sigma_{t=0}^{n_1} \exp[2\pi it a \cdot \mathbf{S}]$ and two similar functions. In fact the presence of diffraction spots on an otherwise blank X-ray film or fluorescent plate can be regarded as the physical appearance of delta functions.

A special term in the Fourier summation of Eq. (4.11) is $F(000) \exp[0]$ $= F(000)$; the phase angle $\alpha(000)$ is zero because there is no phase difference in the scattering by the electrons. The "reflection" (000) is not observable because it is in the line of the direct beam. Nevertheless $F(000)$ adds a constant term to the Fourier summation, which is equal to the total number of electrons in the cell. This requires that $F(000)$ and all other Fs are expressed in electrons. They are then on an *absolute scale*. Very often an arbitrary scale for the Fs is used (see Section 5.2).

All terms other than $F(000)$ have an average value of zero over one full cycle. Therefore the average electron density in the unit cell is zero if $F(000)$ is not incorporated in the Fourier summation. But a constant term can be added to remove negative electron density and the absence of $F(000)$ does not inhibit the interpretation of an electron density map. The limited resolution of a protein X-ray diffraction pattern prevents the calculation of the electron density map at atomic resolution: although amino acid residues can be distinguished, atoms are not separated (Figure

4.23), except in the electron density map of some small proteins at extremely high resolution. Therefore, it seems surprising that the error in the atomic positions is not more than approximately 0.2 Å for a structure derived from a high resolution electron density map. The reason is that the structure of the building blocks—amino acids and small peptides—is known with high accuracy and one can safely assume that the atomic distances and bond angles are the same in the proteins as they are in the small compounds.

4.11. Comparison of $\mathbf{F}(h\ k\ l)$ and $\mathbf{F}(\bar{h}\ \bar{k}\ \bar{l})$

$$\mathbf{F}(h\ k\ l) = V \int_{\text{cell}} \rho(x\ y\ z)\ \exp[2\pi i(hx + ky + lz)]\,dx\,dy\,dz$$

[see Eq. (4.9)]. In the same way we can write for the reflection $(\bar{h}\ \bar{k}\ \bar{l})$:

$$\mathbf{F}(\bar{h}\ \bar{k}\ \bar{l}) = V \int_{\text{cell}} \rho(x\ y\ z)\ \exp[2\pi i(-hx - ky - lz)]\,dx\,dy\,dz \quad (4.19)$$

$\mathbf{F}(h\ k\ l)$ is obtained as the result of a vector summation in which the amplitudes of the constituent vectors are $\rho(x\ y\ z)\,dx\,dy\,dz$ and the phase angles $2\pi(hx + ky + lz)$. For $\mathbf{F}(\bar{h}\ \bar{k}\ \bar{l})$ the amplitudes are the same but the phase angles have just the opposite value: $-2\pi(hx + ky + lz)$. The

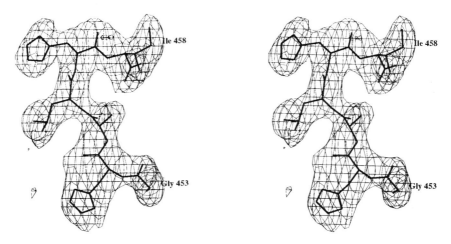

Figure 4.23. Stereo picture for the C-terminal residues 453–458 of the enzyme lipoamide dehydrogenase of *Pseudomonas putida* at 2.45 Å resolution. (Reproduced with permission from the thesis by Andrea Mattevi, University of Groningen, 1992.)

Figure 4.24. Argand diagram for the structure factors of the reflections $F(h\ k\ l)$ and $F(\bar{h}\ \bar{k}\ \bar{l})$.

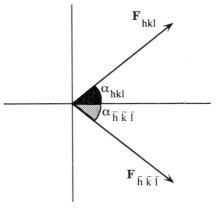

resulting vectors $F(h\ k\ l)$ and $F(\bar{h}\ \bar{k}\ \bar{l})$ also have, therefore, the same length, but opposite phase angles: α and $-\alpha$ in Figure 4.24. The consequence is that Eq. (4.11) reduces to

$$\rho(x\ y\ z) = \frac{1}{V} \sum_{hkl=-\infty}^{+\infty} |F(h\ k\ l)| \cos[2\pi(hx + ky + lz) - \alpha(h\ k\ l)]$$

$$= \frac{2}{V} \sum_{hkl=0}^{+\infty} |F(h\ k\ l)| \cos[2\pi(hx + ky + lz) - \alpha(h\ k\ l)]$$

This expression does not contain an imaginary term but is real, as expected for the electron density as a physical quantity.

Because the intensity of a diffracted beam is proportional to the square of its amplitude [$I(h\ k\ l)$ proportional to $|F(h\ k\ l)|^2$], the intensities $I(h\ k\ l)$ and $I(\bar{h}\ \bar{k}\ \bar{l})$ are also equal. The reflections $(h\ k\ l)$ and $(\bar{h}\ \bar{k}\ \bar{l})$ are called *Friedel* or *Bijvoet*[3] *pairs*. Their equal intensities give rise to a center of symmetry in the diffraction pattern, even if such a center is not present in the crystal structure. The $I(h\ k\ l) = I(\bar{h}\ \bar{k}\ \bar{l})$ equality is usually assumed to be true in crystal structure determinations. It depends, however, on the condition that anomalous scattering is absent (Section 7.8).

4.12. Symmetry in the Diffraction Pattern

In the previous section we noticed that the diffraction pattern from a crystal has a center of symmetry. In addition, more symmetry in the pattern can be present, depending on the symmetry elements in the

---

[3] J.M. Bijvoet, 1892–1980, the famous Dutch crystallographer, was the first to determine the absolute configuration of an organic compound.

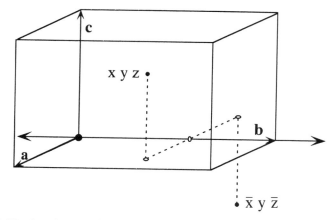

Figure 4.25. A unit cell with a 2-fold axis through the origin and along y. The electron density is equal at positions $x\,y\,z$ and $\bar{x}\,y\,\bar{z}$.

crystal. After the application of a symmetry operation, the crystal structure looks exactly as before. For this reason, and because the diffraction pattern rotates with the crystal, the symmetry of the diffraction pattern must be at least the same as for the crystal. Reflections in the diffraction pattern related by symmetry will have the same intensity and only a portion of all data is unique in terms of intensity.

As we saw in Section 3.3, the only symmetry elements allowed in protein crystals are symmetry axes. In the next section we shall show what the effect on the diffraction pattern is of a 2-fold axis along the y-axis and a 2-fold screw axis along the y-axis.

4.12.1. A 2-Fold Axis Along y

If a 2-fold axis through the origin and along y is present, then the electron density $\rho(x\,y\,z) = \rho(\bar{x}\,y\,\bar{z})$ (Figure 4.25). Therefore

$$\mathbf{F}(h\,k\,l) = V \int_{\substack{\text{asymm} \\ \text{unit}}} \rho(x\,y\,z)\{\exp[2\pi i(hx + ky + lz)]$$

$$+ \exp[2\pi i(-hx + ky - lz)]\}\,dx\,dy\,dz \qquad (4.20)$$

The integration in Eq. (4.20) is over one asymmetric unit (half of the cell), because the presence of the second term under the integral takes care of the other half of the cell.

$$\mathbf{F}(\bar{h}\,k\,\bar{l}) = V \int_{\substack{\text{asymm} \\ \text{unit}}} \rho(x\,y\,z)\{\exp[2\pi i(-hx + ky - lz)]$$

$$+ \exp[2\pi i(hx + ky + lz)]\}\,dx\,dy\,dz \qquad (4.21)$$

It follows that $\mathbf{F}(h\ k\ l) = \mathbf{F}(\bar{h}\ k\ \bar{l})$ and also $I(h\ k\ l) = I(\bar{h}\ k\ \bar{l})$, because the intensities I are proportional to $|F|^2$. Therefore, the diffraction pattern has the same 2-fold axis as the crystal.

4.12.2. A 2-Fold Screw Axis Along y

For a 2-fold screw axis along y (Figure 4.26):

$$\rho(x\ y\ z) = \rho\{\bar{x}(y + 1/2)\bar{z}\}$$

$$\text{term I} \downarrow$$

$$\mathbf{F}(h\ k\ l) = V \int_{\substack{\text{asymm} \\ \text{unit}}} \rho(x\ y\ z)\{\exp[2\pi i(hx + ky + lz)]$$

$$+ \exp[2\pi i(-hx + k(y + 1/2) - lz)]\}\,dx\,dy\,dz \quad (4.22)$$

$$\text{term II} \uparrow$$

$$\text{term III} \downarrow$$

$$\mathbf{F}(\bar{h}\ k\ \bar{l}) = V \int_{\substack{\text{asymm} \\ \text{unit}}} \rho(x\ y\ z)\{\exp[2\pi i(-hx + ky - lz)]$$

$$+ \exp[2\pi i(hx + k(y + 1/2) + lz)]\}\,dx\,dy\,dz \quad (4.23)$$

$$\text{term IV} \uparrow$$

In Eq. (4.22) term II is

$$\exp\{2\pi i[-hx + k(y + 1/2) - lz]\} = \exp[2\pi i(-hx + ky - lz + 1/2k)]$$

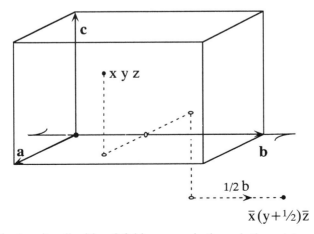

Figure 4.26. A unit cell with a 2-fold screw axis through the origin and along y. The electron density is equal at positions $x\,y\,z$ and $\bar{x}(y + 1/2)\bar{z}$.

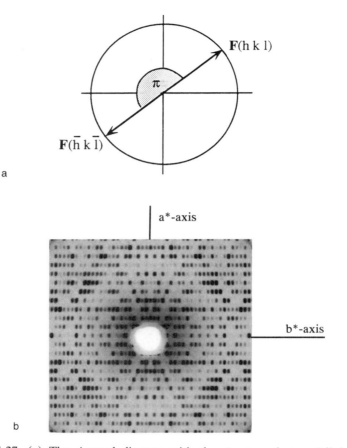

Figure 4.27. (a) The Argand diagram with the structure factors $\mathbf{F}(h\ k\ l)$ and $\mathbf{F}(\bar{h}\ k\ \bar{l})$ for a structure with a 2-fold screw axis along y with k odd. (b) A precession picture of a crystal of the enzyme papain. The crystal belongs to space group $P2_12_12_1$. Note the absence of reflections $(h00)$ for h odd and of reflections $(0k0)$ for k odd.

For k is even this is equal to term III in Eq. (4.23). The same is true for term IV in Eq. (4.23) and term I in Eq. (4.22). Therefore, when k is even: $\mathbf{F}(h\ k\ l) = \mathbf{F}(\bar{h}\ k\ \bar{l})$ and also $I(h\ k\ l) = I(\bar{h}\ k\ \bar{l})$. When k is odd, the terms I and IV have a difference of π in their phase angles: $2\pi(hx + ky + lz)$ and $2\pi(hx + ky + lz + 1/2k)$. The same is true for II and III. If we again regard these exponential terms as vectors in the Argand diagram with a length of 1 and appropriate phase angles, we easily see that when k is odd, $\mathbf{F}(h\ k\ l)$ and $\mathbf{F}(\bar{h}\ k\ \bar{l})$ have equal length but a phase difference of π (Figure 4.27a). But again $I(h\ k\ l) = I(\bar{h}\ k\ \bar{l})$ because $I(h\ k\ l) = |F(h\ k\ l)|^2$.

The result is that a 2-fold screw axis in the crystal is found as a 2-fold axis in the X-ray diffraction pattern. The phase angles of symmetry-related reflections are the same or differ by π, but this cannot be observed in the diffraction pattern. The other possible screw axes also express themselves in the X-ray diffraction pattern as normal nonscrew rotation axes. Although the screw character of a 2-fold screw axis is not detected in the symmetry of the X-ray diffraction pattern, it has an effect on the reflections along the corresponding 2-fold axis in the diffraction pattern. Take again a 2-fold screw axis along y:

$$\mathbf{F}(0\ k\ 0) = V \int_{\substack{\text{asymm} \\ \text{unit}}} \rho(x\ y\ z)\exp\{[2\pi iky] + \exp[2\pi ik(y + 1/2)]\}\, dx\, dy\, dz \tag{4.24}$$

When k is even this is $2 \times V\int\rho(x\ y\ z)\exp[2\pi iky]\, dx\, dy\, dz$. However when k is odd the two terms in Eq. (4.24) cancel and $\mathbf{F}(0\ k\ 0) = 0$ (Figure 4.27b).

The conditions for these reflections are called *serial reflection conditions*, because they apply to a set of reflections lying on a line through the origin in the reciprocal lattice. *Integral reflection conditions* involve all reflections; they are observed for centered lattices as discussed in the next section.

4.13. Integral Reflection Conditions for Centered Lattices

Consider for example, a lattice centered in the *ab*-plane, also called the *C*-plane (Figure 4.28). The following electron density relationship exists:

$$\rho(x\ y\ z) = \rho(x + 1/2, y + 1/2, z)$$

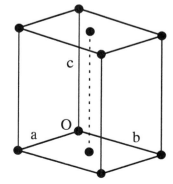

Figure 4.28. A unit cell centered in the *ab*-plane.

The structure factor **F** can now be written as

$$\mathbf{F}(h\ k\ l) = V \int\limits_{\substack{0 \leqslant x < 1 \\ 0 \leqslant y < 1/2 \\ 0 \leqslant z < 1}} \rho(x\ y\ z)\{\exp[2\pi i(hx + ky + lz)]$$

$$+ \exp[2\pi i(h(x + 1/2) + k(y + 1/2) + lz)]\}\ dx\ dy\ dz \quad (4.25)$$

The second exponential term on the right in Eq. (4.25) is equal to

$$\exp\{2\pi i[hx + ky + lz + 1/2(h + k)]\}$$

If $h + k$ is odd the two contributions to **F** cancel each other because of opposite phase angles.

The conclusion is that in the diffraction pattern of a crystal that has its C-face centered, all reflections for which $h + k$ is odd have a zero value for their intensities. The *International Tables* give complete information about the extinction of reflections for all space groups.

4.14. The Projection of Electron Density Along an Axis

The two-dimensional electron density projection along an axis can easily be calculated with a limited number of reflections. For protein structures this is usually not very useful because of the overlap of density and the inability to detect any interesting features in the projected density. Moreover, considering the speed and cost of modern computers and the speed of modern data collection methods, three-dimensional electron density information can easily be obtained. However, one should at least know the existence of the method. We shall discuss the projection of the electron density ρ along the c-axis onto the ab-plane. Expression (4.9) for the structure factor gives for the reflections $(h\ k0)$:

$$\mathbf{F}(h\ k0) = V \int_{xyz} \rho(x\ y\ z)\,dz\ \exp[2\pi i(hx + ky)]\,dx\,dy \quad (4.26)$$

In Eq. (4.26) the integration over z is first performed. Let us assume that the unit cell has an angle of 90° between the c-axis and the ab-plane. The volume of the unit cell V is then equal to $A \times c$, in which A is the surface of the ab-plane. In Eq. (4.26), z and dz are fractional coordinates. Therefore, $V\,dz$ can be written as $A\,c\,dz$ and $\mathbf{F}(h\ k0)$ as

$$\mathbf{F}(h\ k0) = A \int_{xyz} \rho(x\ y\ z)\,c\,dz\ \exp[2\pi i(hx + ky)]\,dx\,dy \quad (4.27)$$

With $\int_z \rho(x\ y\ z)\,c\,dz = \rho(x\ y)$, the electron density in the projected structure in $e/\text{Å}^2$, we obtain

$$\mathbf{F}(h\ k0) = A\int_{xy} \rho(x\ y)\ \exp[2\pi i(hx + ky)]\,dx\,dy \qquad (4.28)$$

The projected electron density ρ is obtained by Fourier inversion:

$$\rho(x\ y) = \frac{1}{A}\sum_h\sum_k \mathbf{F}(h\ k0)\ \exp[-2\pi i(hx + ky)] \qquad (4.29)$$

If the projection is along a 2-fold axis or screw axis along z, the expressions for $\mathbf{F}(h\ k0)$ and $\rho(x\ y)$ are further simplified, because in that
case $\rho(x\ y) = \rho(\bar{x}\ \bar{y})$

$$\mathbf{F}(h\ k0) = \frac{1}{2} A\int_{xy} \rho(x\ y)\{\exp[2\pi i(hx + ky)] + \exp[-2\pi i(hx + ky)]\}\,dx\,dy$$

$$= A\int_{xy} \rho(x\ y)\ \cos[2\pi(hx + ky)]\,dx\,dy \qquad (4.30)$$

and

$$\rho(x\ y) = \frac{1}{2}\frac{1}{A}\sum_h\sum_k \mathbf{F}(h\ k0)\{\exp[-2\pi i(hx + ky)] + \exp[2\pi i(hx + ky)]\}$$

$$= \frac{1}{A}\sum_h\sum_k \mathbf{F}(h\ k0)\ \cos[2\pi(hx + ky)] \qquad (4.31)$$

For such a centrosymmetric case $\mathbf{F}(h\ k0)$ always points along the real axis
in the Argand diagram. It has a positive sign for a phase angle of $0°$ and a
negative sign for a phase angle of $180°$.

4.15. The Intensity Diffracted by a Crystal

Starting from the wave $\mathbf{F}(\mathbf{S})$ diffracted by a unit cell, an expression can be
derived for the integrated intensity $I(\text{int.}, h\ k\ l)$ of the reflection $(h\ k\ l)$.
    The crystal is not perfect; rather it is imperfect and of finite size. These
imperfect crystals can be regarded as being composed of small mosaic
blocks, which can be considered as optically independent fragments
(Figure 4.29). For such an imperfect crystal the intensity profile of a
reflection has a certain width because of the angular spread of the mosaic
blocks; for a protein crystal generally 0.25–$0.5°$. Moreover each tiny
mosaic block has a small intrinsic reflection width (less than $0.01°$) because
it does not strictly obey the reflection condition of an infinite number of
unit cells. This implies that diffraction occurs not only for a sharp point

Figure 4.29. Most crystals are imperfect and can be regarded as being composed of small mosaic blocks.

$(h\ k\ l)$ in the reciprocal lattice, but also for a small region in reciprocal space around the sharp point.

With the assumptions that

1. apart from ordinary absorption, the intensity I_0 of the incident beam is the same throughout the crystal, and
2. the mosaic blocks are so small that a scattered wave is not scattered again (i.e., multiple scattering does not occur)

the expression for I (int., $h\ k\ l$), if the crystal is rotated with an angular velocity ω through the reflection position, is

$$I(\text{int.}, h\ k\ l) = \frac{\lambda^3}{\omega \cdot V^2} \times \left(\frac{e^2}{mc^2}\right)^2 \times V_{\text{cr}} \times I_0 \times L \times P \times A \times |F(h\ k\ l)|^2$$

$$(4.32)$$

The complete scattering Eq. (4.32) not only contains $|F(h\ k\ l)|^2$ but also has terms related to the scattering by the electrons themselves, to the wavelength λ, the volume V_{cr} of the crystal, and the volume V of the unit cell. We shall explain the various terms of Eq. (4.32) instead of deriving it from first principles. I_0 is the intensity of the incident beam and I is the integrated intensity of the reflected beam. e is the charge and m the mass of an electron and c the velocity of light. The Lorentz factor L depends on the data acquisition technique. P is the polarization factor; it will be discussed in Section 4.15.1 and the absorption factor A in Section 4.15.2. With I_0 as the intensity of the incident beam, radiation physics learns that the intensity scattered by a point electron is $(e^2/mc^2)^2 \times P \times I_0$, in which P is related to the polarization of the beam and to the reflection angle θ. If the electron is replaced by a unit cell of the crystal, the scattered amplitude is enhanced by a factor $|F(h\ k\ l)|$ and the intensity by $|F(h\ k\ l)|^2$.

The factor V_{cr}/V^2 in Eq. (4.32) requires some discussion. It depends on the existence of the independently scattering mosaic blocks. The larger the crystal, the more mosaic blocks and, therefore, the proportionality of the integrated intensity with V_{cr}. But why is it proportional to $1/V^2$? In reflection position all unit cells in a mosaic block scatter in phase. For a large unit cell of volume V, the number of unit cells for a given volume of the mosaic blocks is proportional to $1/V$, as is the scattered amplitude. Therefore the intensity is proportional to $1/V^2$.

I (int., $h\,k\,l$) is proportional to λ^3. This can be understood as follows:

- Consider the diffracting region around the reciprocal lattice point P. For a fixed position of the crystal, scattering occurs for the intersection of the diffracting region with the Ewald sphere.
- The intensity scattered by an electron into all directions or, in other words, toward the complete surface $4\pi(1/\lambda)^2$ of the Ewald sphere (radius $1/\lambda$), has a fixed value and is independent of λ. Therefore, the scattering per unit surface, and also the scattering by the intersection considered, is proportional to λ^2.

This λ^2-dependence must be multiplied by a λ-dependent term, which is related to the time t it takes for the complete diffracting region to pass through the Ewald sphere. For the simple case in which the incident and the diffracted beams are perpendicular to the rotation axis, t is found as follows (Figure 4.30):

If the angular speed of rotation is ω, then for the reciprocal lattice point P at a distance $1/d$ from the origin O, the linear speed perpendicular to OP is $v = (1/d)\omega$. Its component $v_\perp$ along PM, and thus perpendicular to the surface of the sphere, should be regarded:

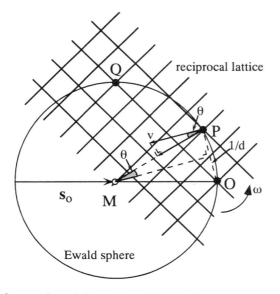

Figure 4.30. If the rotation of the reciprocal lattice is around an axis through the origin O and perpendicular to the plane of the drawing, point P will be in reflection condition much longer than point Q. Note that $OP = 1/d(P)$, $OQ = 1/d(Q)$, and $MP = s(P)$ and $MQ = s(Q)$.

$$v_\perp = \frac{1}{d} \, \omega \cos\theta$$

Because according to Bragg's law $d = \lambda/2 \sin\theta$, we find

$$v_\perp = \frac{2 \sin\theta \cos\theta}{\lambda} \omega = \frac{\sin 2\theta}{\lambda} \omega$$

The time t required to pass the sphere is proportional to

$$\frac{1}{v_\perp} = \frac{1}{\omega} \times \frac{\lambda}{\sin 2\theta}$$

Multiplying by the λ^2 dependence, found above, gives λ^3. The θ-dependent factor $1/\sin 2\theta$ represents the Lorentz factor L for the present case. For other acquisition techniques L may be a more complicated function of $(h \, k \, l)$. Note that for small θ values, $\lambda/\sin 2\theta$ is approximately equal to $\lambda/2 \sin\theta = d$ (error less than 10% for $\theta < 25°$) and λ drops out. This implies that the intensity of reflections from protein crystals, with their small θ values, is not proportional to λ^3, but rather to λ^2.

4.15.1. The Polarization Factor

The polarization factor P in Eq. (4.32) originates from the fact that an electron does not scatter along its direction of vibration. In other directions electrons radiate with an intensity proportional to $(\sin\alpha)^2$ (Figure 4.31a). The effect is that if the incident X-ray beam is unpolarized and then reflected against a plane, the reflected beam is more or less polarized. This affects the intensity. This is illustrated in Figure 4.31b. The unpolarized beam is split into two other beams with equal intensity, one polarized in a direction parallel to the reflecting plane (beam $\|$) and the other one in a direction perpendicular to the first one (beam $\perp$). The polarization direction of incident beam $\perp$ has, on a relative scale, a component $\sin 2\theta$ along the scattering direction (Figure 4.31c). The oscillation of electrons induced by this component does not contribute to the scattered intensity (α in Figure 4.31a is here 0). Only the other component ($\cos 2\theta$) does. Therefore, the scattered intensity is reduced by a factor $(1 - \sin^2 2\theta) = \cos^2 2\theta$. For incident beam $\|$, which is polarized perpendicular to the scattering direction, no reduction of intensity occurs. Combining the intensities of the two reflected beams results in the θ-dependent polarization factor $(1 + \cos^2 2\theta)/2$. It should be emphasized that the polarization factor as given here is valid only if the crystal is radiated with an unpolarized beam. With a monochromator in the incident beam path this is not true and it is certainly not true for synchrotron radiation, which is strongly polarized.

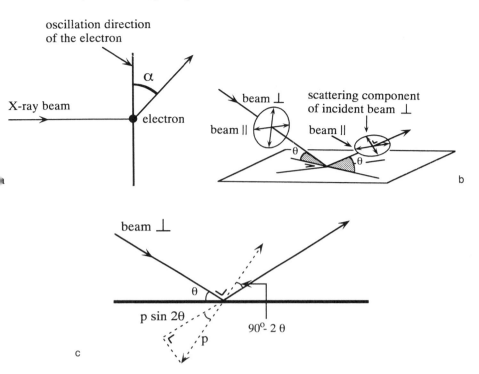

Figure 4.31. An explanation of the polarization factor. (a) The intensity of the radiation scattered by an oscillating electron is proportional to $(\sin \alpha)^2$. (b) The incident beam can be split into two others with the same intensity: one polarized in a direction parallel to the reflecting plane (beam $\|$) and the other one in a direction perpendicular to the first one (beam $\perp$); both polarization directions lie in a plane perpendicular to the direction of the incident beam. (c) The dotted line (p) indicates the polarization direction of incident beam $\perp$. Electrons induced by component $p \sin 2\theta$ do not contribute to the scattering.

4.15.2. Absorption and Extinction

If an X-ray beam passes through matter, its intensity I diminishes as a consequence of absorption: $I = I_0 \exp[-\mu \cdot t]$. t(cm) is the path length in the matter and μ(cm^{-1}) is the total linear absorption coefficient. μ can be obtained as the sum of the atomic mass absorption coefficients μ_a because these are, to a good approximation, additive with respect to the elements composing the material (for a definition of μ_a see the legend to Figure 4.32):

$$\mu = \frac{1}{V} \sum_i n_i (\mu_a)_i$$

where n_i is the number of atoms of element i in volume V. The value of μ_a is more or less independent of the physical state of the material. In general, μ_a is larger for longer wave length and for atoms with a higher atomic number (Figure 4.32). A protein crystal of 0.5 mm has, for Cu radiation, a transmission of approximately 60%. For paper of 0.1 mm and for glass of 0.01 mm thickness, transmission is 93%. Air also absorbs X-ray radiation.

Absorption of X-rays is mainly caused by two effects:

1. Photoelectric absorption: The X-ray photon disappears completely. If the photon energy is sufficient to remove an electron from the atom, the absorption becomes particularly strong.

2. Scattering: The X-ray photon is deflected from its original direction, with or without loss of energy. The first type of scattering is called inelastic or *Compton scattering* and the second type elastic or *Rayleigh scattering*. Between Bragg reflection positions Rayleigh scattering is due to distortions in the regularity of the crystal lattice; it is rather small. However, it can be appreciable at the occurrence of a strong Bragg reflection where it causes an extra reduction of the intensity; this effect is called extinction and is due to a nonperfect mosaicity:

a. The size of the mosaic blocks is so large that multiple scattering occurs within a block, causing interference between the incident and all scattered waves. It is called "primary extinction" (Figure 4.33).

b. The angular spread of the mosaic blocks is too small. Part of the incident beam is reflected by blocks close to the surface before it reaches

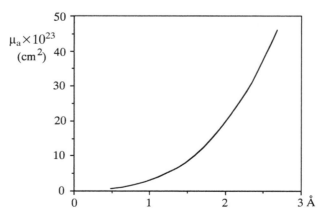

Figure 4.32. The atomic mass absorption coefficient μ_a of the element carbon as a function of the wavelength. The atomic mass absorption coefficient (cm²) for element i is defined as $(\mu_a)_i = \mu_i/\rho_i \times A_i/N$, where μ_i is the linear absorption coefficient, ρ_i the density, and A_i the atomic weight; N is Avogadro's number.

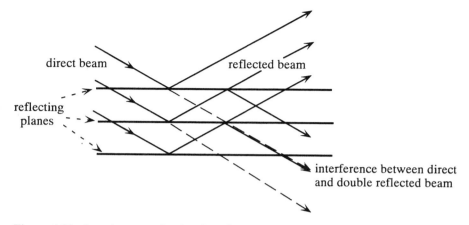

Figure 4.33. In primary extinction interference occurs between the incident and scattered waves. Because at each reflection there is a phase shift of $\pi/2$, the double reflected beam has a phase difference of π with the incident beam and reduces its intensity.

lower lying blocks that are also in reflecting position. This reduces the intensity of the incident beam for the lower lying blocks and consequently also their diffracted intensity; it is called "secondary extinction." For the relatively weak reflections of protein crystals extinction does not play a significant role.

4.16. Choice of Wavelength, Size of Unit Cell, and Correction of the Diffracted Intensity

4.16.1. Choice of Wavelength

The wavelength λ has an appreciable influence on the intensity of the X-rays diffracted by a crystal [Eq. (4.32)]. Using a longer wavelength has the advantage of a stronger diffracted intensity, but the disadvantage of higher absorption. An optimal choice for protein crystallography is the Cu wavelength of $1.5418\,\text{Å}$. However, if high intensity synchrotron radiation is available, a shorter wavelength, e.g., near $1\,\text{Å}$, has the advantage of lower absorption. For an X-ray detector with a fluorescent screen, the optimum wavelength may also be below $1.5\,\text{Å}$, because more visible light is created per X-ray photon. However, part of the shorter wavelength X-ray beam may not be absorbed in the fluorescent layer. There is also more chance that the diffracted beams overlap.

4.16.2. Effect of the Size of the Unit Cell on the Diffraction Intensity

If a crystal is larger, its diffraction (and also its absorption) is stronger. In protein crystallography a crystal size of 0.3–0.5 mm is regarded as optimal. Protein crystals are relatively weak scatterers for two reasons. First, because they consist only or mainly of light atoms: C, N, and O. The second and more important reason is the large size of their unit cells. This we can understand as follows. A crystal with a larger unit cell volume diffracts more weakly but has larger values of $|F(h\ k\ l)|^2$. We can combine these two effects by first calculating the mean square value $\overline{|F(h\ k\ l)|^2}$. Suppose we have the simple situation of a crystal with one kind of atoms, each atom with a scattering factor f and n atoms in the unit cell. $\overline{|F(h\ k\ l)|^2}$ can be calculated by assigning random phases to the contributions f of the individual atoms in the Argand diagram. This problem is analogous to that of the displacement caused by Brownian motion (Figure 4.34): a number of n equal steps of length f gives a root mean square displacement from the origin of $f \times \sqrt{n}$. The root mean square value of $|F(h\ k\ l)|$ is then

$$\sqrt{\overline{|F(h\ k\ l)|^2}} = f \times \sqrt{n} \text{ and } \overline{|F(h\ k\ l)|^2} = f^2 \times n$$

Combining the effect of the unit cell volume V and $|F(h\ k\ l)|$ in the scattering Eq. (4.32) leads to

$$\overline{I(\text{int.}, h\ k\ l)} \text{ is proportional to } \frac{\overline{|F(h\ k\ l)|^2}}{V^2} = \frac{f^2}{V^2} \times n \qquad (4.33)$$

If, through a reorganization of the molecular packing, a unit cell becomes two times as large and the number of molecules per unit cell doubles, V

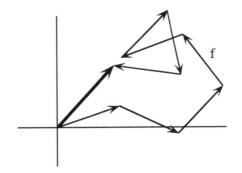

Figure 4.34. The displacement of a particle under the influence of Brownian motion. For n steps, where n is very large and each step has a length f, the final distance to the origin is $f\sqrt{n}$.

would become $2V$ and $n \to 2n$. Applying Eq. (4.33) results in an average intensity for the reflected beams that is half the original one.

4.16.3. Correction of the Measured Intensity

In Eq. (4.32) $(\lambda^3/\omega V^2) \times (e^2/mc^2)^2 \times V_{cr} \times I_0$ is a constant for a given experiment. The intensity $|F(h\,k\,l)|^2$ is obtained on a relative scale by calculating I (int., $h\,k\,l)/(L \times P \times A)$. This is called "correction" of the measured intensity for L, P, and A. In the following the resulting intensity will be called

$$I(h\,k\,l) = |F(h\,k\,l)|^2 \text{ on relative scale} \qquad (4.34)$$

The correction factors L and P are usually incorporated into the software package for the processing of the intensity data. Whether correction for absorption is required depends on the shape of the crystal, the wavelength, and the diffraction technique. For precession and oscillation pictures the pathlength of the primary and secondary beams in the crystal are not very different for all reflections on a particular image plate or film. As a result, the absorption is approximately the same for all those reflections. The absorption correction is then incorporated into the scaling factor for the exposures. It should be noted that inhomogeneously distributed mother liquor around the crystal mounted in the X-ray capillary can also have an appreciable absorption effect. If an absorption correction is applied, it is done in an empirical way in which absorption and extinction are considered simultaneously. For an area detector one can, for example, measure the intensity of symmetry-related reflections that follow different paths in the crystal.

Summary

It requires some simple mathematics to understand the diffraction of X-rays by a crystal. In this chapter it is presented via the addition of waves, the scattering by a simple two-electron system, by an atom, by one unit cell, and by the arrangement of unit cells in a crystal. The crystal periodicity leads to the Laue diffraction conditions

$$\mathbf{a} \cdot \mathbf{S} = h$$
$$\mathbf{b} \cdot \mathbf{S} = k$$
$$\mathbf{c} \cdot \mathbf{S} = l$$

and to Bragg's law:

$$2d \sin\theta = \lambda$$

They tell us that for suitable orientations a crystal diffracts an X-ray beam only in certain specific directions. With the reciprocal lattice formalism the required orientations and diffraction directions can be easily constructed.

A crystal structure is not static: the atoms vibrate around an equilibrium position, some more and others less. As a consequence, the intensity of the diffracted beams is weakened. This is expressed in the temperature factor.

The result of an X-ray structure determination is the electron density in the crystal and the fundamental equation for its calculation is

$$\rho(x\ y\ z) = \frac{1}{V}\sum_h \sum_k \sum_l |F(h\ k\ l)|\ \exp[-2\pi i(hx + ky + lz) + i\alpha(h\ k\ l)]$$

In this equation $\rho(x\ y\ z)$ is expressed as a Fourier transformation of the structure factors $F(h\ k\ l)$. The amplitude of these structure factors is obtained from the intensity of the diffracted beam after application of certain correction factors: $I(h\ k\ l) = |F(h\ k\ l)|^2$. The phase angles $\alpha(h\ k\ l)$ cannot be derived in a straightforward manner, but can be found in an indirect way, which will be discussed in later chapters.

Chapter 5

Average Reflection Intensity and Distribution of Structure Factor Data

5.1. Introduction

A quick glance through this chapter indicates that it is short but that it is mainly of a mathematical nature. However, it is not as difficult as it seems.

In Section 4.16.2 we calculated the average reflection intensity for a structure consisting of identical atoms. In this chapter we shall extend this calculation to structures composed of different atoms and use the result to place the experimentally determined intensities on an absolute scale[1] and obtain a rough estimate of the temperature factor. In later chapters we shall need to know not only the average intensity, but also the probability distribution of the structure factors and their amplitudes. In the derivation of these distribution functions the Gaussian distribution function, also called the Gauss error function, plays an important role. This function is now presented.

The Gauss Error Function

Two Gauss error curves are drawn in Figure 5.1. They obey the equation

$$f(x) = \frac{1}{\sigma\sqrt{2\pi}} \exp\left[\frac{(x-m)^2}{2\sigma^2}\right] \tag{5.1}$$

---

[1] Intensities are on absolute scale if the amplitudes of the structure factors $|F| = \sqrt{I}$ are expressed in electrons.

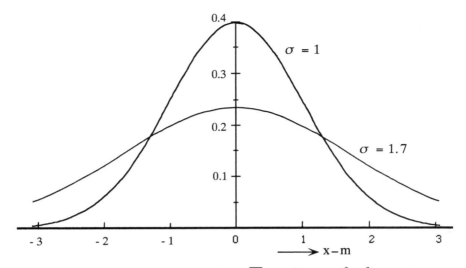

Figure 5.1. Gauss error functions: $(1/\sigma\sqrt{2\pi}) \exp[(x - m)^2/2\sigma^2]$ plotted as a function of $x - m$ for $\sigma = 1$ and $\sigma = 1.7$.

We notice the following:

1. The probability of finding a value between x and $x + dx$ is equal to $f(x) dx$.
2. For $x = m$ the value of the function is given by $f(m) = 1/\sigma\sqrt{2\pi}$.
3. Because it is certain that x lies somewhere between $+\infty$ and $-\infty$, the probability of finding x between $+\infty$ and $-\infty$ is 1 and, therefore,

$$\int_{-\infty}^{+\infty} f(x) dx = 1$$

This is called normalization of the function $f(x)$.

4. The mean value of x is m: $\bar{x} = m$. This follows directly from the symmetry of the function $f(x)$ around m.
5. The spread of the curve is expressed in the variance σ^2 of x, which is defined as the average value of $(x - m)^2$:

$$\overline{(x - m)^2} = \sigma^2 = \int_{x=-\infty}^{+\infty} (x - m)^2 f(x) dx$$

σ is called the standard deviation. Figure 5.1 shows that the width of the curve increases with σ, as expected. The variance σ^2 in Eq. (5.1), is calculated for data x with a frequency distribution $f(x)$ and assuming random errors in the data.

6. In a large set of data with random errors, only a few measurements occur far away from the center, because the curve falls off on either side of the maximum. For a distance $\geq 3\sigma$ from m, the chance of finding a measurement is only 2.7‰. Therefore, it is assumed that a measurement greater than 3σ from m is significantly different from m.

7. If the frequency distribution is not known, we may still have a number of measurements. In such a case, the average $\bar{x}$ of the observations is determined, rather than the mean value m. The variance is then defined as

$$\sigma^2 = \frac{\sum_i (x_i - \bar{x})^2}{N - 1}$$

where N is the number of measurements. The denominator is $N - 1$ and not N, because one degree of freedom is lost in calculating $\bar{x}$ from the measurements.

As an example in which the Gaussian distribution is used, we consider the measurement of an X-ray reflection intensity. Suppose that its actual value is I_{true}, but that values I_i are obtained by measuring the intensity a number of times or by considering the intensity of symmetry-related reflections. Because of experimental errors the values I_i show deviations $I_i - I_{true}$ from the actual value. If only random errors occur, the intensities observed for the particular reflection obey the Gauss error function, which for the present example is

$$f(I) = \frac{1}{\sigma[I]\sqrt{2\pi}} \exp\left[\frac{(I - I_{true})^2}{2(\sigma[I])^2}\right]$$

in which $(\sigma[I])^2$ is the average of $(I - I_{true})^2$. Because in practice the number of measurements is too small to obtain the complete distribution function, we have to be satisfied with best estimates of I_{true} and $\sigma[I]$. For I_{true} the best estimate is the average value $\bar{I}$ of the measured intensities and for $\sigma[I]$ it is given by

$$\sigma_e[I] = \left[\frac{\sum_i (I_i - \bar{I})^2}{N - 1}\right]^{1/2}$$

In practice, the estimated standard deviation σ_e(ESD) is usually called σ. Outliers which differ more than $3\sigma[I]$ from the mean value are usually rejected.

For a small number of intensity measurements σ_e is not a good estimate for σ. However, even if there is only one measurement of the intensity, a standard deviation for the intensity I can be given. This is based on counting statistics and the estimated standard deviation is given as $\sigma_e[I]$ $= \sqrt{I}$; this is explained in Appendix 3.

The precision of the mean $\bar{I}$ is given by the standard error $\sigma[I]/\sqrt{N}$. The standard deviation is also frequently used in electron density plots. In such a plot, peak heights are often given as a multiple of the standard deviation. For instance, the electron density ρ of a significant peak should be at least $3 \times \sigma[\rho]$. Here, $\sigma[\rho]$ is obtained as

$$\sigma[\rho] = \left[\frac{\sum\limits_{i=1}^{N} \{\rho(x_i \, y_i \, z_i) - \bar{\rho}\}^2}{N}\right]^{1/2}$$

5.2. Average Intensity; Wilson Plots

Early in the process of determining a crystal structure it is possible to obtain a rough estimate of the value of the temperature factor and of the factor required for putting the intensities $I(\mathbf{S})$ on an absolute scale. To this end we calculate the average intensity for a series of reflections $\mathbf{S}$, starting from the expression for the structure factor [Eq. (4.3)]:

$$\mathbf{F}(\mathbf{S}) = \sum_{i=1}^{n} f_i \exp[2\pi i \mathbf{r}_i \cdot \mathbf{S}]$$

where the scattering factor f_i of atom i includes the effect of thermal motion, and n is the number of atoms in the unit cell. On an absolute scale the intensity is given by

$$I(\text{abs}, \mathbf{S}) = \mathbf{F}(\mathbf{S}) \cdot \mathbf{F}^*(\mathbf{S}) = |F(\mathbf{S})|^2 = \sum_i \sum_j f_i f_j \exp[2\pi i(\mathbf{r}_i - \mathbf{r}_j) \cdot \mathbf{S}]$$

Suppose that we consider a series of reflections for which $\mathbf{S}$ varies so strongly that the values for the angles $[2\pi(\mathbf{r}_i - \mathbf{r}_j) \cdot \mathbf{S}]$ are distributed evenly over the range $0 - 2\pi$ for $i \neq j$. Then, the average value for all terms with $i \neq j$ will be zero. Only the terms with $i = j$ remain, and we obtain

$$\overline{|F(\mathbf{S})|^2} = \overline{I(\text{abs}, \mathbf{S})} = \sum_i f_i^2 \tag{5.2}$$

We presented this result previously (Section 4.16.2) for a structure with identical atoms. There the equation was not rigorously derived, but was obtained by comparison with Brownian motion. To obtain a rough estimate of the temperature factor and of the scale factor, it is assumed that all atoms in the cell have the same isotropic thermal motion, or

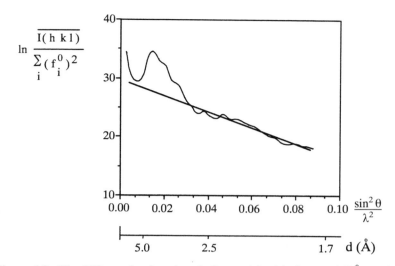

Figure 5.2. The Wilson plot for phospholipase A2 with data to 1.7 Å resolution. Only beyond 3 Å resolution is it possible to fit the curve to a straight line.

$$f_i^2 = \exp\left[-2B\frac{\sin^2\theta}{\lambda^2}\right] \times (f_i^0)^2$$

where f_i^0 is the scattering factor of atom i at rest. Comparison of the calculated values $\overline{I(\text{abs}, \mathbf{S})}$ with the experimental data $\overline{I(\mathbf{S})}$ requires a scale factor C:

$$\overline{I(\mathbf{S})} = C \times \overline{I(\text{abs}, \mathbf{S})} = C \exp\left[-2B\frac{\sin^2\theta}{\lambda^2}\right]\sum_i(f_i^0)^2$$

Both f_i^0 and the temperature factor depend on $\sin\theta/\lambda$. Therefore average intensities are calculated for reflections in shells of (almost) constant $\sin\theta/\lambda$. To determine B and C the equation is written in the form

$$\ln\frac{\overline{I(\mathbf{S})}}{\sum_i(f_i^0)^2} = \ln C - 2B\frac{\sin^2\theta}{\lambda^2} \tag{5.3}$$

and $\ln\overline{I(\mathbf{S})}/\Sigma_i(f_i^0)^2$ is plotted against $(\sin^2\theta)/\lambda^2$. The result should be a straight line—the so-called Wilson plot—from which both the temperature factor and the absolute scale of the intensities can be derived (Figure 5.2). For proteins, the Wilson plot does not give a fully accurate result because the condition that the angles $[2\pi(\mathbf{r}_i - \mathbf{r}_j)\cdot\mathbf{S}]$ are distributed evenly over the $0 - 2\pi$ range is not fulfilled for shells of reflections with (almost) constant $(\sin\theta)/\lambda$ (see below).

The Wilson Plot for a Protein Structure

For practical purposes, the condition that the angles $2\pi(\mathbf{r}_i - \mathbf{r}_j) \cdot \mathbf{S}$ are distributed evenly over the 0 to 2π range is replaced by the more relaxed condition that the range in the angular values should at least be 2π. In proteins, the shortest distance encountered between bonded atoms is approximately $1.5\,\text{Å}$. For this distance and given $\mathbf{S}$, the scalar product varies from $-3\pi|S|$ ($\mathbf{S}$ and $\mathbf{r}_i - \mathbf{r}_j$ antiparallel) to $+3\pi|S|$ ($\mathbf{S}$ and $\mathbf{r}_i - \mathbf{r}_j$ parallel). The condition that the range $6\pi|S|$ should be at least 2π requires that $|S| = 1/d$ is not smaller than $\frac{1}{3}\text{Å}^{-1}$ or $d < 3\,\text{Å}$.

Therefore, we conclude that the Wilson plot gives reliable information only if reflections are used corresponding to Bragg spacings less than $3\,\text{Å}$. For longer distances Figure 5.2 shows deviations from the straight line. For instance, around $d = 4\,\text{Å}$ or $|S| = 0.25\,\text{Å}^{-1}$, there is a maximum that can be ascribed to the presence of many nonbonded distances around $4\,\text{Å}$ in the protein structure. Therefore, the angles $2\pi(\mathbf{r}_i - \mathbf{r}_j) \cdot \mathbf{S}$, with $i \neq j$, tend to cluster around 2π for $|S| = 0.25\,\text{Å}^{-1}$ and terms $\exp[2\pi i(\mathbf{r}_i - \mathbf{r}_j) \cdot \mathbf{S}]$, $i \neq j$, do not average to zero.

5.3. The Distribution of Structure Factors $\mathbf{F}$ and Structure Factor Amplitudes $|F|$

With the information that $\overline{|F(\mathbf{S})|^2} = \Sigma_i f_i^2$ [Eq. (5.2)] it is now easy to derive distribution functions for the structure factors and their amplitudes. However, we shall not need this information before Chapter 8 and, therefore, as an alternative, you can skip it now and read it later.

First we consider for general reflections the probability $p(\mathbf{F})d(\mathbf{F})$ of finding a structure factor between $\mathbf{F}$ and $\mathbf{F} + d\mathbf{F}$. In the two-dimensional Argand diagram $\mathbf{F}$ is expressed as a vector with real component A and imaginary component B: $|F|^2 = A^2 + B^2$. Let A have the probability $p(A)d(A)$ of lying between A and $A + dA$ and similarly for B. Because the components A and B are independent of each other, the probability for $\mathbf{F}$ to point to the volume element $d\mathbf{F} = dA \times dB$ is given by

$$p(\mathbf{F})d(\mathbf{F}) = p(A)d(A) \times p(B)d(B)$$

A protein structure consists of a great many light atoms with an occasional heavy atom. For such a structure a Gaussian distribution can be assumed for the components A and B, if the reflections considered show a sufficiently large variation in their diffraction vectors $\mathbf{S}$. Therefore, the distribution functions of A and B are determined by the average values $\overline{A}$ and $\overline{B}$, and by the variances $\sigma^2[A]$ and $\sigma^2[B]$. Because within the series of reflections all directions for the atomic scattering factors f_i are equally possible, we obtain:

$$\bar{A} = \bar{B} = 0$$

$$\sigma^2[A] = \overline{(A - \bar{A})^2} = \overline{A^2} \quad \text{and} \quad \sigma^2[B] = \overline{(B - \bar{B})^2} = \overline{B^2}$$

$$\overline{A^2} = \overline{B^2} = \frac{1}{2}\overline{|F|^2} = \frac{1}{2}\sum_i f_i^2 \quad \text{(Eq. 5.2)}$$

$$\sigma^2[A] = \sigma^2[B] = \frac{1}{2}\sigma^2[|F|]$$

Because $\sigma^2[A] = \overline{A^2}$, $\frac{1}{2}\sigma^2[|F|]$ is equal to $\frac{1}{2}\sum_{i=1}^{n} f_i^2$. Thus we obtain

$$p(\mathbf{F})d(\mathbf{F}) = \frac{1}{2\pi \times \sigma(A) \times \sigma(B)} \exp\left[-\frac{A^2 + B^2}{2\sigma^2(A)}\right] d(A)\, d(B)$$

$$= \frac{1}{2\pi \times \frac{1}{2}\sigma^2(|F|)} \exp\left[-\frac{|F|^2}{\sigma^2(|F|)}\right] d\mathbf{F}$$

$$= \frac{1}{\pi \times \sum_{i=1}^{n} f_i^2} \exp\left[-\frac{|F|^2}{\sum_{i=1}^{n} f_i^2}\right] d(\mathbf{F})$$

It is now easy to derive $p(|F|)d(|F|)$. This is the probability that the magnitude of a structure factor lies between $|F|$ and $|F| + d|F|$, or that the end of vector **F** in the Argand diagram is in an annulus between $|F|$ and $|F| + d|F|$:

$$p(|F|)\, d|F| = p(\mathbf{F}) \times 2\pi|F|\, d|F| = \frac{2|F|}{\sum_{i=1}^{n} f_i^2} \exp\left[-\frac{|F|^2}{\sum_{i=1}^{n} f_i^2}\right] d|F| \quad (5.4)$$

Note: Because of the decrease of f_i with $\sin\theta/\lambda$, the variance $\frac{1}{2}\sum_{i=1}^{n} f_i^2$ depends on $\sin\theta/\lambda$ and must be taken in shells of $\sin\theta/\lambda$. This problem does not exist if, instead of the structure factors **F(S)**, normalized structure factors **E(S)** are used (Chapter 6):

$$E(S) = \frac{F(S)}{\left(\sum_i f_i^2\right)^{1/2}}$$

In the calculation of normalized structure factors, the atoms are regarded as points and their scattering is independent of $\sin\theta/\lambda$.

Summary

In this chapter we have derived an important equation for the average intensity:

$$\overline{I(\text{abs}, \mathbf{S})} = \sum_i f_i^2$$

We shall need this result frequently. It has already been applied in this chapter in the derivation of distribution functions for the structure factors $\mathbf{F}(\mathbf{S})$ and for their amplitudes $|F(\mathbf{S})|$. The Gauss error function played a central role in the derivation of these functions.

Chapter 6
Special Forms of the Structure Factor

6.1. Introduction

In this chapter some special forms of the structure factor will be presented. It is not essential reading to understand the following chapters, but it does provide an introduction to and definitions of *unitary structure factors* and *normalized structure factors*. The chapter is put in this position in the book because the material can be easily understood using the results presented in the section on the Wilson plot (Section 5.2). However, if this is your first introduction to protein X-ray crystallography, you can skip this chapter for the time being.

6.2. The Unitary Structure Factor

For statistical studies of structure factor amplitude distributions the normal form of the structure factor

$$\mathbf{F}(\mathbf{S}) = \sum_j f_j \exp[2\pi i(\mathbf{r}_j \cdot \mathbf{S})]$$

is not quite suitable. $\mathbf{F}(\mathbf{S})$ decreases with $|S|$ because of the $|S|$ dependence of f_j and because of the temperature factor, and these effects are disturbing and must be eliminated. Therefore, the following modified structure factors have been introduced: the unitary structure factor $\mathbf{U}(\mathbf{S})$ and the normalized structure factor $\mathbf{E}(\mathbf{S})$.

The unitary structure factor is defined as

$$U(S) = \frac{F(S)_{pt}}{\sum_j Z_j} \tag{6.1}$$

where Z_j is the atomic number of atom j and $\Sigma_j Z_j = F(000)$. $F(S)_{pt}$ is the structure factor on an absolute scale with the assumption that the individual scatterers are point atoms. Their scattering is independent of $|S|$ and is equal to the atomic number Z over the entire $|S|$ region. This also excludes any thermal motion. When there is only one type of atom in the unit cell but equal thermal motion for all atoms,

$$F(S)_{pt} = \frac{Z \times \exp[B(\sin^2\theta/\lambda^2)]}{f} \times F_{obs} \tag{6.2}$$

where F_{obs} is the normal structure factor on absolute scale. For more than one type of atom but the same thermal parameter for all atoms, $F(S)_{pt}$ is taken as

$$F(S)_{pt} = \frac{\sum_j Z_j \times \exp[B(\sin^2\theta/\lambda^2)]}{\sum_j f_j} \times F_{obs} \tag{6.3}$$

combining (6.1) and (6.3):

$$U(S) = \frac{\exp[B(\sin^2\theta/\lambda^2)] \times F_{obs}}{\sum_j f_j} \tag{6.4}$$

The exponential term eliminates the effect of the temperature factor and the division by $\Sigma_j f_j$ converts the atoms to point atoms.

Clearly $|U(S)| \leq 1$. For proteins with a great many atoms scattered over the unit cell, the $U(S)$ values are rather small and if probability distributions of structure factors are discussed, it is more convenient to use normalized structure factors. They have the advantage of being independent of scaling factors between sets of reflections.

6.3. The Normalized Structure Factor

The normalized structure factor is

$$E(S) = \frac{F(S)}{\left(\sum_j f_j^2\right)^{1/2}} \tag{6.5}$$

Neither f_j nor $F(S)$ includes the temperature factor.

$$F(S) = F_{obs}(S) \times \exp\left[B\frac{\sin^2\theta}{\lambda^2}\right]$$

with $\mathbf{F}_{obs}(\mathbf{S})$ including the temperature factor. Both $\mathbf{F}(\mathbf{S})$ and $\mathbf{F}_{obs}(\mathbf{S})$ are on an absolute scale here. According to Eq. (5.2)

$$\overline{|F(\mathbf{S})|^2} = \sum_j f_j^2$$

and, therefore

$$\overline{|E(\mathbf{S})|^2} = \frac{\overline{|F(\mathbf{S})|^2}}{\left(\sum_j f_j^2\right)} = \frac{\overline{|F(\mathbf{S})|^2}}{\overline{|F(\mathbf{S})|^2}} = 1$$

Moreover, if $\mathbf{E}(\mathbf{S})$ is written as

$$\mathbf{E}(\mathbf{S}) = \frac{\mathbf{F}(\mathbf{S})}{(\overline{|F(\mathbf{S})|^2})^{1/2}}$$

we see that the scale factor is not important because the numerator and the denominator are on the same scale. $\mathbf{E}(\mathbf{S})$ can be obtained from the experimental data in the following way:

$$\mathbf{E}(\mathbf{S}) = \frac{\mathbf{F}(\mathbf{S})_{exp} \times \exp[B(\sin^2\theta/\lambda^2)]}{(\overline{|F(\mathbf{S})_{exp}|^2})^{1/2}} \tag{6.6}$$

Sometimes a complication exists with the use of $\mathbf{E}(\mathbf{S})$ values in probability distributions of X-ray intensities. This is caused by the fact that for some groups of reflections the E-values are higher than expected. An example will show this: Suppose the structure has an n-fold symmetry axis along the c-axis. For the $(00l)$ reflections only the z-coordinate counts and this is the same for all n symmetry related atoms. Their contribution to the structure factor is

$$n \times f \exp[2\pi i l z]$$

This corresponds to the reflection of a structure with a reduction in the number of atoms by a factor of n, but with each atom having an atomic scattering factor of $n\,f$ instead of f. From Wilson statistics [Eq. (5.2)] the average intensity would be

$$\sum_{j=1}^{N/n} (nf_j)^2 = n \times \sum_{j=1}^{N} f_j^2$$

instead of $\sum_{j=1}^{N} f_j^2$. $\overline{|E|^2}$, where the average is over all reflections, always remains 1. To allow statistical comparison of all reflections, the E-values for reflections belonging to the special groups with too high values of E are reduced by a factor $\sqrt{\varepsilon}$. ε is easily found by a procedure proposed by Stewart and Karle (1976). The more general form of $\mathbf{E}(\mathbf{S})$ is

$$\mathbf{E}(\mathbf{S}) = \frac{\mathbf{F}(\mathbf{S})_{exp} \times \exp[B(\sin^2\theta/\lambda^2)]}{(\varepsilon \times \overline{|F(\mathbf{S})_{exp}|^2})^{1/2}} \tag{6.7}$$

Summary

In this chapter two alternative expression for the structure factor have been introduced:

- The unitary structure factor

$$U(S) = \frac{\exp[B \, \sin^2 \theta / \lambda^2] \times F_{exp} S}{\sum_j f_j}$$

- The normalized structure factor

$$E(S) = \frac{F(S)_{exp} \times \exp[B \, \sin^2 \theta / \lambda^2]}{(\varepsilon \times \overline{|F(S)_{exp}|^2})^{1/2}}$$

They are more convenient in statistical studies of structure factor amplitude distributions than the common form $F(S)$ of the structure factor.

Chapter 7
The Solution of the Phase Problem by the Isomorphous Replacement Method

7.1. Introduction

As we have seen in Chapter 4 the electron density in a crystal can be obtained by calculating the Fourier summation

$$\rho(x\ y\ z) = \frac{1}{V}\sum_{hkl}|F(h\ k\ l)|\exp[-2\pi i(hx + ky + lz) + i\alpha(h\ k\ l)] \qquad (7.1)$$

in which $|F(h\ k\ l)|$ is the structure factor amplitude of reflection $(h\ k\ l)$, including the temperature factor, and $\alpha(h\ k\ l)$ is the phase angle. x, y, and z are coordinates in the unit cell. From the diffraction pattern the values of $I(h\ k\ l)$ are obtained after applying the correction factors L, P, and A. Because $I(h\ k\ l) = |F(h\ k\ l)|^2$ the amplitudes $|F(h\ k\ l)|$ can be found. Unfortunately, no information is available on the phase angles. In principle, four techniques exist for solving the phase problem in protein X-ray crystallography:

1. The isomorphous replacement method, which requires the attachment of heavy atoms (atoms with high atomic number) to the protein molecules in the crystal.
2. The multiple wavelength anomalous diffraction method. It depends on the presence of sufficiently strong anomalously scattering atoms in the protein structure itself. Anomalous scattering occurs if the electrons in an atom cannot be regarded as free electrons.
3. The molecular replacement method for which the similarity of the unknown structure to an already known structure is a prerequisite.
4. Direct methods, the methods of the future, still in a stage of development toward practical application for proteins.

129

Molecular replacement, which will be discussed in Chapter 10, is the most rapid method for determining a protein structure. However, it requires the availability of a known model structure, e.g., of a homologous protein. If this does not exist, isomorphous replacement should be applied. This is the most general method for determining protein phase angles and is used if nothing is, as yet, known about the three-dimensional structure of the protein.

The multiple wavelength anomalous diffraction method does not depend on the attachment of a heavy atom-containing reagent to the protein, but it does require the presence of an anomalously scattering atom and diffraction data collection at a number of X-ray wavelengths, in general, data collection with synchrotron radiation. This method for phase angle determination will be discussed in Section 11.5. In principle, it is an elegant method but technically is not easy to apply.

We shall first discuss the isomorphous replacement method. The initial step in this method requires the attachment of heavy atoms and subsequently the determination of the coordinates of these heavy atoms in the unit cell. A useful role in this process is played by the Patterson function. Therefore, we shall begin by discussing this function and its physical interpretation.

7.2. The Patterson Function

The Patterson function $P(\mathbf{u})$ or $P(u\ v\ w)$ is a Fourier summation with intensities as coefficients and without phase angles, or rather with all phase angles equal to zero.

$$P(u\ v\ w) = \frac{1}{V}\sum_{hkl}|F(h\ k\ l)|^2 \cos[2\pi(h\ u + k\ v + l\ w)] \qquad (7.2)$$

or shorter

$$P(\mathbf{u}) = \frac{1}{V}\sum_{\mathbf{S}}|F(\mathbf{S})|^2 \cos[2\pi\mathbf{u}\cdot\mathbf{S}] \qquad (7.3)$$

u, v, and w are relative coordinates in the unit cell. To avoid confusion with the coordinates x, y, and z in the real cells, we use u, v, and w in the Patterson cell, which, however, has dimensions identical to the real cell. Note that the coefficients in the summations (7.2) and (7.3) are $|F(h\ k\ l)|^2$ and not $|F(h\ k\ l)|$ as in Eq. (7.1).

Further, it can be shown that the Patterson function $P(\mathbf{u})$ can alternatively be written as:

$$P(\mathbf{u}) = \int_{\mathbf{r}_1} \rho(\mathbf{r}_1) \times \rho(\mathbf{r}_1 + \mathbf{u})\,dv \qquad (7.4)$$

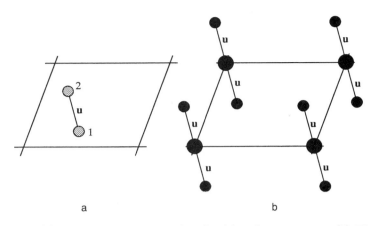

Figure 7.1. (a) A two-dimensional unit cell with only two atoms. (b) The corresponding Patterson cell.

The integration is for r_1 over all positions in the real unit cell. Assuming for the moment that this is true we can use this form of $P(u)$ to understand its physical interpretation: Move through the *real unit cell* with a vector **u**, multiply in every position of **u** the electron density ρ at the beginning of **u** (in position r_1) with the electron density at the end of vector **u** (in position $r_1 + u$) and take the integral of these values. Only if nonzero electron density is present at both the beginning and the end of **u** will the result of the multiplication be nonzero. What this leads to can best be understood from Figure 7.1, in which the real cell contains only two atoms.

$\rho(r_1) \times \rho(r_1 + u)$ has a significant value only if **u** starts in atom 1 and ends in atom 2, or the other way around. In the corresponding Patterson cell the vector **u** starts in the origin of the cell and points either in one direction (atom 1 to atom 2) or in the opposite direction (atom 2 to atom 1). A peak in a Patterson map at position **u** (or $u\ v\ w$), therefore, means that in the real cell atoms occur at a certain position x, y, and z, and at the position $x + u$, $y + v$, and $z + w$, or $x - u$, $y - v$, and $z - w$. So far the real atomic positions are not known, but the vectorial distance between them is clear from the Patterson map.

In simple structures with a limited number of atoms, the atomic positions can be derived fairly straightforwardly from the Patterson map. But this is impossible for complicated structures, like proteins. If a real unit cell contains N atoms, the corresponding Patterson map will show N^2 peaks, because one can draw N vectors from each atom. However, N vectors of the total number of N^2 vectors will have a length 0, because they go from an atom to the same atom. Therefore, the highest peak in a Patterson map is situated in the origin of the cell (Figure 7.2). The

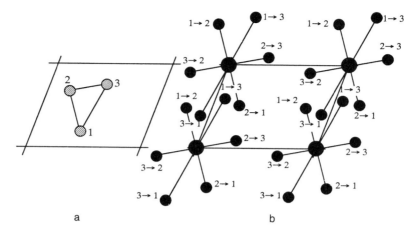

a   b

Figure 7.2. (a) A two-dimensional unit cell with three atoms. (b) The corresponding Patterson map. Note the large increase in the number of Patterson peaks compared with Figure 7.1. The total number of peaks is N^2, but the N self-peaks overlap at the origin and, therefore, $N(N-1)$ nonorigin peaks are found in a Patterson map. Because of the centrosymmetry in the map the number of unique peaks is $[N(N-1)]/2$; in this figure $1 \rightarrow 2$, $1 \rightarrow 3$, and $2 \rightarrow 3$ are unique peaks.

number of nonorigin peaks is $N^2 - N = N(N-1)$. If the unit cell of a protein crystal contains 5000 nonhydrogen atoms, then the number of Patterson peaks would be 25×10^6. It is clear that such a Patterson map is uninterpretable. If, however, a limited number of heavy atoms in the large unit cell must be located, the Patterson function is extremely useful as you can see in Figure 7.4c.

We have presented two different expressions for the Patterson function: Eq. (7.2) or (7.3), which tells us how to calculate it and Eq. (7.4), which facilitates understanding of the physical meaning of the Patterson function.

We shall now prove that

$$P(\mathbf{u}) = \int_{\mathbf{r}_1} \rho(\mathbf{r}_1) \times \rho(\mathbf{r}_1 + \mathbf{u})dv = \frac{1}{V}\sum_{\mathbf{S}}|F(\mathbf{S})|^2 \cos[2\pi\mathbf{u}\cdot\mathbf{S}] \qquad (7.5)$$

and start with

$$\rho(\mathbf{r}_1) = \frac{1}{V}\sum_{\mathbf{S}}|F(\mathbf{S})| \exp[-2\pi i\mathbf{r}_1 \cdot \mathbf{S} + i\alpha(\mathbf{S})] \qquad (7.6)$$

$$\rho(\mathbf{r}_2) = \rho(\mathbf{r}_1 + \mathbf{u}) = \frac{1}{V}\sum_{\mathbf{S}}|F(\mathbf{S}')| \exp[-2\pi i(\mathbf{r}_1 + \mathbf{u}) \cdot \mathbf{S}' + i\alpha(\mathbf{S}')'] \qquad (7.7)$$

In Eq. (7.7) for $\rho(\mathbf{r}_2)$ we use $\mathbf{S}'$, just to distinguish it from $\mathbf{S}$ in the equation for $\rho(\mathbf{r}_1)$.

$$\rho(\mathbf{r}_1) \times \rho(\mathbf{r}_1 + \mathbf{u}) = \frac{1}{V^2}\sum_{\mathbf{S}}\sum_{\mathbf{S'}}|F(\mathbf{S})|\,|F(\mathbf{S'})|\exp[-2\pi i\{\mathbf{r}_1 \cdot (\mathbf{S} + \mathbf{S'})$$
$$+ \mathbf{u} \cdot \mathbf{S'}\} + i\alpha(\mathbf{S}) + i\alpha(\mathbf{S'})] \qquad (7.8)$$

In Section 4.11 we have seen that $|F(h\,k\,l)| = |F(\bar{h}\,\bar{k}\,\bar{l})|$ or $|F(\mathbf{S})| = |F(-\mathbf{S})|$ and also that $\alpha(h\,k\,l) = -\alpha(\bar{h}\,\bar{k}\,\bar{l})$ or $\alpha(\mathbf{S}) = -\alpha(-\mathbf{S})$. Therefore, in Eq. (7.8) the coefficients $|F(\mathbf{S})|\,|F(\mathbf{S'})|$ are equal for $\mathbf{S}$ and $-\mathbf{S}$, as well as for $\mathbf{S'}$ and $-\mathbf{S'}$, whereas the exponential terms have just the opposite sign. This simplifies Eq. (7.8) to a summation of cos terms:

$$\rho(\mathbf{r}_1) \times \rho(\mathbf{r}_1 + \mathbf{u}) = \frac{1}{V^2}\sum_{\mathbf{S}}\sum_{\mathbf{S'}}|F(\mathbf{S})| \cdot |F(\mathbf{S'})|\cos[2\pi\{\mathbf{r}_1 \cdot (\mathbf{S} + \mathbf{S'}) + \mathbf{u} \cdot \mathbf{S'}\}$$
$$- \alpha(\mathbf{S}) - \alpha(\mathbf{S'})] \qquad (7.9)$$

The next step is an integration with $\mathbf{r}_1$ over the entire unit cell. In other words, $\mathbf{r}_1$ assumes different lengths and different directions:

$$P(\mathbf{u}) = \int_{\mathbf{r}_1} \rho(\mathbf{r}_1) \times \rho(\mathbf{r}_1 + \mathbf{u})\,dv$$

$$= \frac{1}{V^2}\sum_{\mathbf{S}}\sum_{\mathbf{S'}}|F(\mathbf{S})| \times |F(\mathbf{S'})| \int_{\mathbf{r}_1} \cos[2\pi\{\mathbf{r}_1 \cdot (\mathbf{S} + \mathbf{S'}) + \mathbf{u} \cdot \mathbf{S'}\}$$
$$- \alpha(\mathbf{S}) - \alpha(\mathbf{S'})]\,dv \qquad (7.10)$$

The integration with $\mathbf{r}_1$ over the entire unit cell means that the constant vector $\mathbf{u}$ must move through the unit cell and has its beginning in every position $\mathbf{r}_1$ of the unit cell. Since $\mathbf{r}_1$ can have different lengths and many different directions, the angles

$$2\pi\{\mathbf{r}_1(\mathbf{S} + \mathbf{S'}) + \mathbf{u} \cdot \mathbf{S'}\} - \alpha(\mathbf{S}) - \alpha(\mathbf{S'})$$

can assume all values between 0 and 2π for $\mathbf{S} + \mathbf{S'} \neq 0$. Therefore, the integration

$$\int_{\mathbf{r}_1} \cos[2\pi\{\mathbf{r}_1 \cdot (\mathbf{S} + \mathbf{S'}) + \mathbf{u} \cdot \mathbf{S'}\} - \alpha(\mathbf{S}) - \alpha(\mathbf{S'})]\,dv$$

will in general lead to zero. However, in the special case when $\mathbf{S} + \mathbf{S'} = 0$ or $\mathbf{S'} = -\mathbf{S}$ and $\alpha(\mathbf{S'}) = -\alpha(-\mathbf{S'})$, a nonzero value will result:

$$P(\mathbf{u}) = \frac{1}{V^2}\sum_{\mathbf{S}}|F(\mathbf{S})|^2 \cos[2\pi\mathbf{u} \cdot \mathbf{S}] \int_{\mathbf{r}_1} dv = \frac{1}{V}\sum_{\mathbf{S}}|F(\mathbf{S})|^2 \cos[2\pi\mathbf{u} \cdot \mathbf{S}] \quad (7.11)$$

because $\int_{\mathbf{r}_1} dv = V$.

The Patterson function has the following properties:

1. The Patterson map has peaks at end points of vectors $\mathbf{u}$ equal to vectors *between* atoms in the real cell.

2. For every pair of atoms in the real cell, there exists a unique peak in the Patterson map.

3. A Patterson map is always centrosymmetric.

4. Screw axes in a real cell become normal axes in a Patterson cell. We shall prove this for a 2-fold screw axis along y.

In Section 4.12.2 we showed that for a 2-fold screw axis along y the diffraction pattern has a 2-fold axis along y:

$$I(h\ k\ l) = I(\bar{h}\ k\ \bar{l})$$

We must now prove that $P(u\ v\ w) = P(\bar{u}\ v\ \bar{w})$.

$$P(u\ v\ w) = \frac{1}{V}\sum_{hkl}|F(h\ k\ l)|^2 \cos[2\pi(hu + kv + lw)]$$

This is exactly equal to:

$$P(u\ v\ w) = \frac{1}{V}\sum_{hkl}|F(\bar{h}\ k\ \bar{l})|^2 \cos[2\pi(\bar{h}u + kv + \bar{l}w)]$$

because the summation is still over all reflections $h\,k\,l$. We know already that $I(\bar{h}\ k\ \bar{l}) = I(h\ k\ l)$ or $|F(\bar{h}\ k\ \bar{l})|^2 = |F(h\ k\ l)|^2$. Therefore, we can write $P(u\ v\ w)$ as

$$P(u\ v\ w) = \frac{1}{V}\sum_{hkl}|F(h\ k\ l)|^2 \cos[2\pi(h\bar{u} + kv + l\bar{w})]$$

and this is precisely $P(\bar{u}\ v\ \bar{w})$. This proves that

$$P(u\ v\ w) = P(\bar{u}\ v\ \bar{w}).$$

5. Symmetry elements can cause a concentration of peaks in certain lines or planes: "Harker lines" or "Harker planes." Examples are given in Figures 7.3 and 7.4.

6. The Patterson function

$$P(\mathbf{u}) = \int_{\mathbf{r}_1} \rho(\mathbf{r}_1) \times \rho(\mathbf{r}_1 + \mathbf{u})\,dv \qquad (7.12)$$

is the convolution of the structure and its inverse. The mathematical definition of the convolution $C(x)$ of two real, periodic functions $f(h)$ and $g(h)$ is

$$C(x) = \int_{\eta=0}^{1} f(\eta)g(x - \eta)\,d\eta \qquad (7.13)$$

The Patterson function can be put into this form as follows: Replacing $\mathbf{r}_1 + \mathbf{u}$ by $\mathbf{r}''$ in Eq. (7.12) gives

$$P(\mathbf{u}) = \int_{\mathbf{r}''} \rho(\mathbf{r}'' - \mathbf{u})\rho(\mathbf{r}'')\,dv \qquad (7.14)$$

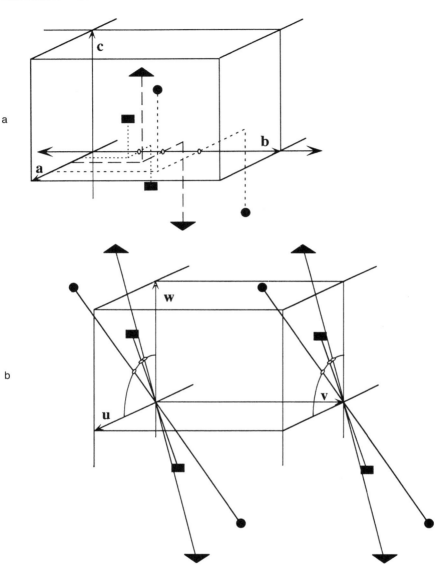

Figure 7.3. (a) A unit cell with a 2-fold axis along y; (b) the corresponding Patterson cell with Harker peaks in the $(u\ 0\ w)$ plane.

With $\rho(\mathbf{r}'' - \mathbf{u}) = \rho_{inv}(\mathbf{u} - \mathbf{r}'')$ where $\rho_{inv}(\mathbf{u} - \mathbf{r}'')$ is the electron density distribution of the inverse structure, (7.14) transforms into

$$P(\mathbf{u}) = \int_{\mathbf{r}''} \rho(\mathbf{r}'')\rho_{inv}(\mathbf{u} - \mathbf{r}'')\,dv \qquad (7.15)$$

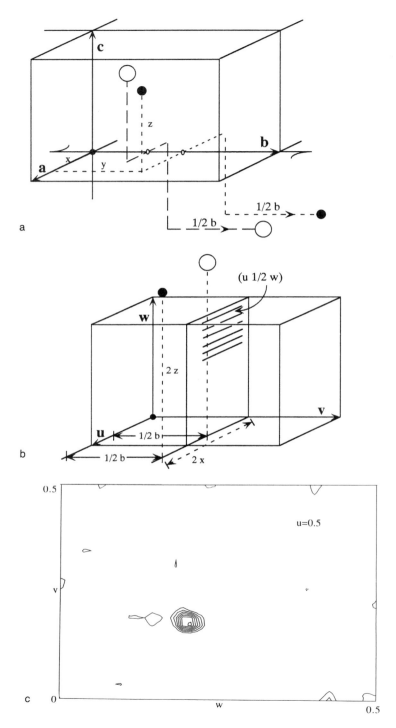

which is of the same form as (7.13) and this proves property 6.

A general property of the Fourier transform of a convolution is the following: If $F(h)$ is the transform of $f(\eta)$ in Eq. (7.13) and $G(h)$ is the transform of $g(\eta)$, then the product $F(h) G(h)$ is the Fourier transform of $C(x)$. Application to Eq. (7.15) gives the following: The product of the transform of $\rho(\mathbf{r}'')$ [which is $\mathbf{F(S)}$] and the transform of $\rho_{inv}(\mathbf{r}'')$ [which is $\mathbf{F}^*(\mathbf{S})$] is equal to the transform of $P(\mathbf{u})$ and, therefore, the transform of $P(\mathbf{u})$ is equal to $\mathbf{F(S)F}^*(\mathbf{S}) = |F(\mathbf{S})|^2$.

7. In locating Patterson peaks of heavy atoms in the isomorphous replacement method, it is useful to realize that the height of a peak is proportional to the product of the atomic numbers of the atoms that are responsible for the peak.

7.3. The Isomorphous Replacement Method

Application of the isomorphous replacement method requires the X-ray diffraction pattern of the native protein crystal as well as that of the crystal of at least one heavy atom derivative. For perfect isomorphism the conformation of the protein and the unit cell parameters in the native and in the derivative crystals must be exactly the same. The intensity differences between the native and the other patterns are then exclusively due to the attached heavy atoms. For an example see Figure 7.5. From these differences the positions of the heavy atoms can be derived and this is the starting point for the determination of the protein phase angles. Perfect isomorphism hardly ever occurs. Errors due to nonisomorphism are usually more serious than errors in the X-ray data. However, a modest change in the protein structure is not a great obstacle. Nonisomorphism often presents itself as a change in the cell dimensions. In a quick data collection one can determine whether the heavy atom has attached itself to the protein, by comparing the intensities of the reflections with those of the native crystal as well as whether this has seriously affected the cell dimensions and the quality of the diffraction pattern. A change in the cell dimensions of $d_{min}/4$, where d_{min} is the resolution limit, is tolerable. In principle nonisomorphism can occur without expressing itself in the cell dimensions, for instance, if a slight rotation of the protein molecules has occurred as a consequence of the

←————————————————————————————

Figure 7.4. (a) A unit cell with a 2-fold screw axis along y; (b) in the $(u\ 1/2\ w)$ plane of the corresponding Patterson cell a concentration of peaks is found; only two Harker peaks are indicated; (c) a realistic example showing the Harker section at $u = 0.5$ with $0 < v < 0.5$ and $0 < w < 0.5$. The high density peak indicates the end of the vector between the mercury atoms from a mercury-containing reagent attached to the protein hevamine. The crystals belong to space group $P2_12_12_1$. (Source: Anke Terwisscha van Scheltinga.)

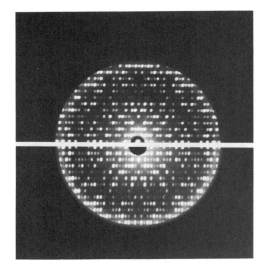

Figure 7.5. A comparison of the precession photographs of the same reciprocal lattice plane for a native papain crystal and a heavy atom derivative in which one mercury atom was attached to each protein molecule. Appreciable differences in intensity between corresponding diffraction spots can be seen.

heavy atom binding. This will later result in a poor refinement of the heavy atom parameters.

The isomorphous replacement method requires the following steps:

1. Preparation of at least one, but preferably a few heavy atom containing derivatives of the protein in the crystalline state. A first check for isomorphism is measuring the cell dimensions.
2. X-ray intensity data must be collected for crystals of the native protein as well as for crystals of the derivatives.
3. Application of the Patterson function for the determination of the heavy atom coordinates.
4. Refinement of the heavy atom parameters and calculation of the protein phase angles.
5. Calculation of the electron density of the protein.

7.3.1. The Attachment of Heavy Atoms

The search for heavy atom derivatives is still basically an empirical method and very often dozens of reagents are tried before a few suitable ones are found. The preferred method is by soaking the protein crystal in a solution of the reagent. The composition of this solution is identical to the mother liquor, except for the added reagent, often with a slight increase of precipitant concentration. Cocrystallization is not commonly used, because of the risk that crystals will not grow or grow nonisomorphously. However, for covalently attached reagents, cocrystallization is sometimes an advantage because of the better control over the stoichiometry and the ability to prevent excess binding.

The soaking procedure depends on the existence of relatively wide pores in the crystal, wide enough to allow the reagent to diffuse into the crystal and to reach the reactive sites on the surface of all protein molecules in the crystal. An extremely high excess of reagent is commonly used, as the following example shows.

Let the protein have a molecular weight of 40,000 and the crystal a size of $0.5 \times 0.5 \times 0.5 \, mm^3$. This crystal contains approximately 2 nmol of protein. If the crystal is soaked in 1 ml solution with a reagent concentration of 10 mM, the amount of reagent in the solution is 10^4 nmol, an enormous excess in molarity of reagent with respect to protein. However, the position of the equilibrium is not determined by the total amount of the reagent and the protein, but by the concentrations of the reagent and the protein, and the value of the equilibrium constant K. For the reaction: reagent + protein → derivative,

$$K = \frac{[\text{derivative}]}{[\text{reagent}] \times [\text{protein}]}$$

The crystallographer is interested in the occupancy of the binding site:

$$\text{occupancy} = \frac{[\text{derivative}]]}{[\text{derivative}] + [\text{protein}]} = \frac{K \times [\text{reagent}]}{\{K \times [\text{reagent}]\} + 1}$$

The occupancy depends only on $K \times$ [reagent] and is close to 100% for $K \times$ [reagent] $> 10^2$. If the binding is not very strong and the occupancy of the protein binding site does not reach 100%, it is tempting to increase the reagent concentration. However, then the danger exists that the reagent will react with more sites and the chances of nonisomorphism or even crystal degradation are high.

The soaking time varies between hours and months. The minimum time required to reach the equilibrium of the reaction is determined by a number of factors. The diffusion of the reagent through the pores in the crystal is the first important step, and depends on the relative size of the pores and the reagent. Second, a slight conformational change in the protein may be required for a snug fitting of the reagent into its binding site. Finally, there is the chemical reaction itself. Sometimes it is an advantage to use a short soaking time, for example, if the protein molecule presents a great many binding sites to the reagent. If some of them are slow binding sites and others are fast, then, if the crystal is soaked for a short time, only the fast binding sites will react and the chances of maintaining the quality of the crystal are higher. In some cases it is better to soak the crystal for a long time, for example, if the reagent or the protein changes while standing and a suitable reagent or a reactive site on the protein develops in the course of weeks or months. For instance, Pt compounds can gradually change their ligands. If K_2PtCl_4 is kept in an ammonium sulfate solution, $[PtCl_4]^{2-}$ can exchange Cl^- for NH_3 and $[Pt(NH_3)Cl_3]^-$ or $[Pt(NH_3)_2Cl_2]$ or even $[Pt(NH_3)_4]^{2+}$, which has an opposite charge, can be formed with a concomitant change in reactivity. Protein modification with time may be caused by a chemical reaction in the protein, such as deamidation of asparagine or glutamine residues, or oxidation of sulfhydryl groups. This changes the overall charge of the protein and may influence its affinity for charged reagents. The solution can also change slowly, for example, if an ammonium sulfate solution loses ammonia.

7.3.2. Site of Attachment of Heavy Atoms

Although the search for a suitable heavy atom reagent is an empirical process, one should employ all available chemical and biochemical properties of the protein. If the protein contains a free sulfhydryl group, it is obvious that mercury-containing compounds should be tried. Even if sulfhydryl groups are absent, mercurials still have a chance. Histidine residues are frequently found as ligands to heavy atoms, but the pH should not be too low because it is the neutral histidine side chain that acts as the ligand. The sulfur atom in methionine is a preferred binding site for platinum compounds.

For proteins containing Ca^{2+} or Mg^{2+} ions, an attempt should always be made to replace the metal ion by a heavier one, notably rare earth ions. If Ca^{2+} is replaced by Sm^{3+}, for example, only the difference in electrons between the two elements is added: 41 and not 59 electrons. But anomalous scattering helps because it is strong for these heavy ions (see Section 7.8). The radius of the ions is also important, because the cavity containing the metal ion is least disturbed if the diameter of the introduced metal ions is close to the diameter of Ca^{2+} or Mg^{2+} ions. In Table 7.1 one can see that Ba^{2+} and Pb^{2+} are much larger than Ca^{2+} and are not good replacements for Ca^{2+}. However, this does not mean that

Table 7.1. Radii of Some Ions with 6-Coordination

	Ca^{2+}	Mg^{2+}	Ba^{2+}	Pb^{2+}
Electrons	18	10	54	80
Radius (pm)	114	86	149	133

	La^{3+}	Pr^{3+}	Sm^{3+}	Eu^{3+}	Gd^{3+}	Dy^{3+}	Er^{3+}	Tm^{3+}	Yb^{3+}
Electrons	54	56	59	60	61	63	65	66	67
Radius (pm)	117	113	110	109	108	105	103	102	101

they can never replace Ca^{2+}, because the flexibility of the binding site also plays a role. Ca^{2+} can best be replaced by one of the first rare earth ions because their radius is close to that of Ca^{2+}. The radius becomes smaller for the higher elements. Sometimes heavy atom derivatives of a biological substrate or cofactor are used, but this is not frequently done.

The pH of the solution should not be neglected. It has already been mentioned that histidine is a better ligand at higher pH values. The pH is also important in the binding of charged reagents such as HgI_4^{2-}, $Au(CN)^{2-}$, $PtCl_6^{2-}$, etc. At higher pH values, where the protein has a higher negative charge, these reagents react less readily with the protein. This is an advantage if the reaction is too strong at lower pH values when too many sites react and nonisomorphism occurs. On the other hand, if these negative ions do not bind at all or bind only poorly, the pH should be lowered a little. This is of course possible only if the protein crystal permits this change. Heavy atom salts which are easily hydrolyzed, such as UO_2^{2+} or Sm^{3+} salts, cannot be used at an alkaline pH.

If the medium is a water–organic solvent mixture, electrostatic forces are stronger because of the lower dielectric constant and the binding of ionic compounds will be stronger. However, the organic solvent might be a chelating agent for the heavy ion; this is true for 2-methyl-2,4-pentanediol (MPD), a popular organic solvent in protein crystallization experiments.

7.3.3. Chemical Modification of the Native Protein

If straightforward soaking does not result in a useful complex, the situation is not completely hopeless. One may still try to modify the protein by covalently attaching a heavy atom containing reagent or a potential heavy atom binder, such as p-iodophenylisothiocyanate or p-iodophenyliso-cyanate. They react with the ε-NH_2 of lysine side chains to form a thiourea or urea derivative, at least at sufficiently high pH. Another chemical reaction is the iodination of tyrosine side chains. They can take up a maximum of three iodine atoms. Iodine has a reasonable number of electrons (53), but despite its successful use in a number of cases, it is not a very popular method. The reason is probably its tendency to react with other groups in the protein.

7.3.4. Genetic Modification of the Protein

Genetic engineering has opened up new areas for protein modification. For the preparation of heavy atom derivatives, it is sometimes useful to replace one of the amino acids by a cysteine (Tucker et al., 1989; Nagai et al., 1990). Of course this replacement helps only if the cysteine residue is not oxidized readily, which is a potential danger. Therefore, mutants should be treated with an antioxidant, such as dithiothreitol, before reaction with the mercury-containing compound (Nagai et al., 1991). The new cysteine residue should of course not disturb the protein structure, and should be accessible. This is difficult to predict beforehand. The best one can do is to replace a residue in a very polar region of the amino acid sequence, which hopefully is a loop at the surface of the molecule.

Another biological modification is to incorporate selenomethionine in place of methionine and solve the structure by the multiple wavelength anomalous diffraction (MAD) technique (see Section 9.5).

7.3.5. Problems Commonly Encountered in the Search for Heavy Atom Derivatives

7.3.5.1. Increased Radiation Damage

X-ray radiation damage is caused by radical formation and subsequent chemical reactions. This process can be slowed down by lowering the temperature of the crystal in the X-ray beam. Even a few degrees lower helps (a temperature of 5°C instead of room temperature, for example).

7.3.5.2. The Insolubility of Phosphates

Phosphate buffers are often used for protein crystallization and soaking. However, some heavy metal phosphates are insoluble, including those of the rare earths and of uranyl ions. In such cases the phosphate buffer should be replaced by a suitable buffer, usually an organic one.

7.3.5.3. Ammonium Sulfate

Ammonium sulfate is a very popular precipitating agent. However, it can prevent the binding of heavy metals in two ways. First, it is in equilibrium with ammonia. At somewhat higher pH values the ammonia concentration in the solution is appreciable and this can act as a ligand for the heavy ion, which might prevent binding to the protein. The solution of this problem is to replace the ammonium sulfate by another salt, such as Li- or Cs-sulfate or K- or Na-phosphate, or by polyethylene glycol (PEG). The other problem with ammonium sulfate is its high ionic strength. This weakens electrostatic interactions and in this way can prevent the binding of a heavy ion. The solution is to change from ammonium sulfate to PEG.

7.4. Effect of Heavy Atoms on X-ray Intensities

Can the attachment of one or a few heavy atoms to a large protein molecule sufficiently change the intensities of the reflections? Suppose we have a protein with a molecular weight of 42,000. Each of its molecules contains about 3000 nonhydrogen atoms or $3000 \times 7 = 21,000$ electrons. In this ocean of 21,000 electrons a mercury atom adds only 80 electrons and yet its attachment changes the intensities of the X-rays diffracted by the crystal of the protein in a measurable way. This seems impossible, but it is nevertheless true, as we shall see.

Crick and Magdoff (1956) estimated the expected intensity changes resulting from heavy atom attachment and arrived at the following result: For centric reflections they found that the relative root mean square intensity change is

$$\frac{\sqrt{\overline{(\Delta I)^2}}}{\overline{I_P}} = 2 \times \sqrt{\frac{\overline{I_H}}{\overline{I_P}}} \qquad (7.16)$$

and for acentric reflections

$$\frac{\sqrt{\overline{(\Delta I)^2}}}{\overline{I_P}} = \sqrt{2} \times \sqrt{\frac{\overline{I_H}}{\overline{I_P}}} \qquad (7.17)$$

where $\overline{I_H}$ is the average intensity of the reflections if the unit cell would contain the heavy atoms only and $\overline{I_P}$ is the average intensity of the reflections for the native protein (see the derivation below).

Crick and Magdoff's Estimation of X-ray Reflection Intensity Changes if Heavy Atoms Are Attached to the Protein

First, centric reflections will be considered. If the origin of the system is placed in the center of symmetry, they have their structure factors **F** pointing along the horizontal axis in the Argand diagram, to the right for phase angle $\alpha = 0'$ and to the left for $\alpha = 180'$. Therefore, **F** can be expressed as a real number, equal to its amplitude, with positive sign for $\alpha = 0'$ and negative sign for $\alpha = 180'$, since for $\alpha = 0'$

$$\mathbf{F} = |F| \exp[i\alpha] = |F| (\cos \alpha + i \sin \alpha) = +F$$

and for $\alpha = 180'$

$$\mathbf{F} = |F| \exp[i\alpha] = |F| (\cos \alpha - i \sin \alpha) = -F$$

In the following discussion, P stands for the native protein, PH for the heavy atom derivative, and H for the heavy atoms. For centric reflections (Figure 7.6):

$$I_{PH} = (F_P + F_H)^2$$

Note that F_P and F_H can be either positive or negative.

$$I_P = F_P^2$$

$$\Delta I = 2F_P F_H + F_H^2$$

$$(\Delta I)^2 = 4F_P^2 F_H^2 + 4F_P F_H^3 + F_H^4$$

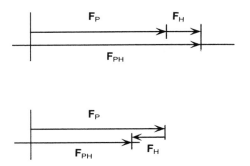

Figure 7.6. Structure factors in the isomorphous replacement method for centric reflections. $\mathbf{F}_P$ is for the protein, $\mathbf{F}_{PH}$ is for the derivative, and $\mathbf{F}_H$ is for the heavy atom contribution.

and the mean square change in intensity is

$$\overline{(\Delta I)^2} = 4\overline{F_P^2 F_H^2} + 4\overline{F_P F_H^3} + \overline{F_H^4}$$

Since F_P and F_H are not correlated, $\overline{F_P F_H^3} = 0$ and $\overline{F_P^2 F_H^2} = \overline{F_P^2} \times \overline{F_H^2}$.

$$\frac{\sqrt{\overline{(\Delta I)^2}}}{\overline{I_P}} = \frac{\sqrt{4\overline{F_P^2} \times \overline{F_H^2} + \overline{F_H^4}}}{\overline{F_P^2}}$$

$$= 2\sqrt{\frac{\overline{F_H^2}}{\overline{F_P^2}}} \sqrt{1 + \frac{\overline{F_H^4}}{4 \times \overline{F_P^2} \times \overline{F_H^2}}} \cong 2\sqrt{\frac{\overline{F_H^2}}{\overline{F_P^2}}} = 2\sqrt{\frac{\overline{I_H}}{\overline{I_P}}}$$

assuming that $\overline{F_H^4} \ll 4\overline{F_P^2} \times \overline{F_H^2}$. We shall now do the same for noncentric reflections (Figure 7.7):

$$\mathbf{F}_{PH} = \mathbf{F}_P + \mathbf{F}_H$$

$$I_{PH} = |\mathbf{F}_P + \mathbf{F}_H|^2 = |F_{PH}|^2 = |F_P|^2 + 2|F_P||F_H|\cos\alpha + |F_H|^2$$

$$\Delta I = 2|F_P||F_H|\cos\alpha + |F_H|^2$$

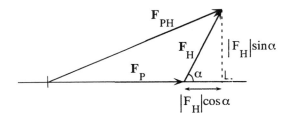

Figure 7.7. Structure factors in the isomorphous replacement method for non-centric reflections; the horizontal direction of $\mathbf{F}_P$ is arbitrary.

$$(\Delta I)^2 = 4|F_P|^2|F_H|^2 \cos^2 \alpha + 4|F_P||F_H|^3 \cos \alpha + |F_H|^4$$

$$\overline{(\Delta I)^2} = 2\overline{|F_P|^2|F_H|^2} + 4\overline{|F_P||F_H|^3 \cos \alpha} + \overline{|F_H|^4}$$

because $\overline{|F_P|}$ and $\overline{|F_H|}$ are not correlated and $\overline{\cos \alpha} = 0$:

$$\overline{(\Delta I)^2} = 2\overline{|F_P|^2} \times \overline{|F_H|^2} + 0 + \overline{|F_H|^4}$$

$$\frac{\sqrt{\overline{(\Delta I)^2}}}{I_P} = \sqrt{\frac{2\overline{|F_P|^2} \times \overline{|F_H|^2} + \overline{|F_H|^4}}{(\overline{|F_P|^2})^2}} = \sqrt{2} \times \sqrt{\frac{\overline{|F_H|^2}}{\overline{|F_P|^2}} + \frac{\overline{|F_H|^4}}{2(\overline{|F_P|^2})^2}}$$

$$= \sqrt{2} \times \sqrt{\frac{\overline{|F_H|^2}}{\overline{|F_P|^2}}} \times \sqrt{1 + \underbrace{\frac{\overline{|F_H|^4}}{2 \times \overline{|F_P|^2} \times \overline{|F_H|^2}}}_{\substack{\text{small with} \\ \text{respect to 1}}}}$$

$$\cong \sqrt{2} \times \sqrt{\frac{\overline{|F_H|^2}}{\overline{|F_P|^2}}} = \sqrt{2} \times \sqrt{\frac{\overline{I_H}}{\overline{I_P}}}$$

In Table 7.2 this result is used to calculate the size of the relative change in intensity that can be expected for the acentric reflections of a protein crystal, if one mercury atom is attached per protein molecule. $\bar{I}$ is obtained with the expression

$$\bar{I} = \sum_i f_i^2$$

(see Section 5.2) f_i is 80 for a mercury atom and on the average 7 for a typical protein atom. If we assume that the intensities can be determined

Table 7.2. Average Relative Change in Intensity for the Acentric Reflections of a Protein Crystal if One Mercury Atom is Attached per Protein Molecule[a]

Molecular Weight of the Protein	100% Occupancy	50% Occupancy
14,000	0.51	0.25
28,000	0.36	0.18
56,000	0.25	0.12
112,000	0.18	0.09
224,000	0.13	0.06
448,000	0.09	0.04

[a] The data are for $(\sin \theta)/\lambda = 0$. With increasing diffraction angle the relative contribution of Hg is somewhat higher because its atomic scattering falls off less rapidly than for the light elements.

with an accuracy of 10%, then the practical limit for $\sqrt{\overline{(\Delta I)^2/I_P}}$ is $0.10 \times \sqrt{2} = 0.14$ (the factor $\sqrt{2}$ stems from the fact that the intensity difference is the result of two measurements). From Table 7.2 we see that this corresponds to a maximum molecular weight of 200,000 for full occupancy by one mercury atom per protein molecule and 50,000 for half occupancy. The changes are of course larger if more than one heavy atom is bound per protein molecule but lower if the binding sites are not fully occupied. The conclusion is that the isomorphous replacement method can be applied successfully for the determination of a protein crystal structure, even for large protein molecules.

7.5. Determination of the Heavy Atom Parameters from Centrosymmetric Projections

In step 3 of the isomorphous replacement method the coordinates of the heavy atoms must be found. This is an easy procedure if the crystal has centrosymmetric projections, e.g., in space group $P2_12_12_1$, where the three projections along the axes of the unit cell are centrosymmetric because of the 2-fold screw axes. For centrosymmetric projections the vectorial summation (Figure 7.6)

$$\mathbf{F}_{PH} = \mathbf{F}_P + \mathbf{F}_H$$

is simplified to

$$|F_{PH}| = |F_P| \pm |F_H|$$
$$|F_H| = |F_{PH}| - |F_H|$$

or

$$|F_H| = |F_P| - |F_{PH}|$$

and

$$|F_H|^2 = (|F_{PH}| - |F_P|)^2$$

We have made the assumption that F_{PH} and F_P have the same sign, either both positive or both negative. With this assumption, the Patterson summation with the coefficients $(|F_{PH}| - |F_P|)^2$ will give a Patterson map of the heavy atom arrangement in the unit cell. For the majority of the reflections the assumption will be true, because in general F_H will be small compared with F_P and F_{PH}. If, however, F_P is small, F_{PH} could have the opposite sign and F_H would be $F_P + F_{PH}$. Fortunately this does not occur often enough to distort the Patterson map seriously.

To calculate $|F_H|$ the structure factor amplitudes $|F_{PH}|$ and $|F_P|$ should of course be put on the same scale. This can be done in an approximate way by applying the Wilson plot and putting the $|F_P|^2$ and $|F_{PH}|^2$ values on an absolute scale [Eq. (5.3)]. This gives the factors C_P and C_{PH} with B_P and B_{PH}. Alternatively, a relative Wilson plot is calculated:

$$\ln \frac{\overline{I_{PH}}}{\sum_i (f_i^0)^2 + (f_H)^2} - \ln \frac{\overline{I_P}}{\sum_i (f_i^0)^2} = \ln \frac{C_{PH}}{C_P} - 2(B_{PH} - B_P) \frac{\sin^2 \theta}{\lambda^2}$$

With the relative value C_{PH}/C_P and the difference between B_P and B_{PH}, $|F_{PH}|^2$ and $|F_P|^2$ can be put on the same scale. For the native protein $\sum_i (f_i^0)^2$ must be calculated for all protein atoms, but for the derivative an estimated heavy atom contribution $(f_H)^2$ should be added. In the subsequent process of refining the heavy atom parameters, the scale factor is refined together with the other parameters. Sometimes the (f_H) contribution to the structure factor $\mathbf{F}_{PH}$ is neglected and the $|F_P|$ and $|F_{PH}|$ values are put on the same scale by minimizing a least squares function E with respect to the relative scale factor (for the method of least squares, see Section 7.14):

$$E = \sum_h \frac{1}{\sigma_F^2} (k|F_{PH}| - |F_P|)^2 \qquad (7.18)$$

where σ_F^2 is the variance to be chosen for either the $|F_{PH}|$ or the $|F_P|$ values and the summation is over all reflections h. The minimization of E with respect to k gives

$$k = \frac{\sum_h \frac{1}{\sigma_F^2} |F_{PH}| \times |F_P|}{\sum_h \frac{1}{\sigma_F^2} |F_{PH}|^2} \qquad (7.19)$$

If the morphology of the crystal(s) used for collecting the native data set differs appreciably from the morphology of the derivative crystals, differences in absorption may affect the comparison of the two data sets. The isomorphous differences and $R_{deriv.}$ (see Appendix 2) appear larger than they really are. Therefore, it is always advisable to correct for absorption, such as by comparing and equalizing symmetry-related reflections within one data set.

It is sometimes observed that after scaling, as just described, reflections that should have the same intensity tend to be stronger in one region of reciprocal space than in another. This can be due to problems of an instrumental nature or to poor absorption correction. In those cases local scaling must be applied, in which reciprocal space is divided into blocks of $h k l$ with an individual scaling factor for each block (Matthews and Czerwinski, 1975).

If the Patterson map of a centrosymmetric projection can be interpreted, it gives two coordinates of the heavy atoms and with a second projection the third coordinate as well. With the positions of the heavy atoms known, the structure factors $\mathbf{F}_H$ can be calculated, including their sign (for centrosymmetric projections) or their phase angle (for acentric reflections). In principle one heavy atom derivative is sufficient to determine the signs of centrosymmetric protein reflections. For example, if $|F_{PH}| > |F_P|$ and the sign of F_H is +, then F_P will have a + sign. For a second heavy atom derivative it is not absolutely necessary to calculate a Patterson map, because the sign of the centric protein reflections in combination with the difference between $|F_P|$ and $|F_{PH}|$ of the second heavy atom derivative, gives the sign of F_H immediately. This allows the calculation of a Fourier summation, resulting in the projection of the heavy atom arrangement from which the coordinates can be obtained.

7.6. Parameters of Heavy Atoms Derived from Acentric Reflections

Not all space groups have centrosymmetric projections. The heavy atom positions can still be found in such cases. The two sets of known data are the amplitudes of the structure factors $\mathbf{F_P}$ and $\mathbf{F_{PH}}$. Their phase angles are not yet known. For each reflection there is a difference in length (Figure 7.8):

$$\Delta|F|_{iso} = |F_{PH}| - |F_P|$$

We will now see that the coordinates of the heavy atoms can generally be derived from a Patterson map calculated with $(\Delta|F|_{iso})^2$. The triangle ABC in Figure 7.8 expresses the vector sum: $\mathbf{F_{PH}} = \mathbf{F_P} + \mathbf{F_H}$. However, for the time being only the lengths of $\mathbf{F_{PH}}$ ($|F_{PH}|$) and that of $\mathbf{F_P}$ ($|F_P|$) are known, but not their directions. For $\mathbf{F_H}$ both the length and direction are unknown.

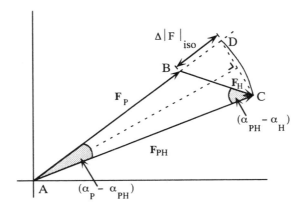

Figure 7.8. The structure factor triangle for isomorphous replacement: $\Delta|F|_{iso} = |F_{PH}| - |F_P|$.

Derivation of $\Delta|F|_{iso}$ (see Figure 7.8)

$$|F_P| = AB \quad \text{and} \quad |F_{PH}| = AC$$

$$\Delta|F|_{iso} = |F_{PH}| - |F_P| = AC - AB = AD - AB = BD$$

$$|F_H| = BC$$

The sin rule applied in triangle BCD gives

$$\frac{BD}{BC} = \frac{\sin \angle BCD}{\sin \angle BDC} \quad \text{or} \quad BD = BC \frac{\sin \angle BCD}{\sin \angle BDC}$$

$$\angle BCD = \angle ACD - \angle ACB = \left(90° - \frac{\alpha_P - \alpha_{PH}}{2}\right) - (\alpha_{PH} - \alpha_H)$$

$$= 90° - \tfrac{1}{2}(\alpha_P + \alpha_{PH}) + \alpha_H$$

$$\angle BDC = 90° - \tfrac{1}{2}(\alpha_P - \alpha_{PH})$$

$$\Delta|F|_{iso} = |F_H| \frac{\sin[90° - \tfrac{1}{2}(\alpha_P + \alpha_{PH}) + \alpha_H]}{\sin[90° - \tfrac{1}{2}(\alpha_P - \alpha_{PH})]}$$

$$= |F_H| \frac{\cos[\tfrac{1}{2}(\alpha_P + \alpha_{PH}) - \alpha_H]}{\cos[\tfrac{1}{2}(\alpha_P - \alpha_{PH})]}$$

For the numerator we can write

$$\cos[\tfrac{1}{2}(\alpha_P - \alpha_{PH}) + (\alpha_{PH} - \alpha_H)]$$
$$= \cos\tfrac{1}{2}(\alpha_P - \alpha_{PH}) \cos(\alpha_{PH} - \alpha_H) - \sin\tfrac{1}{2}(\alpha_P - \alpha_{PH}) \sin(\alpha_{PH} - \alpha_H)$$

The result is that

$$\Delta|F|_{iso} = |F_H| \cos(\alpha_{PH} - \alpha_H) - |F_H| \sin(\alpha_{PH} - \alpha_H) \tan\tfrac{1}{2}(\alpha_P - \alpha_{PH})$$

The following expression for $\Delta|F|_{iso}$ is obtained (see above):

$$\Delta|F|_{iso} = |F_H| \cos(\alpha_{PH} - \alpha_H) - |F_H| \sin(\alpha_{PH} - \alpha_H) \tan\tfrac{1}{2}(\alpha_P - \alpha_{PH})$$

In general $\alpha_P - \alpha_{PH}$ is small, because for most reflections $|F_H| \ll |F_P|$ and $|F_{PH}|$. Therefore, we can safely neglect $|F_H| \sin(\alpha_{PH} - \alpha_H) \tan\tfrac{1}{2}(\alpha_P - \alpha_{PH})$ and obtain

$$\Delta|F|_{iso} = |F_H| \cos(\alpha_{PH} - \alpha_H) \tag{7.20}$$

The result is that a Patterson summation with $(\Delta|F|_{iso})^2$ as the coefficients will in fact be a Patterson summation with coefficients $|F_H|^2 \cos^2(\alpha_{PH} - \alpha_H)$. Since

$$\cos^2(\alpha_{PH} - \alpha_H) = \tfrac{1}{2} + \tfrac{1}{2} \cos 2(\alpha_{PH} - \alpha_H)$$

we obtain

$$|F_H|^2 \cos^2(\alpha_{PH} - \alpha_H) = \tfrac{1}{2}|F_H|^2 + \tfrac{1}{2}|F_H|^2 \cos 2(\alpha_{PH} - \alpha_H)$$

Bec   ~~l~ted the second term on the
rigl   first
ter
on

tw   * Don't send before March 1
It   *   Reprints
n   *   ? nibble off ends
d   ? Protein type
F

If the difference
heavy atom positions, one can try to apply
for phase determination, as they are developed for the X-ray structure
determination of small molecules, because the problem is very similar: for
only a relatively small number of sites in the unit cell, the parameters
must be found.

We are now able to find the parameters of the attached heavy atoms in
the crystal structure. We will discuss how a common origin for the
coordinates of the heavy atoms from different derivatives can be found
and how the heavy atom parameters can be refined. Subsequently the
protein phase angles will be calculated. But before doing so we will
discuss another extremely useful Fourier summation: "the difference
Fourier." We shall also introduce so-called "anomalous scattering,"
because this can contribute to localization of the heavy atoms.

7.7. The Difference Fourier Summation

With this summation we can find the position of reagents attached to
protein molecules in the crystal, either heavy atoms or other reagents,
such as enzyme inhibitors. However, it is necessary that we know protein
phase angles $\alpha_P(h\ k\ l)$!

$$\Delta\rho(x\ y\ z) = \frac{1}{V}\sum_{hkl}\Delta|F(h\ k\ l)|_{iso} \exp[-2\pi i(hx + ky + lz) + i\alpha_P(h\ k\ l)]$$

$$= \frac{1}{V}\sum_{hkl}\Delta|F(h\ k\ l)|_{iso} \cos[2\pi(hx + ky + lz) - \alpha_P(h\ k\ l)]$$

Written more compactly:

$$\Delta\rho(\mathbf{r}) = \frac{1}{V}\sum_{\mathbf{h}}\Delta|F(\mathbf{h})|_{\text{iso}}\exp[-2\pi i\mathbf{h}\cdot\mathbf{r} + i\alpha_P(\mathbf{h})] \qquad (7.22)$$

Thus a difference Fourier summation is calculated with the coefficients $\Delta|F|_{\text{iso}}$ and the phase angles α_P of the protein. Now we shall see what this leads to. Suppose the structure factors of the attached reagent are the still unknown vectors $\mathbf{F_H}$. In Section 7.6 we derived that

$$\Delta|F|_{\text{iso}} \approx |F_H|\cos(\alpha_{PH} - \alpha_H) \qquad (7.20)$$

Because $\exp[i\alpha] = \cos\alpha + i\sin\alpha$ and $\exp[-i\alpha] = \cos\alpha - i\sin\alpha$,

$$\Delta|F|_{\text{iso}} \approx \tfrac{1}{2}|F_H|\{\exp[i(\alpha_{PH} - \alpha_H)] + \exp[-i(\alpha_{PH} - \alpha_H)]\}$$

and

$$\Delta|F|_{\text{iso}}\exp[i\alpha_P] \approx \tfrac{1}{2}|F_H|\{\exp[i(\alpha_{PH} - \alpha_H)] \times \exp[i\alpha_P]$$
$$+ \exp[-i(\alpha_{PH} - \alpha_H)] \times \exp[i\alpha_P]\}$$

For $|F_H|\exp[i\alpha_H]$ we can write $\mathbf{F_H}$, and for $|F_H|\exp[-i\alpha_H]$ we write $\mathbf{F_H^*}$.

$$\Delta|F|_{\text{iso}}\exp[i\alpha_P] = \tfrac{1}{2}\mathbf{F_H}\exp[-i\alpha_{PH}] \times \exp[i\alpha_P]$$
$$+ \tfrac{1}{2}\mathbf{F_H^*}\exp[i\alpha_{PH}] \times \exp[i\alpha_P]$$

Since $\alpha_P \cong \alpha_{PH}$,

$$\Delta|F|_{\text{iso}}\exp[i\alpha_P] = \tfrac{1}{2}\mathbf{F_H} + \tfrac{1}{2}\mathbf{F_H^*}\exp[2i\alpha_P]$$

The term $\tfrac{1}{2}\mathbf{F_H^*}\exp[2i\alpha_P]$ will give noise in the Fourier map, because the vectors $\mathbf{F_H^*}$ and $\exp[2i\alpha_P]$ are not correlated in their direction in the Argand diagram. Therefore,

$$\Delta|F|_{\text{iso}}\exp[i\alpha_P] \approx \tfrac{1}{2}\mathbf{F_H}$$

If this result is combined with Eq. (7.22) then

$$\Delta\rho(\mathbf{r}) = \frac{1}{V}\sum_{h}\frac{1}{2}\mathbf{F_H}\exp[-2\pi i\mathbf{h}\cdot\mathbf{r}]$$

$$= \frac{1}{2}\frac{1}{V}\sum_{h}|F_H(\mathbf{h})|\exp[-2\pi i\mathbf{h}\cdot\mathbf{r} + i\alpha_H] \qquad (7.23)$$

Conclusion: A difference Fourier map shows positive electron density at the site of attached atoms and negative density at the positions of removed atoms. The height of the peaks is only half of what it would be in a normal Fourier map. With a difference Fourier map even small changes in the electron density can be observed, such as the attachment or removal of a water molecule. It is a powerful method, even if only preliminary values for the protein phase angles are known. For example, after the main heavy atom site has been found from a difference Patterson map additional weakly occupied sites can be detected with a difference Fourier map.

An improved difference Fourier map can be calculated if anomalous scattering data are incorporated in the calculation of the protein phase angles, which will be discussed in Chapter 9. Another useful Fourier summation has as coefficients $2|F_{PH}| - |F_P|$ and as phase angles the protein phase angles α_P:

$$\rho(\mathbf{r}) = \frac{1}{V}\sum_h (2|F_{PH}| - |F_P|) \exp[-2\pi i \mathbf{r} \cdot \mathbf{h} + i\alpha_P] \qquad (7.24)$$

The coefficients can be written as

$$2|F_{PH}| - |F_P| = 2(|F_{PH}| - |F_P|) + |F_P| = 2\Delta|F|_{iso} + |F_P|$$

Thus this electron density map wil give the native protein structure and, apart from noise, the electron density of the attached atoms but now at full and not half height.

Structural information in electron density maps is determined to a greater extent by the phase angles than by the Fourier coefficients. Therefore, the electron density maps calculated with native protein phase angles are biased toward the native protein. Read (1986) showed that the bias can be minimized if the electron density is calculated with protein phase angles α_P and as coefficients $2m|F_{PH}| - D|F_P|$, where m is the figure of merit (Section 7.15) and D is a multiplier equal to the Fourier transform of the probability distribution of $\overline{\Delta r}$, the mean error in the atomic positions (see Section 15.6).

The difference Fourier should not be mistaken for the residual Fourier, which can be calculated after the structure determination is almost complete. Its coefficients are $(|F_{PH}| - |F_P + F_H|)$. The values of $|F_{PH}|$ are the amplitudes measured for the derivative; F_P and F_H are the structure factors calculated for the present protein and heavy atom models.

$$\text{Res. Fourier} = \frac{1}{V}\sum_h (|F_{PH}| - |F_P + F_H|) \exp[-2\pi i \mathbf{h} \cdot \mathbf{r} + i\alpha_{PH}] \quad (7.25)$$

The phase angles α_{PH} are calculated for the present model of the derivative. $|F_{PH}| \exp[i\alpha_{PH}]$ represents the actual structure as far as its amplitude is concerned, but its phase corresponds with the present model of the structure. If the difference between the actual structure and the model is not too large, the residual Fourier can be shown to give this difference on half the scale. The map can be used in the search for undetected heavy atom sites.

7.8. Anomalous Scattering

If the absorption by an element, such as copper is plotted as a function of the X-ray wavelength λ, a typical curve is obtained (Figure 7.9). The sharp change in the curve is called an absorption edge. It is caused by photon absorption: an electron is ejected from an atom by the photon energy of the X-ray beam. For copper the K-absorption edge is at $\lambda = 1.380\,\text{Å}$. At this wavelength an electron is ejected from the K-shell to a state in the continuous energy region. Copper emits at its characteristic wavelength of $K_\alpha = 1.5418\,\text{Å}$, somewhat above the K-absorption edge, because now the electron falls back from the L-shell into the K-shell and this is a smaller energy difference. (See Fig. 4.32 for the abs. coeff. of carbon)

So far we have always regarded the electrons in an atom as free electrons. However, this is no longer true if the X-ray wavelength approaches an absorption edge wavelength. From radiation physics it is known that for a free electron the scattered beam differs exactly by 180° in phase from the incident beam. However, the inner electrons in an electron cloud around an atomic nucleus are tightly attached to the nucleus, more than the outer electrons. This is especially true for the heavy elements, which have a high nuclear charge. For these inner shell electrons the diffracted beam does not differ 180° in phase angle from the incident beam. The situation is drawn in Figure 7.10. The atomic scattering

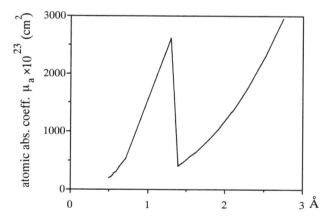

Figure 7.9. The atomic absorption coefficient for copper. The K-absorption edge is at $1.380\,\text{Å}$. The atomic absorption coefficient or "atomic cross-section" for absorption, μ_a (cm^2), is defined by $\mu_a = (\mu/\rho) \times (A/N)$, where μ/ρ is the mass absorption coefficient (cm^2/g), ρ is the density of the absorber, A is its atomic weight, and N is Avogadro's number. μ (cm^{-1}) is the total linear absorption coefficient defined by $I = I_0 \exp[-\mu t]$ with t the thickness of the material in cm, I_0 the intensity of the incident and I the intensity of the transmitted beam.

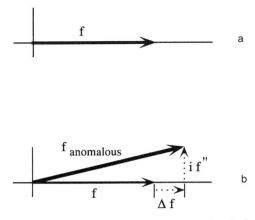

Figure 7.10. The atomic scattering factor for a completely free electron (a) and for a bound electron (b). The anomalous contribution consists of two parts: a real part Δf and an imaginary part if''.

factor for a completely free electron is drawn in Figure 7.10a and for a bound electron in Figure 7.10b; its scattering is anomalous and can be written as

$$f_{anom.} = f + \Delta f + if'' = f' + if''$$

Δf is the change in the electron scattering factor along the horizontal axis in the Argand diagram and if'' along the vertical axis (remember that i indicates a counterclockwise rotation of 90° (Section 4.2). For higher scattering angles the anomalous scattering becomes relatively more important. The reason is that it is nearly constant as a function of $(\sin\theta)/\lambda$, because it stems mainly from the inner electrons (Table 7.3). The effect of anomalous scattering is that in the Argand diagram the atomic scattering vector is rotated counterclockwise. As a consequence the structure factors $\mathbf{F}_{PH}(h\ k\ l)$ and $\mathbf{F}_{PH}(\bar{h}\ \bar{k}\ \bar{l})$ for the heavy atom derivative of the protein are no longer equal in length and have a different phase

Table 7.3. The Anomalous Scattering in Electrons of Hg for Copper Radiation

	$\sin\theta/\lambda$		
	0 $(\infty)^a$	0.4 (Å^{-1}) (1.25 Å)^a	0.6 (Å^{-1}) (0.83 Å)^a
f	80	53	42
Δf	−5	−5	−5
f''	8	8	8

^{a} Corresponding lattice spacing.

angle (Figure 7.11). This difference can be used separately or in combination with the isomorphous replacement method in the search for the heavy atom positions. We define:

$$\Delta |F|_{ano} = \{|F_{PH}(+)| - |F_{PH}(-)|\}\frac{f'}{2f''} \qquad (7.26)$$

$|F_{PH}(+)|$ represents the amplitude of the structure factor for a reflection $(h\ k\ l)$, and $|F_{PH}(-)|$ is the amplitude for the reflection $(\bar{h}\ \bar{k}\ \bar{l}) \equiv (-h, -k, -l)$. $\Delta |F|_{ano}$ is the difference between the amplitudes of the structure factor for the reflections $h\,k\,l$ and $\bar{h}\,\bar{k}\,\bar{l}$ (Bijvoet or Friedel pairs), scaled up with the factor $f'/2f''$.

From the anomalous Patterson map, calculated with $(\Delta |F|_{ano})^2$, the location of anomalous scatterers can be derived. These anomalous scatterers can be either extra heavy atoms attached to the protein or heavy atoms such as copper, iron, or even sulfur that are already present in the native protein structure. The anomalous scattering by sulfur atoms is relatively weak and it can be used only with rather small protein molecules. If the sulfur in the protein can be replaced by selenium the situation is more favorable (see Table 7.4) and even more favorable if a wavelength close to the K-absorption edge of Se (0.98 Å) is chosen. This replacement of sulfur by selenium can be done biologically by incorporation of selenomethionine instead of methionine.

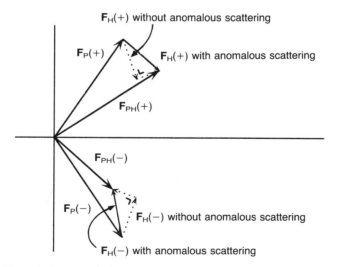

Figure 7.11. $\mathbf{F}_P(+)$ and $\mathbf{F}_P(-)$ are symmetric with respect to the horizontal axis in the Argand diagram, assuming the absence of anomalous scatterers in the protein. Without anomalous scattering, $\mathbf{F}_H(+)$ and $\mathbf{F}_H(-)$ are also symmetric. The imaginary part of the anomalous scattering contribution has been exaggerated. In this example $|F_{PH}(+)| > |F_{PH}(-)|$.

Table 7.4. The Anomalous Scattering in Electrons for
CuK_α Radiation by Mercury, Sulfur, and Selenium for
$\sin \theta/\lambda = 0^a$

	f	Δf	f''
Hg	80	−5.0	7.7
S	16	0.3	0.6
Se	34	−0.9	1.1

^{a} It is assumed that the anomalous scattering is isotropic. This
is not true if the wavelength is close to an absorption edge
corresponding to an electron ejection to an upper state
with nonspherical symmetry; for a detailed discussion see
Templeton and Templeton (1991).

In Sections 9.2 and 9.3 we shall see how information from anomalous
scattering can help in the determination of the protein phase angles if
only one wavelength is used. In Section 9.5 protein phase angles are
derived from multiple wavelength anomalous dispersion. In the next
sections it will be shown that

1. $(\Delta|F|_{ano})^2$ as the coefficients in a Patterson summation will result in a
   Patterson map of the anomalous scatterers (the heavy atoms).
2. $(\Delta|F|_{iso})^2 + (\Delta|F|_{ano})^2$ as coefficients will give the same Patterson map,
   but with less noise in the background than for separate Patterson
   maps.
3. The position of heavy atoms in different derivatives can be found with
   respect to one and the same origin by calculating correlation functions
   containing $\Delta|F|_{iso}$ and $\Delta|F|_{ano}$.

Moreover, as will be shown in Section 9.4, the absolute configuration of
the protein can be determined with $\Delta|F|_{ano}$.

If the protein crystal contains anomalous scatterers it is essential to
differentiate between the reflections $(+h, +k, +l)$ and $(-h, -k, -l)$.
This can be done by applying the following rules:

1. Choose the unit cell angles α, β, and γ between the positive axes ($\mathbf{a}$, $\mathbf{b}$,
   and $\mathbf{c}$) $\geqslant 90°$.
2. Use a right-handed coordinate system (see, for example, Figure 3.3).

As a result, the set of axes is always chosen in the same way with respect
to the content of the unit cell for all crystals of the protein or protein
derivative.

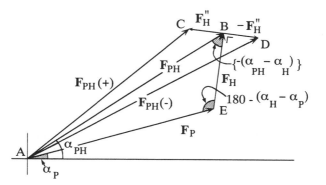

Figure 7.12. In this drawing the structure factors $\mathbf{F_P}(-)$, $\mathbf{F_{PH}}(-)$, $\mathbf{F_H}(-)$, and $\mathbf{F''_H}(-)$ have been reflected with respect to the horizontal axis and combined with the structure factors for the reflection $(h\,k\,l)$. Note that α_H is the phase angle for the nonanomalous part of $\mathbf{F_H}$.

7.9. The Anomalous Patterson Summation

The heavy atom contribution to the structure factor consists of a normal part, $\mathbf{F_H}$, and an anomalous part, $\mathbf{F''_H}$. In Figure 7.12 this is drawn for a reflection $(h\,k\,l)$ and for $(\bar{h}\,\bar{k}\,\bar{l})$. However, for convenience, the structure factors for $(\bar{h}\,\bar{k}\,\bar{l})$ have been reflected with respect to the horizontal axis. It can be derived that a Patterson summation with the coefficients $(\Delta|F|_{ano})^2$ can be approximated by a summation with the coefficients $|F_H|^2 \sin^2(\alpha_{PH} - \alpha_H) = \frac{1}{2}|F_H|^2 - \frac{1}{2}|F_H|^2 \cos 2(\alpha_{PH} - \alpha_H)$. This will give a Patterson map of the anomalous scatterers (the heavy atoms) (see below).

The Patterson Summation with the Coefficients $(\Delta|F|_{ano})^2$

To simplify the derivation, the structure factors $\mathbf{F_P}(-)$, $\mathbf{F_{PH}}(-)$, $\mathbf{F_H}(-)$, and $\mathbf{F''_H}(-)$ have been reflected with repect to the horizontal axis in the Argand diagam and combined with the structure factors for the reflection $h\,k\,l$. The structure factors $\mathbf{F_{PH}}(+)$ and $\mathbf{F_{PH}}(-)$ have the imaginary part of the anomalous scattering included and $\mathbf{F_{PH}}$ has it excluded. The application of the cos rule in triangle ABC gives

$$|F_{PH}(+)|^2 = |F_{PH}|^2 + |F''_H|^2 - 2|F''_H| \times |F_{PH}| \cos\{90° + (\alpha_{PH} - \alpha_H)\}$$
$$= |F_{PH}|^2 + |F''_H|^2 + 2|F''_H| \times |F_{PH}| \sin(\alpha_{PH} - \alpha_H)$$

and in triangle ABD

$$|F_{PH}(-)|^2 = |F_{PH}|^2 + |F''_H|^2 - 2|F''_H| \times |F_{PH}| \cos\{90° - (\alpha_{PH} - \alpha_H)\}$$
$$= |F_{PH}|^2 + |F''_H|^2 - 2|F''_H| \times |F_{PH}| \sin(\alpha_{PH} - \alpha_H)$$
$$|F_{PH}(+)|^2 - |F_{PH}(-)|^2 = 4|F''_H| \times |F_{PH}| \sin(\alpha_{PH} - \alpha_H)$$

but

$$|F_{PH}(+)|^2 - |F_{PH}(-)|^2 = (|F_{PH}(+)| + |F_{PH}(-)|) \times (|F_{PH}(+)| - |F_{PH}(-)|)$$
$$\cong 2|F_{PH}| \times (|F_{PH}(+)| - |F_{PH}(-)|)$$

and it follows that

$$|F_{PH}(+)| - |F_{PH}(-)| = 2|F''_H| \sin(\alpha_{PH} - \alpha_H) \qquad (7.27)$$

The scattering factor of a heavy atom j is $f_j = f'_j + if''_j$. Assuming that the proportion f''_j/f'_j is the same for all heavy atoms in the structure:

$$|\mathbf{F}''_H| = \left|\sum_j f''_j \exp[2\pi i \mathbf{h} \cdot \mathbf{r}_j]\right| = \left|\sum \frac{f''_j}{f'_j} \times f'_j \exp[2\pi i \mathbf{h} \cdot \mathbf{r}_j]\right|$$

$$= \frac{f''_j}{f'_j} \times \left|\sum_j f'_j \exp[2\pi i \mathbf{h} \cdot \mathbf{r}_j]\right| = \frac{f''}{f'} \times |F_H|$$

$$|F_{PH}(+)| - |F_{PH}(-)| = \frac{2f''}{f'}|F_H| \sin(\alpha_{PH} - \alpha_H) \qquad (7.28)$$

or

$$\Delta|F|_{ano} = |F_H| \sin(\alpha_{PH} - \alpha_H) \qquad (7.29)$$
$$(\Delta|F|_{ano})^2 = |F_H|^2 \sin^2(\alpha_{PH} - \alpha_H)$$
$$= \tfrac{1}{2}|F_H|^2 - \tfrac{1}{2}|F_H|^2 \cos 2(\alpha_{PH} - \alpha_H)$$

As in the derivation of the $(\Delta|F|_{iso})^2$ Patterson, we obtain two terms. The second term leads to noise in the Patterson map and the first one leads to the Patterson peaks of the heavy atoms.

It is interesting to compare the coefficients for the isomorphous and the anomalous Patterson:

$$(\Delta|F|_{iso})^2 = |F_H|^2 \cos^2(\alpha_{PH} - \alpha_H)$$
$$\frac{(\Delta|F|_{ano})^2 = |F_H|^2 \sin^2(\alpha_{PH} - \alpha_H)}{(\Delta|F|_{iso})^2 + (\Delta|F|_{ano})^2 = |F_H|^2}$$

It is clear that a Patterson summation calculated with the coefficients

$$(\Delta|F|_{iso})^2 + (\Delta|F|_{ano})^2$$

will give, within the framework of the approximations made, an exact Patterson map of the heavy atoms, or at least a map with lower noise than the isomorphous or anomalous Patterson summation themselves.

7.10. The Matthews Patterson Summation

In the previous paragraphs we have derived that a $|F_H|^2$ Patterson summation can be simulated by a $(\Delta|F|_{iso})^2$ or a $(\Delta|F|_{ano})^2$ Patterson summation or by a combination of the two. In an alternative method, developed by Matthews (1966), $|F_H|^2$ is expressed directly as a function of $|F_P|$, $|F_{PH}|$, $|F_{PH}(+)|$, and $|F_{PH}(-)|$; $|F_{PH}|$ can be taken as the mean value of $|F_{PH}(+)|$ and $|F_{PH}(-)|$. Matthews derived (see below)

$$|F_H|^2 = |F_P|^2 + |F_{PH}|^2$$

$$- 2|F_P| \times |F_{PH}| \left\{ 1 - \left[\frac{(f'/f'')(|F_{PH}(+)| - |F_{PH}(-)|)}{2|F_P|} \right]^2 \right\}^{1/2} \quad (7.30)$$

Derivation of the Matthews Patterson Summation

We start from Eq. (7.28) and apply the sin rule in triangle $A\,B\,E$ in Figure 7.12:

$$\frac{|F_H|}{\sin(\alpha_{PH} - \alpha_P)} = \frac{|F_P|}{\sin - (\alpha_{PH} - \alpha_H)}$$

Combining this with Eq. (7.28)

$$|F_{PH}(+)| - |F_{PH}(-)| = -\frac{2f''}{f'} \times |F_P| \sin(\alpha_{PH} - \alpha_P)$$

or

$$\sin(\alpha_{PH} - \alpha_P) = \frac{(f'/f'')(|F_{PH}(+)| - |F_{PH}(-)|)}{2|F_P|}$$

$$\cos(\alpha_{PH} - \alpha_P) = \pm \left\{ 1 - \left[\frac{(f'/f'')(|F_{PH}(+)| - |F_{PH}(-)|)}{2|F_P|} \right]^2 \right\}^{1/2}$$

Application of the cos rule in triangle $A\,B\,E$ gives

$$|F_H|^2 = |F_P|^2 + |F_{PH}|^2 - 2|F_P| \times |F_{PH}| \cos(\alpha_{PH} - \alpha_P)$$

Because $|\alpha_{PH} - \alpha_P|$ will in general be smaller than $90°$, $\cos(\alpha_{PH} - \alpha_P) > 0$ and

$$|F_H|^2 = |F_P|^2 + |F_{PH}|^2$$

$$-2|F_P| \times |F_{PH}| \left\{ 1 - \left[\frac{(f'/f'')(|F_{PH}(+)| - |F_{PH}(-)|)}{2|F_P|} \right]^2 \right\}^{1/2}$$

[for $\cos(\alpha_{PH} - \alpha_P) < 0$ the minus sign $(2|F_P| \times |F_{PH}| \{...\})$ would become a plus sign]. In this way $|F_H|^2$ is expressed exclusively in the known amplitudes: $|F_P|$, $|F_{PH}|$, $|F_{PH}(+)|$, and $|F_{PH}(-)|$.

A Patterson summation can now be calculated that includes information from the anomalous scattering. It can easily be shown that this result is related to calculating a Patterson summation with coefficients

$$(\Delta|F|_{\text{iso}})^2 + (\Delta|F|_{\text{ano}})^2$$

Equation (7.30) can be somewhat simplified because for most reflections: $(f'/f'')(|F_{\text{PH}}(+)| - |F_{\text{PH}}(-)|) < 2|F_{\text{P}}|$, and since $\sqrt{1 - A^2} \approx 1 - \frac{1}{2}A^2$ for small A,

$$|F_{\text{H}}|^2 \approx |F_{\text{P}}|^2 + |F_{\text{PH}}|^2 - 2|F_{\text{P}}| \times |F_{\text{PH}}|$$

$$+ |F_{\text{P}}| \times |F_{\text{PH}}| \left\{ \frac{(f'/f'')(|F_{\text{PH}}(+)| - |F_{\text{PH}}(-)|)}{2|F_{\text{P}}|} \right\}^2$$

$$= (|F_{\text{P}}| - |F_{\text{PH}}|)^2$$

$$+ |F_{\text{P}}| \times |F_{\text{PH}}| \left\{ \frac{(f'/f'')(|F_{\text{PH}}(+)| - |F_{\text{PH}}(-)|)}{2|F_{\text{P}}|} \right\}^2$$

$$= (\Delta|F_{\text{iso}}|)^2$$

$$+ |F_{\text{P}}| \times |F_{\text{PH}}| \left\{ \frac{(f'/f'')(|F_{\text{PH}}(+)| - |F_{\text{PH}}(-)|)}{2|F_{\text{P}}|} \right\}^2$$

The second term on the right contains information from the anomalous scattering. If we introduce the approximation $|F_{\text{P}}| = |F_{\text{PH}}|$ in this second term, we obtain

$$|F_{\text{H}}|^2 = (\Delta|F|_{\text{iso}})^2 + \left\{ \frac{f'}{2f''} (|F_{\text{PH}}(+)| - |F_{\text{PH}}(-)|) \right\}^2$$

$$= (\Delta|F|_{\text{iso}})^2 + (\Delta|F|_{\text{ano}})^2 \tag{7.31}$$

In the Patterson summation calculated with the coefficients from Eq. (7.30) equal weight is given to the contribution from the isomorphous difference, $(\Delta|F|_{\text{iso}})^2$, and from the anomalous difference,

$$\{(f'/2f'') (|F_{\text{PH}}(+)| - |F_{\text{PH}}(-)|)\}^2$$

$|F_{\text{PH}}| - |F_{\text{P}}|$ will in general be much larger than $|F_{\text{PH}}(+)| - |F_{\text{PH}}(-)|$. Their accuracy in absolute terms will be the same, but the errors in $|F_{\text{PH}}(+)| - |F_{\text{PH}}(-)|$ are upgraded with the factor $f'/2f''$ and this would cause an undesirably large influence of the error in $|F_{\text{PH}}(+)| - |F_{\text{PH}}(-)|$.

Therefore, the anomalous part in Eq. (7.30) should be scaled down by a weighting factor w for which 0.75 is a reasonable value:

$$|F_{\text{H}}|^2 \approx |F_{\text{P}}|^2 + |F_{\text{PH}}|^2 - 2|F_{\text{P}}| \times |F_{\text{PH}}|$$

$$\times \left\{ 1 - \left[\frac{w(f'/f'')(|F_{\text{PH}}(+)| - |F_{\text{PH}}(-)|)}{2|F_{\text{P}}|} \right]^2 \right\}^{1/2} \tag{7.32}$$

The errors in $|F_{\text{PH}}(+)|$ and $|F_{\text{PH}}(-)|$ are relatively large compared with their difference $|F_{\text{PH}}(+)| - |F_{\text{PH}}(-)|$. It seems surprising that w is not smaller than 0.75. However, it should be pointed out that although the anomalous differences are relatively small, they are much less influenced by nonisomorphism, by poor scaling of native and derivative data, and by absorption than the isomorphous differences. For some attached groups of heavy atoms, such as $(PtCl_4)^{2-}$, a theoretical value for f'/f'' cannot easily be determined. This problem was solved by Matthews who derived the expression for an empirical value of f'/f'' in the following way.

We start with Eq. (7.28) and write k for f'/f'':

$$k^{-1}|F_H| \sin(\alpha_{PH} - \alpha_P) = \tfrac{1}{2}\{|F_{PH}(+)| - |F_{PH}(-)|\}$$

$$k^{-1}|F_H| \, |\sin(\alpha_{PH} - \alpha_P)| = \tfrac{1}{2}|\{|F_{PH}(+)| - |F_{PH}(-)|\}|$$

Taking the average on both sides and realizing that the average value for $|\sin(\alpha_{PH} - \alpha_P)|$ over all possible angles $(\alpha_{PH} - \alpha_P)$, or over a great many reflections, is $2/\pi$:

$$k^{-1}\overline{|F_H|} \times \frac{2}{\pi} = \frac{1}{2}\overline{|\{|F_{PH}(+)| - |F_{PH}(-)|\}|}$$

$\overline{|F_H|}$ must be substituted by known parameters. This can be done with Eq. (7.20):

$$\Delta|F|_{iso} = |F_{PH}| - |F_P| = |F_H| \cos(\alpha_{PH} - \alpha_H)$$

$$|\{|F_{PH}| - |F_P|\}| = |F_H| \, |\cos(\alpha_{PH} - \alpha_H)|$$

If this is averaged we obtain

$$|F_H| \times \frac{2}{\pi} = \overline{|\{|F_{PH}| - |F_P|\}|}$$

It follows that

$$k_{emp} = 2 \frac{\overline{|\{|F_{PH}| - |F_P|\}|}}{\overline{|\{|F_{PH}(+)| - |F_{PH}(-)|\}|}}$$

The average value must be determined in shells of resolution and k_{emp} is then obtained as a function of $(\sin \theta)/\lambda$.

7.11. One Common Origin for all Derivatives

If a number of heavy atom derivatives have been used for the phase determination, the position of the heavy atoms in all derivatives should be determined with respect to the same origin. In some space groups it is not a serious problem to find a common origin because crystal symmetry limits the choice of origin. An example is given in Figure 7.13. The origin can be chosen in the positions I, II, III, or IV at $z = 1/4$ or $3/4$. The

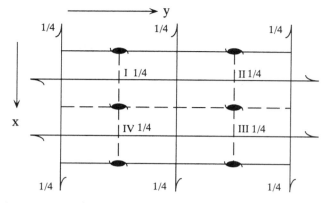

Figure 7.13. A unit cell (space group $2_12_12_1$) with origin at the midpoint of three nonintersecting pairs of parallel 2-fold screw axes: at position I, II, III, or IV at $z = 1/4$ or $3/4$.

choice has an effect on the phase angles. For instance, for the $(h\ k\ 0)$ reflections:

Origin in I:

$$\mathbf{F}_{hk0} = \sum_j f_j \exp[2\pi i(hx_j + ky_j)]$$

Origin in II:

$$\mathbf{F}_{hk0} = \sum_j f_j \exp\left[2\pi i\left(hx_j + k\left\{y_j - \frac{1}{2}\right\}\right)\right]$$

$$= \sum_j f_j \exp[2\pi i(hx_j + ky_j) - i\pi k]$$

The phase angles stay the same if k is even but change by π when k is odd. By comparing the sets of protein phase angles obtained from different heavy atom derivatives, one can easily determine a common origin. In another method, the protein phase angles are derived for a centrosymmetric projection from one derivative and then a difference Fourier is calculated for a second derivative. These preliminary heavy atom positions are now also fixed with respect to the same origin. For space groups with lower symmetry the origin problem is different. For instance, in monoclinic space groups with the 2-fold axis along b, a common origin can easily be found in the x, z plane, but not along y. It is somewhere between $y = 0$ and 1. A very straightforward method of finding a common origin is to calculate a difference Fourier summation with $\{|F_{PH_2}| - |F_P|\}$ $\exp[\alpha_P]$, where the phase angles α_P are derived from derivative 1. $|F_{PH_2}|$ are the structure factor amplitudes for derivative 2. The "common origin" problem could also be solved, at least in principle, if a derivative could be prepared in which heavy atoms of type 1 and type 2 are jointly attached to the protein. A difference Patterson summation would then correspond to a structure containing both the heavy atoms 1 and 2. The coefficients for calculating this Patterson summation are

$$\mathbf{F}_{H_1+H_2}\mathbf{F}^*_{H_1+H_2} = |\mathbf{F}_{H_1+H_2}|^2 = (\mathbf{F}_{H_1} + \mathbf{F}_{H_2})(\mathbf{F}^*_{H_1} + \mathbf{F}^*_{H_2})$$

$$= \mathbf{F}_{H_1}\mathbf{F}^*_{H_1} + \mathbf{F}_{H_2}\mathbf{F}^*_{H_2} + \mathbf{F}_{H_1}\mathbf{F}^*_{H_2} + \mathbf{F}^*_{H_1}\mathbf{F}_{H_2} \quad (7.33)$$

$$- \text{I} \underline{\hspace{1cm}} \text{II} \underline{\hspace{1cm}} \text{IIIa} \underline{\hspace{1cm}} \text{IIIb} -$$

The coefficients I give rise to the self-Patterson peaks of the heavy atoms 1, the coefficients II to the self-Patterson peaks of the atoms 2, and the coefficients III to cross-Patterson peaks between 1 and 2. IIIa leads to cross-peaks on positions $\mathbf{r}_{H_1} - \mathbf{r}_{H_2}$ and IIIb to the centrosymmetrically related cross-peaks $\mathbf{r}_{H_2} - \mathbf{r}_{H_1}$. For the derivation see below.

The Peaks in a Patterson Map if Two Kinds of Heavy Atoms Have Been Attached to the Protein Simultaneously

To obtain the value of the Patterson at position $\mathbf{u}$ we scan in principle through the electron density in the real unit cell with a vector $\mathbf{u}$ and calculate

$$P(\mathbf{u}) = \int_{\mathbf{r}} \rho(\mathbf{r}) \times \rho(\mathbf{r} + \mathbf{u})\, dv$$

$P(\mathbf{u})$ has a high value (a peak), if at both $\mathbf{r}$ and $\mathbf{r} + \mathbf{u}$ the electron density is high. For the cross-peaks, $P(\mathbf{u})$ is high if the vector $\mathbf{u}$ begins at a high density in the first heavy atom structure and ends at a high density in the second heavy atom structure.

$$P(\mathbf{u}) = \int_{\mathbf{r}_1} \rho_1(\mathbf{r}_1) \times P_2(\mathbf{r}_2)\, dv$$

with

$$\mathbf{r}_2 = \mathbf{r}_1 + \mathbf{u} \quad \text{or} \quad \mathbf{u} = \mathbf{r}_2 - \mathbf{r}_1$$

$$\rho_1(\mathbf{r}_1) = \frac{1}{V}\sum_{\mathbf{S}}\mathbf{F}_1(\mathbf{S}) \exp[-2\pi i \mathbf{r} \cdot \mathbf{S}]$$

$$\rho_2(\mathbf{r}_1 + \mathbf{u}) = \frac{1}{V}\sum_{\mathbf{S}'}\mathbf{F}_2(\mathbf{S}') \exp[-2\pi i(\mathbf{r}_1 + \mathbf{u})\mathbf{S}']$$

Replace $\mathbf{S}'$ by $-\mathbf{S}'$ and $\mathbf{F}_2(-\mathbf{S}')$ by $\mathbf{F}^*_2(\mathbf{S}')$:

$$\rho_2(\mathbf{r}_1 + \mathbf{u}) = \frac{1}{V}\sum_{\mathbf{S}'}\mathbf{F}^*_2(\mathbf{S}') \exp[2\pi i(\mathbf{r}_1 + \mathbf{u})\mathbf{S}']$$

$$\rho_1(\mathbf{r}_1) \times \rho_2(\mathbf{r}_1 + \mathbf{u}) = \frac{1}{V^2}\sum_{\mathbf{S}}\sum_{\mathbf{S}'}\mathbf{F}_1(\mathbf{S})\mathbf{F}^*_2(\mathbf{S}') \exp[2\pi i \mathbf{r}_1(\mathbf{S}' - \mathbf{S}) + 2\pi i \mathbf{u} \cdot \mathbf{S}']$$

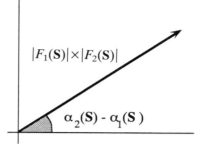

Figure 7.14. A cross-Patterson function between two heavy atom derivatives has Fourier terms with coefficients $|F_1(\mathbf{S})| \times |F_2(\mathbf{S})| \exp[-i\{\alpha_2(\mathbf{S}) - \alpha_1(\mathbf{S})\}]$.

$$\int_{\mathbf{r}_1} \rho_1(\mathbf{r}_1) \times \rho_2(\mathbf{r}_1 + \mathbf{u}) \, dv = P(\mathbf{u})$$

$$= \frac{1}{V^2} \sum_{\mathbf{S}} \sum_{\mathbf{S}'} \mathbf{F}_1(\mathbf{S}) \mathbf{F}_2^*(\mathbf{S}') \exp[2\pi i\mathbf{u} \cdot \mathbf{S}'] \int_{\mathbf{r}_1} \exp[2\pi i\mathbf{r}_1(\mathbf{S}' - \mathbf{S})] \, dv$$

The integral on the right is 0, unless

$$\mathbf{S}' - \mathbf{S} = 0 \quad \text{or} \quad \mathbf{S}' = \mathbf{S}$$

Therefore,

$$P(\mathbf{u}) = \frac{1}{V^2} \sum_{\mathbf{S}} \mathbf{F}_1(\mathbf{S}) \mathbf{F}_2^*(\mathbf{S}) \exp[2\pi i\mathbf{u} \cdot \mathbf{S}] \int_{\mathbf{r}'} 1 \, dv$$

$$= \frac{1}{V} \sum_{\mathbf{S}} \mathbf{F}_1(\mathbf{S}) \mathbf{F}_2^*(\mathbf{S}) \exp[2\pi i\mathbf{u} \cdot \mathbf{S}]$$

$$= \frac{1}{V} \sum_{\mathbf{S}} \mathbf{F}_1^*(\mathbf{S}) \mathbf{F}_2(\mathbf{S}) \exp[-2\pi i\mathbf{u} \cdot \mathbf{S}]$$

$\mathbf{S}$ has been replaced by $-\mathbf{S}$ because a Fourier summation is calculated with $\exp[-2\pi i\mathbf{u} \cdot \mathbf{S}]$. The coefficients in this Fourier summation are

$$\mathbf{F}_1^*(\mathbf{S}) \mathbf{F}_2(\mathbf{S}) = |F_1(\mathbf{S})| \times |F_2(\mathbf{S})| \exp[i\{\alpha_2(\mathbf{S}) - \alpha_1(\mathbf{S})\}]$$

(see Figure 7.14). This result tells us that the Fourier summation will give a noncentrosymmetric structure of $P(\mathbf{u})$ with peaks at the positions $\mathbf{u} = \mathbf{r}_2 - \mathbf{r}_1$. If we use the coefficients

$$\mathbf{F}_1(\mathbf{S}) \mathbf{F}_2^*(\mathbf{S}) = |F_1(\mathbf{S})| \times |F_2(\mathbf{S})| \exp[-i\{\alpha_2(\mathbf{S}) - \alpha_1(\mathbf{S})\}]$$

then $P(\mathbf{u})$ has no peaks at the positions $\mathbf{r}_2 - \mathbf{r}_1$ but instead at the centrosymmetrically related positions $\mathbf{r}_1 - \mathbf{r}_2$.

Summarizing the four coefficients of the Patterson summation for the structure that would contain the heavy atoms of type 1 and type 2:

I. $\mathbf{F}_{H_1}\mathbf{F}_{H_1}^*$: phase angle 0; Patterson of atoms 1 → 1.

II. $\mathbf{F}_{H_2}\mathbf{F}_{H_2}^*$: phase angle 0; Patterson of atoms 2 → 2.

IIIa. $\mathbf{F}_{H_1}\mathbf{F}_{H_2}^*$: phase angle $\alpha_1 - \alpha_2$; Fourier with peaks at the end of the vectors $\mathbf{u}$ that begin at a density on position $\mathbf{r}_2$ in structure 2 and have their end on position $\mathbf{r}_1$ in structure 1: $\mathbf{u} = \mathbf{r}_1 - \mathbf{r}_2$.

IIIb. $\mathbf{F}_{H_1}^*\mathbf{F}_{H_2}$: phase angle $\alpha_2 - \alpha_1$; Fourier with peaks at the end of the vectors $\mathbf{u} = \mathbf{r}_2 - \mathbf{r}_1$.

Usually derivatives that contain type 1 and type 2 heavy atoms simultaneously cannot be obtained. However, Rossmann (1960) and Kartha and Parthasarathy (1965) have developed method for finding a common origin based on the Patterson functions just outlined.

7.12. The Rossmann Method

In Figure 7.15 the angle ϕ between the structure factors of two different heavy atom derivatives is very small for most reflections. Therefore, the length of the vector $\mathbf{F}_{PH_2} - \mathbf{F}_{PH_1}$ can be approximated by $|F_{PH_2}| - |F_{PH_1}|$ and a Patterson summation calculated with the coefficients $(|F_{PH_2}| - |F_{PH_1}|)^2$ will be very similar to a Patterson summation calculated with the coefficient

$$
\begin{aligned}
|\mathbf{F}_{PH_2} - \mathbf{F}_{PH_1}|^2 &= |\mathbf{F}_P + \mathbf{F}_{H_2} - \mathbf{F}_P - \mathbf{F}_{H_1}|^2 = |\mathbf{F}_{H_2} - \mathbf{F}_{H_1}|^2 \\
&= (\mathbf{F}_{H_2} - \mathbf{F}_{H_1})(\mathbf{F}_{H_2}^* - \mathbf{F}_{H_1}^*) \\
&= \mathbf{F}_{H_2}\mathbf{F}_{H_2}^* + \mathbf{F}_{H_1}\mathbf{F}_{H_1}^* - \mathbf{F}_{H_1}\mathbf{F}_{H_2}^* - \mathbf{F}_{H_1}^*\mathbf{F}_{H_2} \\
&\quad -\text{I} \;\;\;\text{---}\;\;\; \text{II} \;\;\;\text{---}\;\;\; \text{IIIa} \;\;\text{---}\;\; \text{IIIb} -
\end{aligned}
$$

This equation is similar to Eq. (7.33), except that the terms IIIa and IIIb now have a negative sign. Coefficient I will give the self-Patterson of the heavy atoms 2, coefficient II the self-Patterson of the heavy atoms 1, and coefficients IIIa and IIIb the cross-Patterson peaks corresponding to the vectors from the atoms 2 to 1 with the centrosymmetrically related peaks from 1 to 2. However, because of their negative sign, the cross-Patterson peaks will appear with a negative density in the Patterson and, therefore, are easy to recognize. The Patterson coefficients in the Rossmann (1960) method are $(|F_{PH_2}| - |F_{PH_1}|)^2$, which is equal to

$$
\{(|F_{PH_2}| - |F_P|) - (|F_{PH_1}| - |F_P|)\}^2 = \{(\Delta|F|_{iso})_2 - (\Delta|F|_{iso})_1\}^2
$$

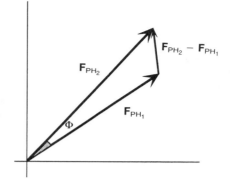

Figure 7.15. The structure factors $\mathbf{F}_{PH_1}$ and $\mathbf{F}_{PH_2}$, for one reflection and two heavy atom derivatives, $\mathbf{F}_{PH_1}$ and $\mathbf{F}_{PH_2}$, will in general point in approximately the same direction.

7.13. Other "Common Origin" Methods

Kartha and Parthasarathy (1965) have introduced a method for the location of a common origin, combining information from isomorphous replacement and anomalous scattering, which, however, has not become very popular. They calculate a Patterson map using the coefficients

$$(\Delta|F|_{\text{iso}})_1 \times (\Delta|F|_{\text{iso}})_2 - (\Delta|F|_{\text{ano}})_1 \times (\Delta|F|_{\text{ano}})_2 = \tfrac{1}{2}\mathbf{F}_{H_1}\mathbf{F}_{H_2}^* + \tfrac{1}{2}\mathbf{F}_{H_1}^*\mathbf{F}_{H_2}$$

In principle this should result in a Patterson map with appreciably reduced noise.

7.14. Refinement of the Heavy Atom Parameters

After the heavy atom structure has been derived from a Patterson map, the heavy atom parameters can be improved (refined) by modifying them in such a way that $|F_{PH}(\text{obs})|$ and $|F_{PH}(\text{calc})|$ approach each other as close as possible. This refinement is carried out by means of the method of least squares and, therefore, this method will be discussed briefly.

The Method of Least Squares

In crystallography the measured data set has for each reflection $(h\,k\,l)$ an intensity $I(h\,k\,l)$ from which the amplitude of the structure factor $|F_{\text{obs}}(h\,k\,l)|$ can be derived. From the preliminary model, values for the structure factors $\mathbf{F}_{\text{calc}}(h\,k\,l)$ can be calculated and in the refinement procedure the values of $|F_{\text{calc}}(h\,k\,l)|$ should be brought as close as possible to $|F_{\text{obs}}(h\,k\,l)|$ for all reflections $(h\,k\,l)$. $|F_{\text{calc}}|$ can be varied by changing the parameters of the model. For some reflections $|F_{calc}|$ will be larger than $|F_{obs}|$ and for others it is just the other way around. We assume that the $|F_{obs}|$ values are distributed as in a Gaussian error curve (see Section 5.1) around their real values $|F_{real}|$, which means that the probability P of finding a value $|F_{obs}(h\ k\ l)|$ for the reflection $(h\ k\ l)$ between $|F_{obs}(h\ k\ l)|$ and $|F_{obs}(h\ k\ l)| + d|F_{obs}(h\ k\ l)|$ is

$$P(h\ k\ l) = \frac{1}{\sigma\sqrt{2\pi}} \exp\left[-\frac{\{|F_{obs}(h\ k\ l)| - |F_{real}(h\ k\ l)|\}^2}{2\sigma^2}\right] d|F_{obs}(h\ k\ l)|$$

σ^2 is the variance caused by arbitrary errors in the measurements:

$$\sigma^2 = \int_{-\infty}^{+\infty} \{|F_{obs}(h\ k\ l)| - \overline{|F_{obs}(h\ k\ l)|}\}^2 P(h\ k\ l)\, d|F_{obs}(h\ k\ l)|$$

Normalization requires

$$\int_{-\infty}^{+\infty} P(h\ k\ l)\, d\{|F_{obs}(h\ k\ l)|\} = 1$$

With the assumption that the errors in the $|F_{obs}(h\ k\ l)|$ values for different reflections are independent of each other, the total probability P for finding a certain set of $|F_{obs}(h\ k\ l)|$ is

$$P = \prod_{hkl} P(h\ k\ l)$$

$$= \prod_{hkl} \frac{1}{\sigma(h\ k\ l)\sqrt{2\pi}} \exp\left[-\frac{\{|F_{obs}(h\ k\ l)| - |F_{real}(h\ k\ l)|\}^2}{2\sigma^2(h\ k\ l)}\right] d|F_{obs}(h\ k\ l)|$$

$$= \exp\left[-\sum_{hkl} \frac{\{|F_{obs}(h\ k\ l)| - |F_{real}(h\ k\ l)|\}^2}{2\sigma^2(h\ k\ l)}\right] \times$$

$$\prod_{hkl} \frac{1}{\sigma(h\ k\ l)\sqrt{2\pi}} d|F_{obs}(h\ k\ l)|$$

The problem is that the real values of the $F(h\ k\ l)$s are unknown. However, it is assumed that these real values can be approximated by the calculated values. The goal is to bring the set of $|F_{calc}|$s as close as possible to the $|F_{obs}|$s. In the method of least squares this is defined as occurring at the maximum value of P. In other words, the optimal set of $|F_{calc}|$s is the one that has the highest probability P. A maximum for P is obtained for a minimum of

$$\sum_{hkl} \frac{\{|F_{obs}(h\ k\ l)| - |F_{calc}(h\ k\ l)|\}^2}{2\sigma^2(h\ k\ l)}$$

This is the principle of least squares.

The least squares minimum is found by varying the $|F_{calc}(h\ k\ l)|$s. This is done by differentiating with respect to the parameters of the atoms and setting the derivatives equal to zero.

7.14.1. Refining the Heavy Atom Parameters without Knowledge of the Protein Phase Angles

7.14.1.1. Without Anomalous Scattering Contribution

Suppose the positions of the heavy atoms have been found with a $(\Delta|F|_{iso})^2$ Patterson. In the calculation of the Patterson, $(\Delta|F|_{iso})^2$ was used instead of the actual, but unknown, squared structure factor amplitudes $|F_H|^2$. In the least-squares refinement according to Rossmann (1960), the difference between $|(\Delta|F|_{iso})|^2$ and $|F_H|^2_{calc}$, calculated for the present heavy atom structure, is minimized. In principle this is not correct because $\Delta|F|_{iso}$ and $|F_H|$ do not necessarily have the same length (see Figure 7.8).

$$|\Delta|F|_{iso}| = ||F_{PH}| - |F_P|| \cong |F_H \cos(\alpha_{PH} - \alpha_H)|$$

Especially small $|\Delta|F|_{iso}|$s can deviate considerably from $|F_H|$. For example, in Figure 7.8 if $\mathbf{F}_H$ is perpendicular to $\mathbf{F}_{PH}$, $|\Delta|F|_{iso}| = 0$ irrespective of the value of $|F_H|$. If, on the other hand, $|\Delta|F|_{iso}|$ is large, $\cos(\alpha_{PH} - \alpha_H)$ is likely to be small and the probability that $|\Delta|F|_{iso}|$ approximates $|F_H|$ is large. Therefore, a weighting factor $w(h\ k\ l) = |\Delta|F|_{iso}(h\ k\ l)|^2$ is introduced, because the larger the difference is between $|F_{PH}|$ and $|F|_P$ the better the chance is that $\mathbf{F}_H$ points in the same direction as $\mathbf{F}_{PH}$ and $\mathbf{F}_P$.

The minimization is then for

$$\varepsilon = \sum_{hkl} w(h\ k\ l)[(\Delta|F|_{iso})^2 - k|F_H|^2_{calc}]^2$$

With the factor k the value of $|F_H|^2_{calc}$ can be corrected to a theoretically more acceptable value; k is arbitrarily chosen between 1 and $1/2$.

7.14.1.2. Including Anomalous Scattering Contribution

It was shown previously (Sections 7.9 and 7.10) that difference Patterson maps could be improved by including the contribution from anomalous scattering. This can also be applied here. For instance, the Matthews Eq. (7.30) can be used for calculating an "observed" value for $|F_H|$ from $|F_P|$, $|F_{PH}(+)|$ and $|F_{PH}(-)|$, and to reduce the difference between this $|F_H|_{obs}$ and $|F_H|_{calc}$ by minimizing

$$\varepsilon = \sum_{hkl} w(|F_H|_{obs} - |F_H|_{calc})^2$$

(Dodson and Vijayan, 1971). The incorporation of anomalous scattering in the calculation of a value for $|F_H|$ also suggests an improvement in the calculation of a difference Fourier map (Section 7.7) for locating heavy atom positions. Of course this is possible only if (preliminary) values for the protein phase angles are known.

Without anomalous scattering the difference Fourier map is calculated with the coefficients $\Delta|F|_{iso}$ and phase angles α_P:

$$\Delta|F|_{iso} \times \exp[i\alpha_P] \approx \underline{\tfrac{1}{2}\mathbf{F}_H + \tfrac{1}{2}\mathbf{F}_H^* \exp[2i\alpha_P]}$$
$$\text{noise}$$

If instead $(\Delta|F|_{iso} - i\Delta|F|_{ano}) \exp[i\alpha_P]$ is chosen, the noise will nearly disappear. This can be understood as follows: It was shown earlier that

$$\Delta|F|_{iso} = |F_H| \cos(\alpha_{PH} - \alpha_H) \tag{7.20}$$

and

$$\Delta|F|_{ano} = |F_H| \sin(\alpha_{PH} - \alpha_H) \tag{7.29}$$

$$(\Delta|F|_{iso} - i\Delta|F|_{ano}) = |F_H| \cos(\alpha_{PH} - \alpha_H) - i|F_H| \sin(\alpha_{PH} - \alpha_H)$$
$$= |F_H| \exp[-i(\alpha_{PH} - \alpha_H)]$$
$$= |F_H| \exp[-i\alpha_{PH}] \exp[i\alpha_H]$$

and, therefore,

$$(\Delta|F|_{iso} - i\Delta|F|_{ano}) \exp[i\alpha_P] = \underline{\mathbf{F}_H \exp[-i\alpha_{PH}] \exp[i\alpha_P]}$$
$$\cong 1$$

7.14.2. Refining the Heavy Atom Parameters with Knowledge of (Preliminary) Protein Phase Angles

For the refinement of the heavy atom positions as discussed in the previous sections, no knowledge of the protein phase angles was required. These methods give satisfactory results, but at the end of the refinement process all heavy atom parameters can be further improved with the "lack of closure" method. This requires preliminary values for the protein phase angles α_P. With the value of α_P known, the vector triangle $\mathbf{F}_P + \mathbf{F}_H = \mathbf{F}_{PH}$ (Figure 7.16a) can be drawn for each reflection. The length and direction of $\mathbf{F}_P$ and $\mathbf{F}_H$ are known and $\mathbf{F}_{PH}$ is then pointed to the end of vector $\mathbf{F}_H$. In practice the observed amplitude $|F_{PH}|$ will be too short or too long to exactly reach the endpoint of $\mathbf{F}_H$ (Figure 7.16b). The difference is called the "lack of closure error" ε. The goal of the refinement is to make these errors ε as small as possible. For each reflection, $|F_{PH}|_{calc}$ is calculated with the cosine rule:

$$|F_{PH}|_{calc} = \{|F_P|^2 + |F_H|^2 + 2|F_P| \times |F_H| \cos(\alpha_H - \alpha_P)\}^{1/2}$$

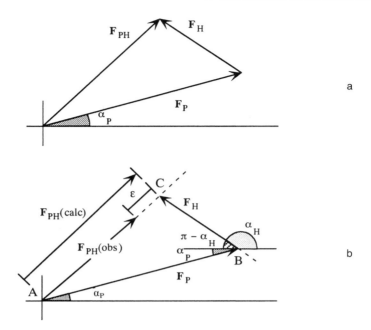

Figure 7.16. (a) The ideal isomorphous situation in which the vector triangle $\mathbf{F_P} + \mathbf{F_H} = \mathbf{F_{PH}}$ closes exactly. Normally, this is not true and the observed and calculated values of $|F_{PH}|$ differ by the lack of closure error ε (b).

For the heavy atom derivative j, ε_j is defined as

$$\varepsilon_j = \{k_j(|F_{PH}|_{obs})_j - (|F_{PH}|_{calc})_j\} \tag{7.34}$$

where k_j is a scaling factor. The function to be minimized is

$$E_j = \sum_{hkl} m_{hkl}\varepsilon_j(h\ k\ l)^2 \tag{7.35}$$

The variables are the parameters of the heavy atoms in derivative j: atomic coordinates, occupancy, temperature factor. Their value determines the length and direction of $\mathbf{F_H}$ and therefore its endpoint in the Argand diagram. Moreover the scale factor k_j can be refined. m_{hkl} is a weighting factor that indicates the quality of the phase angle; m is the figure of merit, defined in the next section. After one or a few refinement cycles new values for the protein phase angles α_P are calculated as will be described in the next section. It is advised to calculate the protein phase angles without using the isomorphous derivative j under consideration. Otherwise the result depends to some extent on the input data. This is especially important if one derivative dominates the phase angle determination.

7.15. Protein Phase Angles

After the refinement of heavy atom positions, protein phase angles can be determined. The principle, due to Harker (1956), is as follows. Draw a circle with radius $|F_P|$. From the center of the circle vector $-\mathbf{F}_H$ is drawn and next a second circle with radius $|F_{PH}|$ and with its center at the end of vector $-\mathbf{F}_H$ (Figure 7.17). The intersections of the two circles correspond to two equally probable protein phase angles, because for both points the triangle $\mathbf{F}_{PH} = \mathbf{F}_P + \mathbf{F}_H$ closes exactly. With a second heavy atom derivative one can, in principle, distinguish between the two alternatives. However, because of errors an exact intersection of the three circles with radii $|F_P|$, $|F_{PH_1}|$, and $|F_{PH_2}|$ will usually not be obtained, and some uncertainty as to the correct phase angle α_P remains. The errors are introduced in X-ray intensity data collection or by poor isomorphism. In practice more than two derivatives are used, if they are available, and, therefore, the method is called multiple isomorphous replacement (MIR).

For mathematical reasons the best procedure to follow is the following: The vector triangle, $\mathbf{F}_{PH} = \mathbf{F}_P + \mathbf{F}_H$, closes exactly only at the two intersection points of the circles with radii $|F_P|$ and $|F_{PH}|$ (see Figure 7.17). These intersection points correspond to two values of α_P. For all other values of α_P a closure error remains:

$$\varepsilon = A C - |F_{PH}|_{obs}$$

(see Figure 7.16b). It is assumed that all errors concern the length of $\mathbf{F}_{PH}$ and that both $\mathbf{F}_H$ and $\mathbf{F}_P$ are error-free. For every value of the protein phase angle α_P, the length of $A C$ in Figure 16b can be calculated with the cosine rule in triangle $A B C$, because $|F_P|$ and $\mathbf{F}_H$ are known. $\varepsilon(\alpha)$ is the difference between this calculated $A C$ and the observed value for $|F_{PH}|$

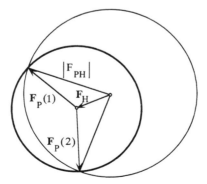

Figure 7.17. Harker construction for protein phase determination. In the isomorphous replacement method each heavy atom derivative gives two possibilities for the protein phase angle α_P, corresponding to the two vectors $\mathbf{F}_P(1)$ and $\mathbf{F}_P(2)$.

for a protein phase angle α. If $\varepsilon(\alpha)$ is smaller, chances for having the correct protein phase angle α are higher.

A Gaussian probability distribution is assumed for ε, and for each reflection in the diffraction pattern of one derivative:

$$P(\alpha) = P(\varepsilon) = N \exp\left[-\frac{\varepsilon^2(\alpha)}{2E^2}\right]$$

N is a normalization factor. It is related to the fact that the phase angle α is somewhere between 0 and 2π:

$$\int\limits_{\alpha=0}^{2\pi} P(\alpha)\, d\alpha = 1$$

E^2 is the "mean square" value of ε. If E is small, the probability curves will have sharp peaks and the protein phase angle is well-determined, but for large E-values they are very poorly determined. For each reflection, $P(\alpha)$ can be calculated as a function of α. A curve is obtained that is symmetrical around a point D in Figure 7.18. The two equally high peaks to the left and right of D correspond to the intersection points of the circles with radii $|F_P|$ and $|F_{PH}|$. These curves can be calculated for each reflection and each of the n heavy atom derivatives. The total probability for each reflection is obtained by multiplying the separate probabilities (see below):

$$P(\alpha) = \prod_{j=1}^{n} P_j(\alpha) = N' \exp\left[-\sum_j \frac{\varepsilon_j^2(\alpha)}{2E_j^2}\right] \tag{7.36}$$

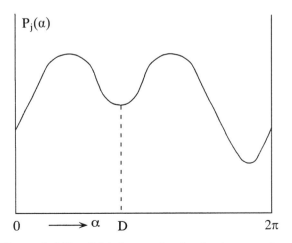

Figure 7.18. The probability $P_j(\alpha)$ for a reflection having α as the correct phase angle derived from derivative j is shown as a function of all angles between 0 and 2π.

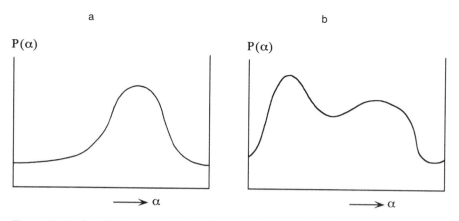

Figure 7.19. (a, b) Two examples of the total probability $P(\alpha)$ for the phase angle α of a reflection as derived from more than one derivative.

The total $P(\alpha)$ curve will normally not show the symmetry of Figure 7.18, but will look like Figure 7.19a or b.

The fundamental rule for the combination of probabilities is as follows:

If events are independent of each other, the probability of their occurring at the same time is the *product* of the probabilities of their separate occurrence.

Probabilities should be *added* if the events exclude each other. For instance, the chance that a particular plane of a dice is on top is 1/6, but the chance that a 1 or a 5 is on top is 1/6 + 1/6 = 1/3.

If an electron density map for a protein is calculated with a certain set of phase angles $\alpha(h\ k\ l)$, the probability that the particular map is correct is equal to $\Pi_{hkl}P_{hkl}(\alpha_{hkl})$. But how can we find the best Fourier map? At first thought, one would choose for each reflection the value $\alpha(h\ k\ l)$ for which $P_{hkl}(\alpha_{hkl})$ has a maximum and, therefore, their product $\Pi_{hkl}P_{hkl}(\alpha_{hkl})$ also has a maximum value. Accepting the maximum value of $\Pi_{hkl}P_{hkl}(\alpha_{hkl})$ would result in the most probable electron density map. However, this most probable map is not necessarily the best electron density map. This is defined as the map with the minimum mean square error in the electron density due to errors in the phase angles. The reason is that the function

$$P_{hkl}(\alpha) = \prod_{j=1}^{n} P_j(\alpha_{hkl})$$

does not always have a single maximum, but sometimes two, or is asymmetric around its maximum (Figure 7.19). In calculating the most probable electron density map, this is completely neglected. The best solution for this problem is as follows. For the structure factor $\mathbf{F}_{hkl} = |F_{hkl}| \exp[i\alpha_{hkl}]$ the amplitude is known, whereas from the experimental data of the derivatives the probability distribution $P_{hkl}(\alpha)$ for the phase angle α can be derived. The probability for the structure factor $\mathbf{F}_{hkl}$ to be $|F_{hkl}| \exp[i\alpha]$ is thus $P_{hkl}(\alpha)$. The best estimate, $\mathbf{F}_{hkl}(\text{best})$, for the actual structure factor on the basis of the present experimental data is given by the least-squares criterium (Section 7.14):

$$Q = \int_\alpha \{P_{hkl}(\alpha)|F_{hkl}| \exp[i\alpha] - \mathbf{F}_{hkl}(\text{best})\}^2 \, d\alpha$$

should be a minimum. With

$$\frac{dQ}{d\{\mathbf{F}_{hkl}(\text{best})\}} = 0$$

it is found that

$$\mathbf{F}_{hkl}(\text{best}) = \int_\alpha \{P_{hkl}(\alpha)|F_{hkl}| \exp[i\alpha]\} \, d\alpha = |F_{hkl}|\mathbf{m} \qquad (7.37)$$

with

$$\mathbf{m} = \int_\alpha \{P_{hkl}(\alpha) \exp[i\alpha]\} \, d\alpha; \quad 0 \leqslant |m| \leqslant 1$$

As a result, the best value of $\mathbf{F}_{hkl}$ is obtained by taking the weighted average over the range of possible $\mathbf{F}_{hkl}$s. $\mathbf{F}_{hkl}(\text{best})$ points to the center of gravity ("centroid") of the probability distribution of $\mathbf{F}$ (Figure 7.20). In practice the integration is replaced by a summation in steps of, say, 5° and

$$\mathbf{F}_{\text{best}} = \frac{\Sigma P(\alpha)\mathbf{F}(\alpha)}{\Sigma P(\alpha)} \qquad (7.38)$$

With $\mathbf{m} = m \exp[i\alpha(\text{best})]$ Eq. (7.37) becomes

$$\mathbf{F}_{hkl}(\text{best}) = |F_{hkl}|m \exp[i\alpha(\text{best})] \qquad (7.39)$$

and

$$m = \frac{|F_{hkl}(\text{best})|}{|F_{hkl}|} \qquad (7.40)$$

m is called the "figure of merit."

If the $\mathbf{F}_{hkl}(\text{best})$ values are used in the calculation of the electron density distribution, a map is obtained that minimizes the mean square error in the electron density due to errors in the phase angles. The interpretation of the isomorphous replacement map in terms of a polypeptide chain produces a first model of the protein molecular structure that is certainly not the final model. That final model is obtained after refinement whose aim is adjusting the model to find a closer agreement between the structure factors calculated on the basis of the model and the observed structure factors (Chapter 13). In the procedure described above, which is due to Blow and Crick (1959), errors in the intensity measurements and in the heavy atom model are lumped together and treated as Gaussian errors in the measured $|F_{PH}|$.

This is of course an approximation and more detailed treatments of the propagation of the various errors into the protein phase angles have been given (Read, 1990a). The difference between these other procedures, which include errors, and the Blow and Crick procedure with sharp circles is schematically represented in Figure 7.21.

7.16. The Remaining Error in the Best Fourier Map

The isomorphous replacement method provides us with a preliminary model of the protein structure; a final model is obtained only after refinement of the structure. Therefore, from a practical point of view we are not particularly interested in the errors that are present in a best Fourier map as calculated in the previous section. From an instructional point of view, however, it is worthwhile to consider these errors.

In Figure 7.20 phase circles are drawn with radius $|r| = 1$. The curve that describes the probability that the phase angle is correct is drawn on the circle as a baseline. The centroid of the probability distribution is not on the circle, but at C somewhat closer to the center of the circle. If the probability distribution is sharp, as in Figure 7.20a, the centroid is nearly on the circle and the phase angle is well defined. If the distribution is as shown in Figure 7.20c, the centroid is near the center of the circle and the phase angle is extremely poorly defined. m is the vector from the center of the circle to the centroid C; α(best) is the best phase angle. If α is an arbitrary phase angle

$$\mathbf{F}(\text{best}) = \frac{\Sigma P(\alpha)\mathbf{F}(\alpha)}{\Sigma P(\alpha)}$$

dividing by $|F|$ gives

$$m \cdot \exp[i\alpha(\text{best})] = \mathbf{m} = \frac{\Sigma P(\alpha)\mathbf{r}(\alpha)}{\Sigma P(\alpha)}$$

and because $\mathbf{r}(\alpha) = 1 \cdot \exp[i\alpha]$,

$$\mathbf{m} = \frac{\Sigma P(\alpha) \exp[i\alpha]}{\Sigma P(\alpha)} \qquad (7.41)$$

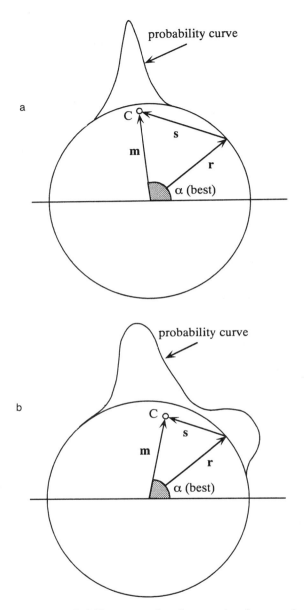

Figure 7.20. Three probability curves for the protein phase angle. The baseline for the curves is the circle with radius $|r| = 1$. C is the centroid of the probability distribution and **m** the vector that connects the center of the circle with C. In other words, the more spread-out the probability curve is, the poorer is the determination of the phase angle, and the shorter is **m**. (a) The sharp peak of the probability curve positions point C close to the circle; (b) it is somewhat further away; (c) it is close to the center of the circle.

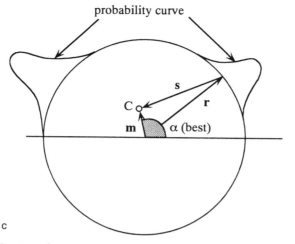

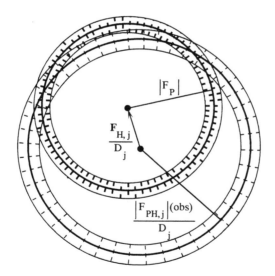

Figure 7.21. Schematic representation of the combination of information from native and derivative data. The shaded areas give an impression of the Gaussian distribution for errors in $|F_P|$ and $|F_{PH}|$. Where the shaded areas cross, a high joint probability exists for the true structure factor conditional on the observed structure factor amplitude for the native protein (dark dashes) and conditional on the observed structure factor amplitude $|F_{PH,j}|$ and the calculated structure factor $\mathbf{F}_{H,j}$ for the heavy atom derivative j (light dashes). D_j is a multiplication factor that is 1 for perfect isomorphism, but is usually less than 1; D_j will be discussed in Section 15.6.

The real part of vector $\mathbf{m}$ is its projection on the horizontal axis in the Argand diagram:

$$m \cos \alpha(\text{best}) = \frac{\Sigma P(\alpha) \cos(\alpha)}{\Sigma P(\alpha)}$$

and its imaginary part is

$$m \sin \alpha(\text{best}) = \frac{\Sigma P(\alpha) \sin(\alpha)}{\Sigma P(\alpha)}$$

If for every reflection the origin is moved from $\alpha = 0$ to $\alpha = \alpha(\text{best})$, then $\cos \alpha(\text{best}) \rightarrow 1$ and $\sin \alpha(\text{best}) \rightarrow 0$

$$m = \frac{\Sigma P(\alpha) \cos\{\alpha - \alpha(\text{best})\}}{\Sigma P(\alpha)} = \overline{\cos\{\alpha - \alpha(\text{best})\}} \qquad (7.42)$$

For reflections with a very well-defined phase angle both m and $\overline{\cos\{\alpha - \alpha(\text{best})\}} \cong 1$. In other words $\{\alpha - \alpha(\text{best})\}$ is very small for phase angles α, which have a high value of $P(\alpha)$. If the curve for $P(\alpha)$ shows a large spread, the value of $\overline{\cos\{\alpha - \alpha(\text{best})\}}$ and of m is much smaller than 1. We can interpret m as the weighted mean of the cosine of the error in the phase angle.

Let us now estimate the error in the electron density map. Suppose that for reflection hkl the true structure factor is $\mathbf{F}_{hkl}(\text{true})$. However, because of errors in our data set, it has been determined as $\mathbf{F}_{hkl}(\text{best})$. For $\bar{h}\bar{k}\bar{l}$ we have $\mathbf{F}^*(\text{best})$ instead of $\mathbf{F}^*(\text{true})$. The incorrect structure factors cause errors in the electron density map. The contribution to the error by reflections hkl and $\bar{h}\bar{k}\bar{l}$ is, if we write $\mathbf{F}_b$ for $\mathbf{F}_{hkl}(\text{best})$ and $\mathbf{F}_T$ for $\mathbf{F}_{hkl}(\text{true})$:

$$\Delta\rho_{hkl} = \frac{1}{V}\{(\mathbf{F}_b - \mathbf{F}_T) \exp[-2\pi i(hx + ky + lz)]$$

$$+ (\mathbf{F}_b^* - \mathbf{F}_T^*) \exp[2\pi i(hx + ky + lz)]\}$$

$$(\Delta\rho_{hkl})^2 = \frac{1}{V^2}\{\cdots\}^2 \qquad (7.43)$$

Equation (7.43) contains the following terms in the right part:

$$(\mathbf{F}_b - \mathbf{F}_T)^2 \exp[-4\pi i(hx + ky + lz)] = (\mathbf{F}_b - \mathbf{F}_T)^2\{\cos[\cdots] - i \sin[\cdots]\}$$

$$(\mathbf{F}_b^* - \mathbf{F}_T^*)^2 \exp[4\pi i(hx + ky + lz)] = (\mathbf{F}_b^* - \mathbf{F}_T^*)^2\{\cos[\cdots] + i \sin[\cdots]\}$$

$$2(\mathbf{F}_b - \mathbf{F}_T)(\mathbf{F}_b^* - \mathbf{F}_T^*) = 2|\mathbf{F}_b - \mathbf{F}_T|^2$$

If the average is taken over all positions x, y, and z in the unit cell, the mean square value of $\Delta\rho_{hkl}$ is obtained: $\overline{(\Delta\rho_{hkl})^2}$. Averaging over x, y, and z makes all cosine and sin terms in Eq. (7.43) equal to 0 and the equation for $\overline{(\Delta\rho_{hkl})^2}$ simplifies to

$$\overline{(\Delta\rho_{hkl})^2} = \frac{2}{V^2} |\mathbf{F}_b - \mathbf{F}_T|^2 \tag{7.44}$$

$\mathbf{F}_b = \mathbf{F}(best)$ has a fixed length and phase angle but $\mathbf{F}_T$ is unknown and, therefore, also $|\mathbf{F}_b - \mathbf{F}_T|^2$. The best value is the weighted average over all possible phase angles for $\mathbf{F}_T$:

$$\overline{(\Delta\rho_{hkl})^2} = \frac{2}{V^2} \times \frac{\displaystyle\int_{\alpha=0}^{2\pi} P_{hkl}(\alpha)[|\mathbf{F}_{best} - \mathbf{F}(\alpha)|^2]\, d\alpha}{\displaystyle\int_{\alpha=0}^{2\pi} P_{hkl}(\alpha)\, d\alpha} \tag{7.45}$$

Equation (7.45) tells us that the mean square error in the electron density is equal to $(2/V^2) \times$ the variance in $\mathbf{F}(\alpha)$ (see Section 5.1 on the Gauss error curve).

As before the integration is replaced by a summation and using

$$\left.\begin{array}{c} \mathbf{F}(best) = |F| \times \mathbf{m} \\ \mathbf{F}(\alpha) = |F| \times \mathbf{r} \\ |r| = 1 \end{array}\right\}$$

$$\overline{(\Delta\rho_{hkl})^2} = \frac{2|F|^2}{V^2} \times \frac{\displaystyle\sum_\alpha P(\alpha)|\mathbf{m} - \mathbf{r}|^2}{\displaystyle\sum_\alpha P(\alpha)}$$

$$= \frac{2|F|^2}{V^2} \times \frac{\displaystyle\sum_\alpha P(\alpha)|s|^2}{\displaystyle\sum_\alpha P(\alpha)} \tag{7.46}$$

Applying the cosine rule gives for $|s|^2$ (see Figure 7.20):

$$|s|^2 = |m|^2 + 1 - 2|m| \cos\{\alpha(best) - \alpha\}$$

Writing m for $|m|$ and substituting $|s|^2$ in Eq. (7.46):

$$\overline{(\Delta\rho_{hkl})^2} = \frac{2|F|^2}{V^2} \times \left\{ \frac{\displaystyle\sum_\alpha P(\alpha)}{\displaystyle\sum_\alpha P(\alpha)} (m^2 + 1) - \frac{2m\displaystyle\sum_\alpha P(\alpha)\cos\{\alpha(best) - \alpha\}}{\displaystyle\sum_\alpha P(\alpha)} \right\}$$

$$= \frac{2|F|^2}{V^2} \times \{m^2 + 1 - 2m^2\} = \frac{2|F|^2}{V^2} \times (1 - m^2) \tag{7.47}$$

This is the contribution to the mean square error in the electron density caused by errors in one reflection and its Bijvoet mate. Adding the contributions from all reflections:

$$\overline{(\Delta\rho)^2} = \frac{2}{V^2}\sum_h\sum_k\sum_l|F|^2_{hkl}(1 - m^2_{hkl}) \tag{7.48}$$

where the summation is over the reflections in half of reciprocal space. It can be derived that for difference Fourier maps a similar equation is valid:

$$\overline{\{\Delta(\Delta\rho)\}^2} = \frac{2}{V^2}\sum_h\sum_k\sum_l(\Delta|F|_{hkl})^2(2 - m^2_{hkl}) \tag{7.49}$$

The extra $(\Delta|F|_{hkl})^2$ is due to the intrinsic error in difference Fourier maps, which is due to the fact that the direction of $\mathbf{F_H}$ is not known.

Suppose the average m is 0.8 and $m^2 = 0.64$. For the normal Fourier map we obtain

$$\overline{(\Delta\rho)^2} = 0.36 \times \left[\frac{2}{V^2}\sum_h\sum_k\sum_l|F|^2_{hkl}\right]$$

and

$$[\overline{(\Delta\rho)^2}]^{1/2} = 0.6 \times \left[\frac{2}{V^2}\sum_h\sum_k\sum_l|F|^2_{hkl}\right]^{1/2}$$

and for the difference Fourier map:

$$(\overline{\{\Delta(\Delta\rho)\}^2}) = 1.36 \times \left[\frac{2}{V^2}\sum_h\sum_k\sum_l(\Delta|F|_{hkl})^2\right]$$

If $\Delta|F|$ is of the order of $0.1 \times |F|$, and, therefore,

$$(\Delta|F|)^2 = 0.01 \times |F|^2$$

the error in the difference Fourier map is

$$\overline{\{\Delta(\Delta\rho)\}^2} = 1.36 \times 0.01 \times \left[\frac{2}{V^2}\sum_h\sum_k\sum_l(|F|_{hkl})^2\right]$$

$$= 0.0136 \times \left[\frac{2}{V^2}\sum_h\sum_k\sum_l(|F|_{hkl})^2\right]$$

$$(\overline{\{\Delta(\Delta\rho)\}^2})^{1/2} = 0.12 \times \left[\frac{2}{V^2}\sum_h\sum_k\sum_l(|F|_{hkl})^2\right]^{1/2}$$

This comparison between the errors in a Fourier and a difference Fourier map shows that the errors in a difference Fourier map are appreciably smaller than in a normal Fourier map. This is the reason that reasonably accurate data can be derived from a difference Fourier map.

7.17. The Single Isomorphous Replacement Method (SIR)

A single heavy atom derivative gives two equally possible protein phase angles corresponding with the structure factors $\mathbf{F_P}(1)$ and $\mathbf{F_P}(2)$ (Figure 7.17). Only one of them is the correct phase angle. With a second heavy atom derivative the choice can be made, but suppose only one derivative is available. If the protein electron density map is then calculated with $\mathbf{F_P}(1) + \mathbf{F_P}(2)$, one can expect that the correct structure factors will lead to an acceptable map, whereas the incorrect ones will lead to noise in the map. The use of $\mathbf{F_P}(1) + \mathbf{F_P}(2)$ in the single isomorphous replacement method is in fact the method of calculating the best electron density map. $\mathbf{F_P}(1)$ and $\mathbf{F_P}(2)$ each has a probability of 0.5 of being the correct structure factor. Therefore,

$$\mathbf{F_P}(\text{best}) = \tfrac{1}{2}[\mathbf{F_P}(1) + \mathbf{F_P}(2)]$$

This best structure factor, $\mathbf{F_P}(\text{best})$, points along $\mathbf{F_H}$ (Figure 7.17) in the same or the opposite direction of $\mathbf{F_H}$. It has either the phase angle α_H of $\mathbf{F_H}$ or $\alpha_H + \pi$, with $\mathbf{F_P}(\text{best})$ within the smallest angle between $\mathbf{F_P}(1)$ and $\mathbf{F_P}(2)$.

The SIR method can work quite satisfactorily by producing sufficiently accurate protein phase angles for calculating an acceptable first electron density map. Its main problem is in a possible pseudocentrosymmetric relationship between the heavy atom positions. If the heavy atom arrangement has an exact center of symmetry, then for each reflection the phase angles of $\mathbf{F_P}(1)$ and $\mathbf{F_P}(2)$ are symmetric to each other with respect to the real axis in the Argand diagram. A set of structure factors, all having a phase angle opposite to the correct one, will lead to an electron density map that is centrosymmetric to the correct map. Instead of having the correct map with noise superimposed, we have the correct map with the centrosymmetric map superimposed. As a result, the interpretation of the map is impossible. Although protein structures themselves have no center of symmetry, the set of heavy atoms can have a pseudocenter of symmetry. This causes the appearance of the (undesirable) centrosymmetric protein structure in the electron density map. The result of the SIR method is appreciably improved if anomalous scattering by the heavy atoms is also taken into account in the phase determination of the protein (Section 9.2).

Summary

1. The X-ray intensities of the native and the derivative structures should be measured as accurately as possible, because the method depends

on relatively small differences between these intensities, especially if anomalous differences are used.

2. The scaling of the data sets is critical. If there are absorption differences due to the nonspherical shape of the crystals, or the solvent around the crystal, or the capillary, a correction for absorption must be applied.

3. It is an advantage to have a low number of sites with a high occupancy, because it simplifies the interpretation of the difference Patterson map. Additional sites with low occupancy can be added later, after their location is determined from difference Fourier maps.

4. After determining the position of the heavy atom sites, it should be checked whether the interatomic vectors correspond with peaks in the Patterson map. Calculation of an anomalous Patterson map and comparison with the isomorphous map give an indication of the significance of the anomalous signal.

5. If it is known that noncrystallographic symmetry is present (such as a 5-fold axis of symmetry within one molecule), this symmetry may also be present between the heavy atom sites. If it is, a vector search in the difference Patterson map should reveal it.

Chapter 8
Phase Improvement

8.1. Introduction

After a first set of protein phases is obtained with the isomorphous replacement method, the molecular replacement method, or the multiple wavelength anomalous dispersion method and an electron density map calculated, the next step is the interpretation of the map in terms of the polypeptide chain. If this is successful and the major part of the chain can indeed be followed in the electron density map, refinement of the structure can begin. However, insufficient quality of the electron density map might hamper a complete and unambiguous tracing of the polypeptide chain, increasing the risk of introducing errors in the model, which cannot be easily removed during refinement. In such a case refinement should be preceded by a process to improve the quality of the map through improvement of the protein phase angles. During phase improvement, all available information on the structure should be used. This information may be in one of the following forms:

1. The structure is partially known.
2. The protein molecules distinguish themselves as relatively high regions of electron density and their boundaries can be estimated. The electron density between them is then set to a constant value.
3. Noncrystallographic symmetry within the asymmetric unit is present and is known from molecular replacement. As in 2, molecular boundaries must then be determined and the solvent region set to a constant value. Moreover, the density of all molecules (or subunits of a molecule) related by noncrystallographic symmetry is averaged.

Methods 2 and 3 are examples of density modification methods. Usually application of these methods improves the electron density map to such an extent that the interpretation is no longer a problem. The crystallographer is not necessarily restricted to the resolution limits set by the isomorphous or molecular replacement method. If the X-ray pattern of the native protein crystals allows, the data limit can be moved very gradually to higher resolution. We shall now discuss these phase improvement methods in some detail.

8.2. The OMIT Map with and without Sim Weighting

Frequently the interpretation of part of an electron density map is somewhat doubtful. For instance, a loop at the surface of the molecule cannot be traced satisfactorily. In such cases it is useful to calculate an OMIT map, that is, an electron density map with the observed structure factor amplitudes ($|F|$) and with phase angles α_K, calculated only for the part of the structure that is known correctly. This part should then show up in full height in the map, whereas the missing part is expected to show up at only about half of the actual height. Because phase angles dominate electron density maps more than the amplitudes, such a map is biased toward the correctly known part of the structure. The picture of the troublesome part can be improved by introducing a suitable weighting factor. A low weight should be given to the amplitudes of reflections for which the phase angles α_K can be expected to differ appreciably from the correct phase angles, and more weight given to reflections for which this difference can be expected to be small. It is assumed that the best weights are those that minimize the mean square error in electron density due to the errors in the phase angles. Recall that this criterion is also applied in the derivation of the best Fourier map. It was shown by Sim (1959, 1960) that the best weights are

$$w = \frac{I_1(X)}{I_0(X)}$$

for noncentric reflections and

$$\tanh\left(\frac{X}{2}\right)$$

for centric reflections, where

$$X = \frac{2|F| \times |F_K|}{\sum\limits_{1}^{n} f_i^2} \tag{8.1}$$

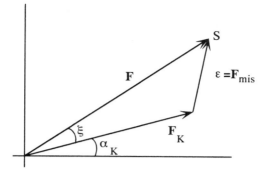

Figure 8.1. The structure factors involved in the calculation of an Omit map. **F** is the total structure factor for the reflection with an observed structure amplitude $|F|$ and a phase angle $\alpha_K + \xi$. $\mathbf{F_K}$ is the structure factor for the known part of the structure with phase angle α_K. The structure factor for the missing part is $\varepsilon = \mathbf{F}_{mis}$.

$I_0(X)$ and $I_1(X)$ are modified Bessel functions of order zero and one, respectively. $|F|$ is the observed structure factor amplitude. $|F_K|$ is the amplitude for the known part of the structure (Figure 8.1). If f_is are atomic scattering factors for n missing atoms, then $\Sigma_1^n f_i^2$ can be estimated from the structure factor amplitudes $|F|$ and $|F_K|$. Bricogne (1976) suggested $||F|^2 - |F_K|^2|$, whereas Read (1986) proposed $n(|F| - |F_K|)^2$ with $n = 1$ for centric and $n = 2$ for noncentric reflections.

The weighting factor w for the noncentric reflections can be derived in the following way. For one reflection, let the structure factor of the known part have an amplitude $|F_K|$ and a phase angle α_K. The correct structure factor for the entire structure has an amplitude $|F|$ and a phase angle $\alpha = \alpha_K + \xi$. $\varepsilon = \mathbf{F}_{mis}$ is the structure factor of the missing part. A single reflection $(h\,k\,l)$ and its Friedel mate $(\bar{h}\,\bar{k}\,\bar{l})$ contribute to the correct electron density ρ at position x, y, z with

$$\rho_{hkl}(x\,y\,z) = \frac{2}{V}|F|\cos[2\pi(hx + ky + lz) - \alpha]$$

$$= \frac{2|F|}{V}\cos\Psi \tag{8.2}$$

If electron density is calculated with correct $|F|$ but erroneous phase angle α_K, then α is replaced by $\alpha_K = \alpha - \xi$ and Ψ by $\Psi + \xi$ in Eq. (8.2). In this case, if a weighting factor w is applied to the amplitude of reflection $(h\,k\,l)$, the error in the electron density is

$$\Delta\rho_{hkl}(x\ y\ z) = \frac{2}{V}|F|[\cos\Psi - w\cos(\Psi + \xi)]$$

$$= \frac{2}{V}|F|[\cos\Psi - w\cos\Psi\cos\xi + w\sin\Psi\sin\xi]$$

$$= \frac{2}{V}|F|[\cos\Psi(1 - w\cos\xi) + w\sin\Psi\sin\xi]$$

$$\{\Delta\rho_{hkl}(x\ y\ z)\}^2 = \frac{4|F|^2}{V^2}[\cos^2\Psi(1 - w\cos\xi)^2 + w^2\sin^2\Psi\sin^2\xi$$

$$+ 2\cos\Psi\sin\Psi(1 - w\cos\xi)w\sin\xi]$$

The mean value for $\{\Delta\rho_{hkl}(x\ y\ z)\}^2$ over all x, y, z is obtained by averaging over Ψ:

$$\overline{\{\Delta\rho_{hkl}(x\ y\ z)\}^2} = \frac{2}{V^2}|F|^2[(1 - w\cos\xi)^2 + w^2\sin^2\xi]$$

$$= \frac{2}{V^2}|F|^2(1 - 2w\cos\xi + w^2)$$

The minimum of $\overline{\{\Delta\rho_{hkl}(x\ y\ z)\}^2}$ with respect to w is found by differentiation:

$$\frac{d\overline{\{\Delta\rho_{hkl}(x\ y\ z)\}^2}}{dw} = \frac{4}{V^2}|F|^2(w - \cos\xi) = 0 \qquad (8.3)$$

It follows from Eq.(8.3) that the best value of w is $w = \cos\xi$. But the phase error ξ is unknown and the best that can be done is to use its average value, given by

$$w = \int_0^{2\pi} p(\xi)\cos\xi\ d\xi \qquad (8.4)$$

where $p(\xi)$ is the probability of finding the phase angle error between ξ and $\xi + d\xi$. Note that w is equal to the figure of merit m as originally defined by Blow and Crick in their calculation of the "best" Fourier map. In Section 7.16 it was shown that m is the weighted mean of the cosine of the error in the phase angle, just as w is.

$p(\xi)$ can be derived from Figure 8.1 in the following way. In Section 5.3 it was found that

$$p(\mathbf{F})d(\mathbf{F}) = \frac{1}{\pi \times \sum\limits_{j=1}^{n} f_j^2}\exp\left[-\frac{|F|^2}{\sum\limits_{j=1}^{n} f_j^2}\right]d(\mathbf{F}) \qquad (8.5)$$

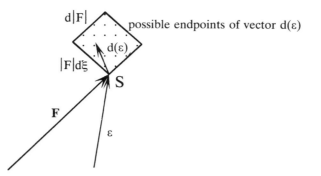

Figure 8.2. The possible endpoints of vector $d(\varepsilon)$ are found in a rectangle bounded by $|F|d\xi$ and $d|F|$.

If the f_js are the atomic scattering factors for the n missing atoms, $\sum_{j=1}^{n} f_j^2$ is the average value expected for $|F_{mis}|^2$ of the missing atoms and the distribution function for the noncentrosymmetric reflections [Eq.(8.5)] is

$$p(\varepsilon)d(\varepsilon) = \frac{1}{\pi \times \sum\limits_{j=1}^{n} f_j^2} \exp\left[-\frac{|\varepsilon|^2}{\sum\limits_{j=1}^{n} f_j^2}\right] d(\varepsilon) \qquad (8.6)$$

With $d(\varepsilon) = |F|d\xi d|F|$ (Figure 8.2):

$$p(\varepsilon)d(\varepsilon) = p(\varepsilon)|F|d\xi d|F| = \frac{|F|}{\pi \times \sum\limits_{j=1}^{n} f_j^2} \exp\left[-\frac{|\varepsilon|^2}{\sum\limits_{j=1}^{n} f_j^2}\right] d|F|d\xi$$

$p(\varepsilon)$ is equal to the probability of finding the measured $|F|$ with a certain ξ. Application of the cosine rule in Figure 8.1 gives the conditional probability:

$$p(\xi; |F|)\,d\xi = \frac{|F|}{\pi \times \sum\limits_{j=1}^{n} f_j^2} \exp\left[-\frac{(|F|^2 + |F_K|^2)}{\sum\limits_{i=1}^{n} f_i^2}\right] \exp\left[\frac{2|F| \times |F_K| \cos\xi}{\sum\limits_{i=1}^{n} f_i^2}\right] d\xi$$

Normalization requires

$$\int\limits_{\xi=0}^{2\pi} N \times p(\xi; |F|)\,d\xi = 1$$

where N is a normalization constant.

$$2 \times N \times \frac{|F|}{\pi \times \sum\limits_{j=1}^{n} f_j^2} \exp\left[-\frac{(|F|^2 + |F_K|^2)}{\sum\limits_{i=1}^{n} f_i^2}\right] \times \int\limits_{0}^{\pi} \exp\left[\frac{2|F| \times |F_K| \cos\xi}{\sum\limits_{i=1}^{n} f_i^2}\right] d\xi = 1$$

$$(8.7)$$

The integral is a modified Bessel function of order 0. The general form for a modified Bessel function of order n is

$$I_n(x) = \frac{1}{\pi} \int_{\xi=0}^{\pi} \exp[x \cos \xi] \cos n\xi \, d\xi$$

$$I_0(x) = \frac{1}{\pi} \int_{\xi=0}^{\pi} \exp[x \cos \xi] \, d\xi$$

Therefore, N can be written as

$$N = \left\{ 2 \times \frac{|F|}{\sum_{j=1}^{n} f_j^2} \exp\left[-\frac{(|F|^2 + |F_K|^2)}{\sum_{i=1}^{n} f_i^2} \right] \times I_0\left(\frac{2|F| \times |F_K|}{\sum_{i=1}^{n} f_i^2} \right) \right\}^{-1}$$

and the normalized distribution function becomes

$$p(\xi; |F|) \, d\xi = \left\{ \exp\left[\frac{2|F| \times |F_K| \cos \xi}{\sum_{i=1}^{n} f_i^2} \right] d\xi \right\} \Big/ \left\{ 2\pi I_0\left[\frac{2|F| \times |F_K|}{\sum_{i=1}^{n} f_i^2} \right] \right\}$$

$$= \frac{\exp[X \cos \xi] \, d\xi}{2\pi I_0(X)} \tag{8.8}$$

where

$$X = \frac{2|F| \times |F_K|}{\sum_{1}^{n} f_i^2}$$

Or, because $\alpha_K = \alpha - \xi$ and α_K is a constant,

$$p_{\text{par}}(\alpha; |F|) \, d\alpha = \frac{1}{2\pi I_0(X)} \exp[X \cos(\alpha - \alpha_K)] \, d\alpha \tag{8.9}$$

The weighting factor w [Eq. (8.4)] becomes

$$w = \int_0^{2\pi} p(\xi) \cos \xi \, d\xi = \frac{\int_0^{2\pi} \exp[X \cos \xi] \cos \xi \, d\xi}{2\pi I_0(X)} = \frac{I_1(X)}{I_0(X)}$$

As mentioned before $w = I_1(X)/I_0(X)$ is equal to the figure of merit $m = \overline{\cos \xi}$, where ξ is the deviation from the phase angle α_K. In the calculation of w it was assumed that the known part of the structure is exactly known and has no errors in the parameters of the atoms. In that case

$$X = \frac{2|F| \times |F_K|}{\sum\limits_{1}^{n} f_i^2}$$

However, in practice, the known part of the structure does have error. X must then be taken (Srinivasan, 1966) as

$$X = \frac{2\sigma_A|E| \times |E_K|}{1 - \sigma_A^2}$$

$|E|$ and $|E_K|$ are normalized structure factors and σ_A will be defined in Section 15.6. It often occurs that phase information from different sources must be combined in a joint probability curve. In Chapter 14 a convenient method for doing this will be presented. The contribution from partial structure information is then $p_{par}(\alpha)$ [Eq. (8.9)].

$I_0(X)$ depends on known quantities only: $|F|$, $|F_K|$, and $\Sigma_1^n f_i^2$, and can be put into a normalizing constant: $p(\xi) = N^* \times \exp[X \cos \xi]$ and

$$p_{par}(\alpha) = N^* \times \exp[X \cos(\alpha - \alpha_K)] \tag{8.9a}$$

In Chapter 14 it will be shown how this probability curve is combined with probability curves from other sources.

8.3. Solvent Flattening

The principle of this method is fairly simple. From highly refined protein crystal structures it is known that the electron density map is rather flat in the solvent region between the protein molecules. This is due to the liquid character of the solvent molecules in those regions. This does not mean that no solvent molecules can be observed. However, the more static solvent molecules are found only internally in the protein molecules, or as a monolayer or double layer at their surface. The rest of the solvent has a dynamic nature and its time-averaged electron density has a low constant value. If the region occupied by the protein molecules can be identified, a nonoptimal electron density map shows noise peaks in the solvent region and they are removed, simply by setting the electron density in this region to a low constant value.

The simplest method for defining a molecular envelope around the protein molecules is by visual inspection of the preliminary electron density map. However, this is rather subjective for a noisy map. An automated method proposed by Wang (1985) and modified by Leslie (1987) is more objective and much easier to apply. In the Wang method the noisy electron density map is smoothed in the following way:

A three-dimensional grid is superimposed on the unit cell. At each grid point j, the electron density is replaced by a new value that is proportional to the weighted sum of the densities within a sphere of radius R with the center in that grid point. R is typically on the order of $10\,\text{Å}$.

$$\rho'_j = K\sum_i^R w_i\rho_i$$

with $w_i = 0$ for $\rho_i < 0$ and $w_i = 1 - (r_{ij}/R)$ for $\rho_i > 0$. The summation is over the grid points i within the sphere. r_{ij} is the distance between the grid points i and j. K is an arbitrary constant. A grid spacing of $1/3$ of the resolution is adequate. The molecular boundary is revealed in the new map by tracing a threshold density level. In the beginning of the process the threshold is usually chosen such that the volume of solvent in the map is a little smaller (e.g., $10-15\%$) than the known or estimated volume fraction of the solvent (estimated using the formula given in Section 3.9). Also, only low resolution data should be used because the phase angles of the high resolution data are still very poor. If necessary, the envelope can be polished, e.g., by removing internal voids. One must also be careful that no overlap with symmetrically related envelopes occurs. During the next cycles of solvent flattening the solvent fraction can gradually be increased up to, e.g., 5% below the estimated value. With the slightly smaller solvent region there are fewer chances that outer loops of the protein molecule are cut off. Moreover, the envelope should be updated in these cycles, because the electron density map improves and this allows us to trace a better envelope. In the solvent region (outside the envelope), the average value of the solvent density is assigned to each grid point. Structure factor amplitudes and phases are calculated for this new map (a process known as map inversion), using the fast Fourier transform technique (Section 13.3).

In the next step an electron density map is calculated with *observed* structure factor amplitudes and with phase angles either from the solvent flattening procedure alone or by combining them with phase angles from isomorphous or molecular replacement or any other phase information. The choice depends on the quality of the initial phases, the resolution limit and the solvent content. If, at the present resolution, no further improvement is obtained, data at higher resolution can be added in small steps.

For the protein phase angles a probability curve $p_{SF}(\alpha)$ is chosen similar to $p_{par}(\alpha)$ in the Sim weighting procedure [Eq. (8.9a)]. The argument is that the solvent flattened structure can be regarded as the "known" part of the structure in the Sim conception.

$$p_{SF}(\alpha) = N\,\exp[X'\,\cos(\alpha_P - \alpha_{calc})] \qquad (8.10)$$

where N is a normalizing constant, α_P is the protein phase angle, α_{calc} is the phase angle calculated for the map with the flattened solvent density, and $X' = 2|F_{obs}| \times |F_{calc}|/\overline{|I_{obs} - I_{calc}|}$. $\overline{|I_{obs} - I_{calc}|}$ is the mean intensity contributed by the unknown part of the structure. It replaces $\Sigma_{j=1}^{n} f_j^2$ in the Sim procedure. The closer the solvent flattened structure is to the true structure, the smaller $|I_{obs} - I_{calc}|$ is and the stronger the phase indication. Appropriate scaling of the calculated to the observed structure factors is of course required. $|I_{obs} - I_{calc}|$ is calculated in shells of increasing resolution.

From the phase probability curve—either the solvent flattened alone or a combined one—the "best" phases and figures of merit can be derived and used in the calculation of a "best" electron density map. The entire method can be repeated until no further improvement of the map is obtained. For a schematic representation of the method see Scheme 8.1 and for an example Figure 8.3. Leslie has given a reciprocal space method for calculating the smoothed electron density map, which is computationally much faster than Wang's real space method. The density for the smoothed map is

$$\rho'(i) = \sum_{r=0}^{R} \rho(i + r) \times \left(1 - \frac{r}{R}\right) \tag{8.11}$$

with $r \leq R$. Equation (8.11) is a convolution of the function ρ with the function $[1 - (r/R)]$ [see Eq. (7.13)]. Therefore, the transform of the function $\rho'(i)$ is equal to the product of the transform of $\rho(i)$ and the transform of $[1 - (r/R)]$. The transform of $\rho(i)$ is easily calculated with a fast Fourier program. The transform of $[1 - (r/R)]$ is the transform of 1 minus the transform of r/R. The transform of a function that has a constant value of 1 in the region $r \leq R$ and is 0 outside that region is the transform of a sphere with radius R. We shall meet this transform (the G-function) again in discussing the rotation function (Section 10.2). It has the form

$$G(x) = \frac{3(\sin x - x \cos x)}{x^3} \quad \text{with} \quad x = \frac{4\pi R \sin \theta}{\lambda}$$

The transform of the function which is r/R in the region $r \leq R$ and 0 for $r > R$, is

$$L(x) = \frac{3}{x^4}\{2x \sin x - (x^2 - 2) \cos x - 2\}$$

The total transform of $[1 - (r/R)]$ is then $G(x) - L(x)$.

The following steps for calculating the smoothed map should be performed:

1. Calculate the structure factors for the original electron density $\rho(r)$, including all low angle reflections, because they depend much more on the shape of the solvent region that the higher resolution reflections.
2. Multiply them by $G(x) - L(x)$.

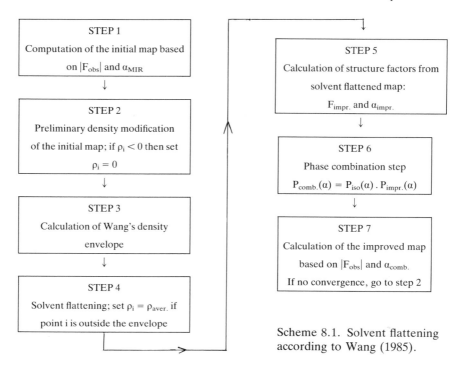

STEP 1
Computation of the initial map based on $\lvert F_{obs}\rvert$ and α_{MIR}

↓

STEP 2
Preliminary density modification of the initial map; if $\rho_i < 0$ then set $\rho_i = 0$

↓

STEP 3
Calculation of Wang's density envelope

↓

STEP 4
Solvent flattening; set $\rho_i = \rho_{aver.}$ if point i is outside the envelope

STEP 5
Calculation of structure factors from solvent flattened map: $F_{impr.}$ and $\alpha_{impr.}$

↓

STEP 6
Phase combination step $P_{comb.}(\alpha) = P_{iso}(\alpha) \cdot P_{impr.}(\alpha)$

↓

STEP 7
Calculation of the improved map based on $\lvert F_{obs}\rvert$ and $\alpha_{comb.}$ If no convergence, go to step 2

Scheme 8.1. Solvent flattening according to Wang (1985).

3. Use these modified structure factors for calculating the smoothed electron density map ρ'.

See Scheme 8.2 for a schematic representation. Solvent flattening is most powerful for crystals with a high solvent content.

8.4. Molecular Averaging

From the first characterization of a protein crystal, it usually becomes clear how many protein molecules or subunits are contained in the asymmetric unit. If there is more than one and they are equal, the molecular replacement method (Chapter 10) can give us the relative position and orientation of the molecules or subunits (the noncrystallographic symmetry).

The electron density in the molecules (subunits), related by this non-crystallographic symmetry, is essentially equal, although the difference in

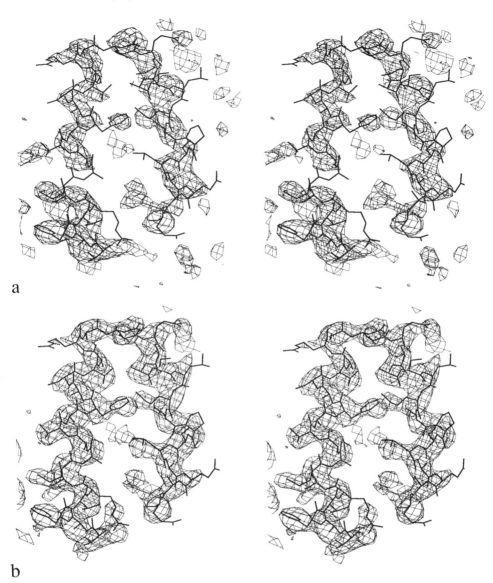

Figure 8.3. Stereo pairs of part of the electron density map of the *E. coli* enzyme soluble lytic transglycosylase at 3.3 Å resolution. The crystal contained 60% solvent. (a) The map as obtained with the multiple isomorphous replacement method, using two derivatives and including anomalous scattering by the heavy atoms. (b) The solvent flattened map. Disconnected parts of density before solvent flattening are nicely connected in (b). (Source: Dr. A.M.W.H. Thunnissen.)

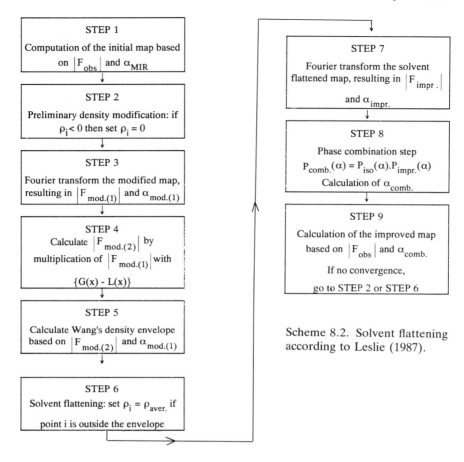

Scheme 8.2. Solvent flattening according to Leslie (1987).

the contact with neighbors may cause some deviation from exact equality. The equal density in the molecules related by the noncrystallographic symmetry imposes a constraint on the protein structure factors and, therefore, on the protein phase angles. Reciprocal space methods to derive these phase relationships were proposed by Rossmann and Blow (1963), Main (1967), and Crowther (1969). They were not very successful, but a real space approach, developed by Bricogne (1974), has found wide application. It consists of the following steps:

1. First the envelope of the molecules in the asymmetric unit must be defined in the electron density map, calculated with the available phase information. The envelope should contain as much protein density as

possible, but it is sometimes chosen slightly smaller than the actually observed one, because of the possible difference between the molecules in the contact with their neighbors.

2. The electron density of the molecules in the asymmetric unit is averaged, the solvent region flattened, and its density set equal to the average electron density in that region; then the asymmetric unit is reconstituted.

3. Phase angles for this new model are calculated by back-transforming the electron density map.

4. If necessary, this phase information is combined with previously known phase information and "best" phases and figures of merit are obtained.

5. A new and improved electron density map is calculated with observed structure factor amplitudes and phase information from step 4.

6. The procedure is repeated, starting from step 1.

Bricogne (1976) developed a complete set of programs for the application of this method. Another program has been described by Johnson (1978). More recently, Rossmann et al. (1992) presented a new program for the execution of the method, based on previous experience and using improved computer technology. Rossmann and co-workers applied averaging and phase extension with great success for the structure determination of several spherical viruses (Rossmann, 1990; McKenna et al., 1992). Rayment (1983) studied the use of noncrystallographic symmetry and solvent flattening as a phase constraint on model structure factors of icosahedral particles. He found that the phase angles can be successfully refined against low resolution data. He also pointed out that it is important to include calculated values for unrecorded data in the refinement.

The phase information is derived from this averaging procedure in the same way as in the solvent flattening method and is based on Sim's phase probability function. The average structure is regarded as the known part in Sim's conception and $p_{average}(\alpha_P)$ has the same form as $P_{SF}(\alpha_P)$ [Eq. (8.10)]:

$$P_{average}(\alpha_P) = N \exp[X' \cos(\alpha_P - \alpha_{calc})] \tag{8.12}$$

with $X' = 2|F_{obs}| \times |F_{calc}|/|I_{obs} - I_{calc}|$.

The method of averaging is most powerful in cases of high noncrystallographic symmetry, such as viruses, but it can also give excellent improvement of a density map at lower noncrystallographic symmetry; an example is shown in Figure 8.4. Moreover, the averaging method is not restricted to noncrystallographic symmetry within one crystal, but can be used equally well if proteins crystallize in more than one crystal form.

8.5. Further Considerations Concerning Density Modification

Density modification procedures start with a poor electron density map that has been calculated with structure factors having the correct amplitude $|F_{obs}|$, but a wrong phase angle α_{wr}. This structure factor can be thought of as composed of a contribution by the protein part of the crystal structure $[\mathbf{F}_{wr}(pr)]$ and a contribution by the solvent part $[\mathbf{F}_{wr}(s)]$. The designation $\mathbf{F}_{wr}$ means that the protein and also the solvent contribution are both incorrect in this stage. Flattening the solvent part in the structure means that $\mathbf{F}_{wr}(s)$ is replaced by an improved $\mathbf{F}_{impr}(s)$ (Figure 8.5). A new and improved electron density map is then calculated with the structure factor $\mathbf{F}_{impr}$ (total) having the amplitude $|F_{obs}|$ and the improved phase angle α_{impr}. From this new map an improved envelope can be derived and the process repeated. Usually, several cycles of density modification are required to shift the protein phase angles close enough to their correct value to allow an interpretation of the electron density map in terms of the polypeptide chain. If in the process, the solvent area becomes flatter, the amplitudes of the $\mathbf{F}(s)$ contributions become smaller, except for the low order reflections (see Section 13.1). The shape of the envelope is mainly determined by these reflections and they should be incorporated as much as possible in solvent flattening. If the solvent content of the crystal is high, the contribution of $\mathbf{F}(s)$ to the total structure factor is also relatively high and solvent flattening is more powerful.

In solvent flattening the driving force is the gradual improvement of $\mathbf{F}(s)$. In the averaging procedure, two density modifications are applied in each step: (1) averaging the electron densities of the noncrystallographically related molecules and (2) solvent flattening. Therefore, both $\mathbf{F}_{wr}(s)$ and $\mathbf{F}_{wr}(pr)$ are replaced by improved structure factor contributions: $\mathbf{F}_{impr}(s)$ and $\mathbf{F}_{impr}(pr)$. This speeds up the process considerably compared with solvent flattening alone. As a result it is much more powerful, particularly if the number of symmetry-related molecules is higher.

$\longrightarrow$

Figure 8.4. Example of the effect of 5-fold averaging of the B_5 subunits in the structure determination of the AB_5 complex of heat-labile enterotoxin. Electron densities calculated between 15 and 3.1 Å. Stereo pairs are shown for (a) electron density from isomorphous replacement, including anomalous scattering from three heavy atom derivatives (MIRAS); (b) F(obs) electron density after 5-fold averaging; and (c) Sim weighted F(obs) electron density after seven cycles of averaging, with phase combination of the average phases with the MIRAS phases after each cycle. (Source: Dr. Titia Sixma.)

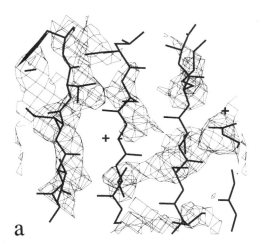
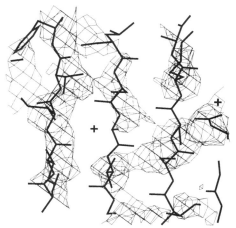

a

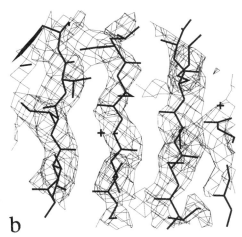
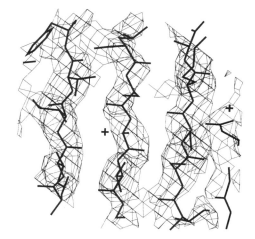

b

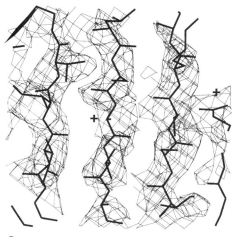
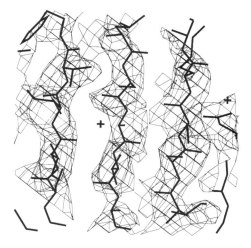

c

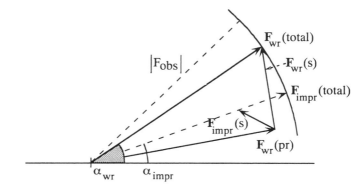

Figure 8.5. Structure factors in solvent flattening. The electron density maps are always calculated with observed structure factor amplitudes $|F_{obs}|$. For the starting map the poor protein phase angles α_{wr} are used for the structure factors $\mathbf{F}_{wr}(\text{total})$. This structure factor is composed of a protein contribution, $\mathbf{F}_{wr}(\text{pr})$, and a solvent contribution, $\mathbf{F}_{wr}(s)$. The flattening does not change the protein contribution, but improves the solvent contribution, replacing $\mathbf{F}_{wr}(s)$ by $\mathbf{F}_{impr}(s)$. The next electron density map is then calculated with structure factors having the same amplitudes as before, $|F_{obs}|$, but improved protein phase angles α_{impr}.

Summary

The interpretation of an electron density map in terms of the polypeptide chain is based on the chemical structure of the protein. Additional information is the higher electron density in the protein compared with the rather flat electron density in the solvent region between the protein molecules and noncrystallographic symmetry, if present. The application of this additional information (density modification) can make all the difference for the interpretation of a hitherto uninterpretable map. Moreover, the resolution can often be increased in small steps. Usually several cycles of density modification and model building are required, using calculated model phases combined with previous phase information. For this procedure the fast Fourier transform algorithm is indispensible. If only part of the electron density map, e.g., rather mobile loops, cannot satisfactorily be interpreted, OMIT maps, preferably with Sim weighting, should be calculated.

Chapter 9
Anomalous Scattering in the Determination of the Protein Phase Angles and the Absolute Configuration

9.1. Introduction

Anomalous scattering is not a new subject having already been introduced in Chapter 7. There, you learned that anomalous scattering by an atom is due to the fact that its electrons cannot be regarded as completely free electrons. This effect depends on the wavelength, but it is in general stronger for the heavier atoms than for the light atoms in the upper rows of the periodic system. If heavy atoms are present in a protein structure, the consequence of their anomalous scattering is that the intensities of a reflection hkl and its Bijvoet mate $\bar{h}\bar{k}\bar{l}$ are no longer equal. In Chapter 7 this effect was used in combination with the isomorphous replacement differences in the search for the heavy atom positions and in the refinement of these positions. In this chapter it will be shown how anomalous scattering information can help to determine the phase angle of the protein reflections and the absolute configuration of the protein structure. Moreover, it will be discussed how anomalous scattering is exploited for protein phase angle determination by the multiple wavelength anomalous dispersion (MAD) method.

9.2. Protein Phase Angle Determination with Anomalous Scattering

In principle the anomalous scattering by heavy atoms contributes to the determination of the protein phase angles as much as the isomorphous replacement does. This can best be explained in Figure 9.1. Three circles are drawn in that figure, with radii F_P, $F_{PH}(+)$, and $F_{PH}(-)$; the $(+)$ and the $(-)$ indicate a Bijvoet pair of reflections. The F_P circle has its center at O. For the $F_{PH}(+)$ circle the center is at the end of the vector $-\mathbf{F}_H(+)$ and for the $F_{PH}(-)$ circle at the end of the vector $-\mathbf{F}_H(-)$. The two intersections of the F_P and $F_{PH}(+)$ circles at α_1 and α_2 indicate two possible protein phase angles. Two other possibilities are found at the two intersections of the circles F_P and $F_{PH}(-)$: α_1' and α_2'. Since the reflections $(h\,k\,l)$ and $(\bar{h}\,\bar{k}\,\bar{l})$ of the native protein crystal have opposite phase angles (Section 4.11) the correct choice is for the phase angles α_1 for $(h\,k\,l)$ and α_1' for $(\bar{h}\,\bar{k}\,\bar{l})$. This is illustrated in a simpler way in Figure 9.2. Here the vector $-\mathbf{F}_H(-)$ is drawn with the opposite phase angle (mirror image with respect to the horizontal axis). Now the correct phase angle is found at the intersection of the three circles F_P, F_{PH} $(+)$ and $F_{PH}(-)$, assuming that the data are error-free. The conclusion is that

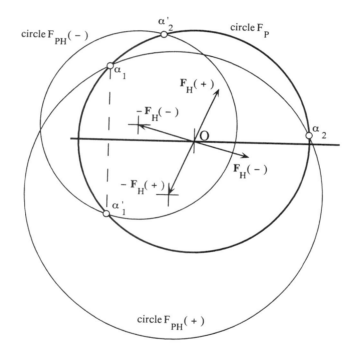

Figure 9.1. The Harker diagram for protein phase angle determination by anomalous scattering. $|F_P|$ is the structure factor amplitude for the native protein and $|F_{PH}(+)|$ and $|F_{PH}(-)|$ for the Friedel mates of the heavy atom derivative. The contribution to the structure factor by the heavy atom is $\mathbf{F}_H(+)$ for one member of the Friedel pair and $\mathbf{F}_H(-)$ for the other member. These two structure factors are not symmetric with respect to the horizontal axis because of an anomalous component. The positions of the intersection points α_1 and α_1' do have a position symmetric with respect to the horizontal axis because the structure factor of the native protein has no anomalous component.

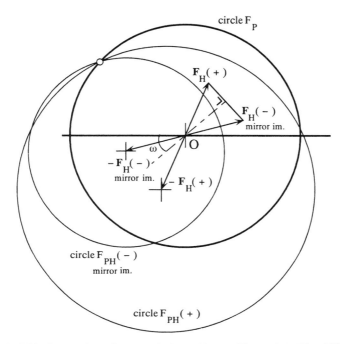

Figure 9.2. This figure gives the same information as Figure 9.1. The difference is that the vector $-\mathbf{F}_H(-)$ is now drawn with the opposite phase angle (mirror image with respect to the horizontal axis). The consequence is a different position for the $F_{PH}(-)$ circle. The advantage of this drawing is that the three circles have one common point of intersection. The dashed line indicates the direction of the nonanomalous scattering part of the heavy atoms.

in principle, the protein phase angle problem can be solved with one isomorphous heavy atom derivative if anomalous scattering is incorporated (SIRAS).

9.3. Improvement of Protein Phase Angles with Anomalous Scattering

From the isomorphous replacement method a probability curve for the protein phase angle is obtained for each reflection: $P_{iso}(\alpha)$. The information from the anomalous scattering data could easily be combined with the $P_{iso}(\alpha)$ curve if it could also be expressed in a probability curve: $P_{ano}(\alpha)$. The combined probability would then be

$$P(\alpha) = P_{iso}(\alpha) \times P_{ano}(\alpha)$$

This can be done in the following way:

$$|F_{PH}(+)| - |F_{PH}(-)| = \Delta PH_{obs}$$

In Section 7.9 it was derived [Eq. (7.28)] that

$$|F_{PH}(+)| - |F_{PH}(-)| = \frac{2f''}{f'}|F_H|\sin(\alpha_{PH} - \alpha_H)$$

or

$$|F_{PH}(+)| - |F_{PH}(-)| = 2\frac{|F_H|}{k}\sin(\alpha_{PH} - \alpha_H) \tag{9.1}$$

where

$$k = \frac{f'}{f''} = \frac{|F_H|}{|F''_H|}$$

ΔPH_{calc} must be expressed as a function of the protein phase angle α_P.
In triangle ABE in Figure 7.12 the sine rule gives

$$\frac{\sin - (\alpha_{PH} - \alpha_H)}{|F_P|} = \frac{\sin(\alpha_H - \alpha_P)}{|F_{PH}|}$$

or
$$\sin - (\alpha_{PH} - \alpha_H) = \frac{|F_P|}{|F_{PH}|}\sin(\alpha_H - \alpha_P)$$

$$\Delta PH_{calc} = \frac{2|F_H|}{k}\sin(\alpha_{PH} - \alpha_H) = -\frac{2|F_P| \times |F_H|}{k|F_{PH}|}\sin(\alpha_H - \alpha_P)$$

In the ideal case $\Delta PH_{calc} = \Delta PH_{obs}$. In practice for each reflection a value $\varepsilon_{ano}(\alpha) = \Delta PH_{obs} - \Delta PH_{calc}$ is found depending on the phase angle α_P of the protein. This is comparable with the lack of closure error ε in the isomorphous replacement phase triangle of the protein. Here also a Gauss probability distribution is assumed:

$$P_{ano}(\alpha) = N' \exp\left[-\frac{\varepsilon_{ano}^2(\alpha)}{2(E')^2}\right] \tag{9.2}$$

N' is a normalization constant and $(E')^2$ is the mean square value of ε. Because anomalous scattering data are taken from the same crystal, lack of isomorphism does not cause errors in the values of $|F_{PH}(+)| - |F_{PH}(-)|$. Therefore, although these differences are small, the errors in $|F_{PH}(+)| - |F_{PH}(-)|$ are inherently smaller than errors in $|F_{PH}| - |F_P|$, and E' is smaller than E and can be taken as, e.g., $\frac{1}{3}E$. Equation (9.2) can now be combined with $P_{iso}(\alpha)$ [Eq. (7.36)]. One should be careful to combine the anomalous data with the correct set of isomorphous data, that is, the set that gives the electron density of the protein in the absolute configuration (see next section) and not to combine it with the wrong set.

If the multiple isomorphous replacement method includes anomalous scattering information, it is called the MIRAS method. It should be stressed that in collecting anomalous scattering data, great care should be taken, because the difference in intensity between the Bijvoet pairs is very small. One generally prefers to collect Bijvoet pairs close in time to avoid experimental errors.

9.4. The Determination of the Absolute Configuration

Without anomalous scattering the isomorphous replacement method results in either the correct protein structure or its enantiomorph (mirror image). If the resolution in the electron density map is sufficiently high and the configuration at the C_α position in the amino acid residues can be observed, it can easily be checked whether the configuration is correct with the amino acid residues having the L-configuration. And if α-helices appear in the map, they should be right-handed for the correct configuration of the protein. However, the absolute configuration of the protein can be derived more straightforwardly from the intensity differences between the two members of the Bijvoet pairs. This will be discussed below.

In Figures 9.1 and 9.2 the situation was presented with the correct set of heavy atom positions and $|F_{PH}(+)| > |F_{PH}(-)|$. In Figure 9.3 the situation is drawn with a correctly chosen set of axes, $|F_{PH}(+)| > |F_{PH}(-)|$, but the choice of the heavy atom positions was incorrect, because from the difference Patterson map the wrong set of the two equally possible centrosymmetrically related sets of positions was chosen (see Section 7.6). The consequence is that the entire set of vectors $F_H(+)$, $-F_H(+)$, $F_H(-)$, and $-F_H(-)$ is reflected with respect to the horizontal axis. This causes a rotation of the circles $F_{PH}(+)$ and $F_{PH}(-)$ by angle 2ω around the center O of the F_P circle. As a result an incorrect value for the phase angle of F_P will be found, which is different from the correct one by the value 2ω. If the anomalous information is combined with each of the two possibilities from the isomorphous data, the correct combination will give an electron density map of the protein that is superior to the map calculated with the incorrect combination.

An alternative method to find the absolute configuration is the following. Use the single isomorphous replacement method with anomalous scattering (SIRAS), as just described, for the calculation of two sets of phase angles, corresponding to the two centrosymmetrically related sets of heavy atoms. With these two sets of protein phase angles two dif-

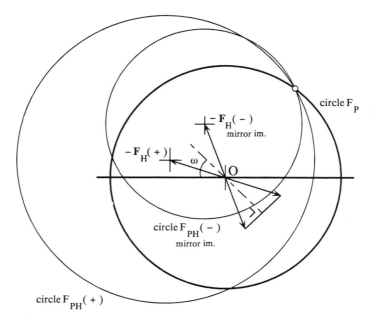

Figure 9.3. In this figure the crystallographic axes are chosen as in Figure 9.2, but the wrong (the centrosymmetric) set of heavy atom positions is chosen. The dashed line is the mirror image of the dashed line in Figure 9.2 and with respect to this dashed line the vectors $\mathbf{F}_H(+)$ and $\mathbf{F}_H(-)$ (mirror im.) are drawn.

ference Fourier maps are calculated for a second heavy atom derivative, PH(2):

1. amplitudes $|F_{PH(2)}| - |F_P|$ and one set of SIRAS phase angles and
2. amplitudes $|F_{PH(2)}| - |F_P|$ and the alternative set of SIRAS phase angles.

The difference Fourier map calculated with the correct set of phase angles (and the correct set of heavy atom positions) will show the highest peaks. This fixes the absolute configuration.

A somewhat simpler way to derive the absolute configuration of the protein from the anomalous scattering is as follows. According to Eq. (9.1), $|F_H|$ can be expressed as

$$|F_H| = \frac{k}{2 \sin(\alpha_{PH} - \alpha_H)}[|F_{PH}(+)| - |F_{PH}(-)|] \qquad (9.3)$$

$|F_{PH}(+)|$ and $|F_{PH}(-)|$ are observed values and $(\alpha_{PH} - \alpha_H)$ can be derived from isomorphous data without anomalous scattering. $|F_H|$ should now be calculated with Eq. (9.3) as a positive number. If the inverted image of the heavy atom set was chosen α_H and α_{PH} as well as $(\alpha_{PH} - \alpha_H)$

would have a value opposite to their correct value. $|F_H|$ would then be calculated as a negative number. If for a number of reflections, for which the heavy atom contribution is relatively strong, $|F_H|$ is calculated, the choice can easily be made. It can also be done by using all reflections and calculating a Fourier map with the amplitudes $|F_H|$ obtained with Eq. (9.3) and phase angles α_H as found from the isomorphous replacement. With the correct choice of the heavy atom positions, positive peaks will appear at the correct heavy atom positions. If the inverted set of heavy atom positions had been chosen, negative peaks would appear at these inverted positions. The coefficients used in the calculation of this Fourier map are

$$|F_H| \exp[i\alpha_H] = \frac{k}{2 \sin(\alpha_{PH} - \alpha_H)}[|F_{PH}(+)| - |F_{PH}(-)|] \exp[i\alpha_H]$$

In another method the following coefficients are used:

$$\tfrac{1}{2}(|F_{PH}(+)| - |F_{PH}(-)|) \exp[i\alpha_{PH}]$$

In this expression (compare with Eq. 7.29)

$$\frac{1}{2}(|F_{PH}(+)| - |F_{PH}(-)|) = \frac{1}{k}|F_H| \sin(\alpha_{PH} - \alpha_H) \qquad (9.1)$$

Here also the correct or incorrect sign of $(\alpha_{PH} - \alpha_H)$ determines whether the peaks in the Fourier map will be positive or negative at the positions assumed for the heavy atoms.

9.5. Multiple Wavelength Anomalous Dispersion (MAD)

If the protein has anomalous scatterers in its molecule, the difference in intensity between the Bijvoet pairs, $|F_h(+)|^2$ and $|F_h(-)|^2$, can profitably be exploited for the protein phase angle determination. In the multiple wavelength method the wavelength dependence of the anomalous scattering is used. The principle of this method is rather old but it was the introduction of the tunable synchrotron radiation sources that made it a technically feasible method for protein structure determination. Hendrickson and colleagues (Hendrickson et al., 1988; Krishna Murthy et al., 1988) were the first to take advantage of this method and to use it for solving the structure of a protein (see also Guss et al., 1988). Of course, the protein should contain an element that gives a sufficiently strong anomalous signal. Therefore, the elements in the upper rows of the periodic system are not suitable. Hendrickson showed that the presence of one Se atom (atomic numer 34) in a protein of not more than approximately 150 amino acid residues is sufficient for a successful applica-

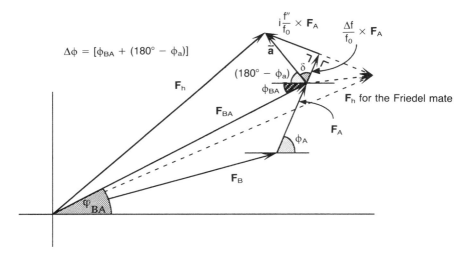

Figure 9.4. The structure factor diagram for the reflection of a protein crystal that contains one kind of anomalously scattering atoms. F_B is the contribution to the structure factor by the nonanomalously scattering atoms, F_A is the nonanomalous contribution of the anomalously scattering atoms, and the complete nonanomalous part is $F_{BA} = F_B + F_A$. $\Delta f/f_0 \times F_A + i(f''/f_0) \times F_A = a$ is the anomalous contribution of the anomalously scattering atoms. The anomalous component is exaggerated in this figure. The dotted lines are for the mirror image of the Friedel mate.

tion of MAD (Hendrickson et al., 1990; Leahy et al., 1992); however, this depends very much on the quality of the data. With more Se atoms the size of the protein can, of course, be larger. One way to introduce Se into a protein is by growing a microorganism on a Se-methionine substrate instead of a methionine-containing substrate. Condition for application of the method is that the wavelengths are carefully chosen to optimize the difference in intensity between Bijvoet pairs and between the diffraction at the selected wavelengths. The most frequently occurring situation in which there is one type of anomalously scattering atoms will be discussed here; this discussion is based on Karle's treatment of the problem (Karle, 1980), which has the advantage that the nonanomalous scattering of all atoms in the structure is separated from the wavelength-dependent part. Each anomalously scattering atom has an atomic scattering factor of $f = f_0 + \Delta f + if''$ (Section 7.8). In Figure 9.4 F_B is the contribution to the structure factor by the nonanomalously scattering atoms, F_A is the nonanomalous contribution of the anomalously scattering atoms, and the complete nonanomalous part is $F_{BA} = F_B + F_A$. The anomalous scattering contribution is

$$\frac{\Delta f}{f_0} \times F_A + i\frac{f''}{f_0} \times F_A = a$$

ϕ_{BA} is the phase angle of F_{BA}, ϕ_A of vector F_A, and ϕ_a of vector $\mathbf{a}$. $\Delta\phi = \phi_{BA} + (180° - \phi_a) = (180° + (\phi_{BA} - \phi_a))$.

Writing $|F|$ for $|F(h)|$ and applying the cosine rule:

$$|F|^2 = |F_{BA}|^2 + |a|^2 - 2|F_{BA}| \times |a| \times \cos\Delta\phi$$

with

$$|a|^2 = \frac{(\Delta f)^2 + (f'')^2}{f_0^2} \times |F_A|^2$$

$$|F|^2 = |F_{BA}|^2 + \frac{(\Delta f)^2 + (f'')^2}{f_0^2} \times |F_A|^2$$

$$+ 2\frac{\Delta f}{f_0} \cos\delta \, |F_{BA}| \times |F_A| \cos(\phi_{BA} - \phi_a)$$

$$+ 2\frac{f''}{f_0} \sin\delta \, |F_{BA}| \times |F_A| \cos(\phi_{BA} - \phi_a)$$

$$\phi_a = \phi_A + \delta; \quad \cos(\phi_{BA} - \phi_a) = \cos(\phi_{BA} - \phi_A - \delta)$$

Because ϕ_{BA} and ϕ_A are independent of the wavelength λ, whereas δ is, the cosine will be split into

$$\cos(\phi_{BA} - \phi_A) \cos\delta + \sin(\phi_{BA} - \phi_A) \sin\delta$$

$$|F|^2 = |F_{BA}|^2 + \frac{(\Delta f)^2 + (f'')^2}{f_0^2} \times |F_A|^2$$

$$+ 2\frac{\Delta f}{f_0}|F_{BA}| \times |F_A| \times \{\cos^2\delta \cos(\phi_{BA} - \phi_A)$$

$$+ \sin\delta \cos\delta \sin(\phi_{BA} - \phi_A)\}$$

$$+ 2\frac{f''}{f_0}|F_{BA}| \times |F_A| \times \{\sin\delta \cos\delta \cos(\phi_{BA} - \phi_A)$$

$$+ \sin^2\delta \sin(\phi_{BA} - \phi_A)\}$$

Grouping together the $\cos(\phi_{BA} - \phi_A)$ terms and also the $\sin(\phi_{BA} - \phi_A)$ terms:

$$|F|^2 = |F_{BA}|^2 + \frac{(\Delta f)^2 + (f'')^2}{f_0^2} \times |F_A|^2$$

$$+ |F_{BA}| \times |F_A| \times \left\{2\frac{\Delta f}{f_0} \cos^2\delta + 2\frac{f''}{f_0} \sin\delta \cos\delta\right\} \cos(\phi_{BA} - \phi_A)$$

$$+ |F_{BA}| \times |F_A| \times \left\{2\frac{\Delta f}{f_0} \sin\delta \cos\delta + 2\frac{f''}{f_0} \sin^2\delta\right\} \sin(\phi_{BA} - \phi_A)$$

Because

$$\left(\frac{\Delta f}{f_0} \cos\delta + \frac{f''}{f_0} \sin\delta\right) \cos\delta = \frac{\Delta f}{f_0}$$

and

$$\left(\frac{\Delta f}{f_0} \cos \delta + \frac{f''}{f_0} \sin \delta\right) \sin \delta = \frac{f''}{f_0}$$

we finally obtain

$$|F|^2 = |F_{BA}|^2 + p|F_A|^2 + |F_{BA}| \times |F_A|$$
$$\times [q \cos(\phi_{BA} - \phi_A) + r \sin(\phi_{BA} - \phi_A)]$$

with

$$p = \frac{(\Delta f)^2 + (f'')^2}{f_0^2}, \quad q = 2\frac{\Delta f}{f_0}, \quad \text{and} \quad r = 2\frac{f''}{f_0}$$

p, q, and r are functions of λ and are known from atomic scattering factor curves. The $|F|^2$ values are different for the Friedel mates but they can be determined experimentally. The unknown quantities are $|F_{BA}|$, $|F_A|$, and $(\phi_{BA} - \phi_A)$, all three independent of λ and equal for Friedel mates, except for the sign of $(\phi_{BA} - \phi_A)$. Therefore, a data set for one value of λ gives two sets of equations for these three unknowns and in principle measurements at two different wavelengths are sufficient to find $|F_{BA}|$, $|F_A|$, and $(\phi_{BA} - \phi_A)$ for each reflection. To calculate the electron density map of the protein, ϕ_{BA} is needed. This is obtained by solving the A-structure, that is, locating the anomalously scattering atoms from a Patterson map with coefficients $|F_A|^2$ or by direct methods. From the A-structure ϕ_A can be calculated and then ϕ_{BA} from the known value of $(\phi_{BA} - \phi_A)$.

Because no anomalous scattering is taken into account for the calculation of the A-structure, the real structure or its enantiomorph is obtained. The solution of this problem is to calculate ϕ_A angles for both structures. This gives two sets of ϕ_{BA} angles and two protein electron density maps from which the best one must be selected. An advantage of this method is that nonisomorphism does not play a role here. All data can be collected from a single crystal if the lifetime of the crystal allows this.

From the practical point of view the MAD method requires that great care be exercised in the collection and processing of the X-ray diffraction intensities, because the intensity differences are rather small. The choice of wavelengths should be such that the differences between $|F(h\ k\ l)|$ and $|F(\bar{h}\ \bar{k}\ \bar{l})|$ as well as the dispersive differences $\Delta F = \overline{|F(\lambda_i)|} - \overline{|F(\lambda_j)|}$ should be optimized. $\overline{|F(\lambda_i)|}$ is the average of $|(F(h\ k\ l)|$ and $|F(\bar{h}\ \bar{k}\ \bar{l})|$ at wavelength λ_i.

The anomalous contribution to the atomic scattering factor is a function of the atomic absorption coefficient for the anomalously scattering element and can be derived from the experimental values of this coefficient. The absorption coefficient must be measured at the absorption edge of the element and at some distance from the edge. Because the precise position of the absorption edge depends on the chemical environment of the element, the spectrum of the atomic absorption coefficient as a function of the X-ray wavelength (or photon energy) should be measured on the crystal itself. This can conveniently be done by measuring the fluorescence from the element when radiated by an incident beam. Fluorescence is a product of the absorption, because in absorption an electron is removed from its atomic orbital and fluorescent radiation is emitted when the empty position is filled up by another electron. The wavelength of the fluorescent radiation is characteristic for the irradiated element. In converting the fluorescence spectrum to the atomic absorption spectrum, background and scaling corrections are made in such a way that the experimental values for the atomic absorption coefficient fit their theoretical values. The latter cannot be calculated accurately inside the edge region, but it can be done outside the edge region.

$$\mu_a = s \times R - (a + b\Delta + c\Delta^2)$$

μ_a is the atomic absorption coefficient, R is the fluorescence ratio $I_{fl}(E)/I_0(E)$, in which $I_{fl}(E)$ is the fluorescent intensity, and $I_0(E)$ is the intensity of the incident beam. E is the energy of the incident photons. $\Delta = E - E_0$, where E_0 corresponds with the photon energy at the absorption edge. s is a scale factor that is assumed to be independent of E. s, a, b, and c are chosen such that the experimental and theoretical curves fit as closely as possible to each other.

The anomalous contribution to the atomic scattering factor can be derived from the values for the atomic absorption coefficient μ_a, applying relationships given in the literature, for instance, in James (1965) and Hendrickson et al. (1988).

Conclusion concerning MAD: In principle MAD is an excellent method to determine protein phase angles. It requires the presence of an anomalously scattering atom in the protein. Although it has been used successfully in a number of structure determinations, it is not an easy method, due to the complications, like tuning synchrotron radiation and painful data measurements. The method must be carried out with extreme care and is, therefore, not as popular as MIR, MIRAS, or molecular replacement. Its great advantage is that the measurements can be done on one crystal, so that one deals with perfect isomorphism.

Summary

The most tightly bound electrons in an atom cause measurable anomalous scattering of X-rays. For light atoms (C, N, and O) the effect is negligible but for heavier atoms (from S onward for the commonly used X-ray wavelengths) a measurable effect does occur and this causes a difference in intensity between Friedel pairs of reflections. Because this difference is very small, it is important to measure the intensities with extreme accuracy.

From anomalous scattering data two kinds of information can be derived:

1. the choice between a structure and its enantiomorph and
2. phase angle information: this can be additional to the isomorphous replacement information, or by collecting data at suitably chosen X-ray wavelengths, it can supply phase information for a native protein crystal if this does contain an anomalously scattering atom.

Chapter 10
Molecular Replacement

10.1. Introduction

With the isomorphous replacement method a preliminary set of protein phases and a first model of the protein structure can be obtained. As we shall see in Chapter 13 such a model can be refined by minimizing the difference between the observed $|F|$-values and the $|F|$-values calculated from the model. An easier way to obtain a first model can be followed if the structure of a protein with a homologous amino acid sequence has already been established. The structure of this homologous protein is—as it were—borrowed by the protein for which the structure must be determined and serves as a very first model that can subsequently be refined. This procedure is based on the observation that proteins, homologous in their amino acid sequence, have a very similar folding of their polypeptide chain. Also, if for another reason two structures can be expected to be similar, one known and the other unknown, the procedure can be applied.

The problem is to transfer the known protein molecular structure from its crystalline arrangement to the crystal of the protein for which the structure is not yet known. The solution is the molecular replacement method, which was initiated in pioneering studies by Rossmann and Blow (1962). Placement of the molecule in the target unit cell requires its proper orientation and precise position. In short, it involves two steps: rotation and translation. In the rotation step the spatial orientation of the known and unknown molecule with respect to each other is determined while in the next step the translation needed to superimpose the now correctly oriented molecule onto the other molecule is calculated. The molecular replacement method can also serve another purpose: If a crystal structure has more than one protein molecule or a number of equal subunits in the asymmetric unit, then their relative position can be determined. This noncrystallographic symmetry is useful information in the process of improving protein phase angles by molecular averaging (Section 8.4).

The basic principle of the molecular replacement method can be understood by regarding the Patterson function of a protein crystal structure. The Patterson map is a vector map: vectors between atoms in the real structure show up as vectors from the origin to maxima in the Patterson map. If the pairs of atoms belong to the same molecule, then the corresponding vectors are relatively short and their end-points are found not too far from the origin in the Patterson map; they are called *self-Patterson vectors*. If there were no intermolecular vectors (*cross-Patterson vectors*), this inner region of the Patterson map would be equal for the same molecule in different crystal structures, apart from a rotation difference. For homologous molecules it is not exactly equal but very similar. Therefore, the self-Patterson vectors can supply us with the rotational relationship between the known and the unknown molecular structures.

10.2. The Rotation Function

We shall first consider how the angular relationship between identical units within one asymmetric unit (*self-rotation function*) or between equal or closely related molecules in two different crystal forms (*cross-rotation function*) can be derived from the X-ray data. This will be discussed following the original Rossmann and Blow procedure. It is true that in many of the software packages available to calculate the rotational orientation the conventional Rossmann and Blow procedure is replaced by the mathematically more elegant Crowther's fast rotation function (Crowther, 1972). However, the principle of the method can be best understood with the Rossmann and Blow procedure.

The self-Patterson peaks all lie in a volume around the origin with a radius equal to the dimension of the molecule (or subunit). If a number of identical molecules (or subunits) lie within one asymmetric unit, the self-Patterson vector distribution is exactly the same for all these molecules, except for a rotation that is the same as their noncrystallographic rotational symmetry in real space. Therefore, if the Patterson function is superimposed on a correctly rotated version, maximum overlap between the two Patterson maps will occur. Similarly, for two different lattices, the two different Patterson maps must be superposed to maximum overlap by a rotation of one of the two maps.

We assume that the crystal system has orthogonal axes. An atom in one system is located at position $\mathbf{x} = x_1\mathbf{a}_1 + x_2\mathbf{a}_2 + x_3\mathbf{a}_3$ in a crystallographic lattice with axes $\mathbf{a}_1$, $\mathbf{a}_2$, and $\mathbf{a}_3$. Rotation of the axial system, keeping the same origin, leads to a new set of axes: $\mathbf{a}_{r,1}$, $\mathbf{a}_{r,2}$ and $\mathbf{a}_{r,3}$. With respect to the new axes the position of the particular atom in position $\mathbf{x}$ is $\mathbf{x}_r = x_{r,1}\mathbf{a}_{r,1} + x_{r,2}\mathbf{a}_{r,2} + x_{r,3}\mathbf{a}_{r,3}$ and the relationship between the two sets of coordinates is

$$\left.\begin{array}{l} x_{r,1} = c_{11}x_1 + c_{12}x_2 + c_{13}x_3 \\ x_{r,2} = c_{21}x_1 + c_{22}x_2 + c_{23}x_3 \\ x_{r,3} = c_{31}x_1 + c_{32}x_2 + c_{33}x_3 \end{array}\right\} \quad \text{or in matrix notation } \mathbf{x}_r = [C]\mathbf{x}$$

A rotation of the axes has the same effect as a rotation of the structure in the opposite direction. If the structure rotates, its Patterson map rotates in the same way. Applying the rotation $[C]$ to the Patterson function $P(\mathbf{u})$ gives the rotated Patterson function $P_r(\mathbf{u}_r)$. An overlap function R of $P(\mathbf{u})$ with the rotated version, $P_r(\mathbf{u}_r)$, of the same crystal lattice (self-rotation function) or a different crystal lattice (cross-rotation function) is defined as

$$R(\alpha, \beta, \gamma) = \int_U P(\mathbf{u}) \times P_r(\mathbf{u}_r)\, d\mathbf{u} \tag{10.1}$$

U is the volume in the Patterson map where the self-Patterson peaks are located. The product function R depends on the rotation angles (related to $[C]$) and will have a maximum value for correct overlap. $P(\mathbf{u})$ can be expanded in a Fourier series:

$$P(\mathbf{u}) = \frac{1}{V}\sum_\mathbf{h}|F(\mathbf{h})|^2 \exp[-2\pi i\mathbf{h}\mathbf{u}]$$

For $P_r(\mathbf{u}_r)$ can be written

$$P_r(\mathbf{u}_r) = \frac{1}{V}\sum_{\mathbf{h}'}|F(\mathbf{h}')|^2 \exp[-2\pi i\mathbf{h}'\mathbf{u}_r]$$

Because $\mathbf{u}_r = [C]\mathbf{u}$

$$P_r(\mathbf{u}_r) = \frac{1}{V}\sum_{\mathbf{h}'}|F(\mathbf{h}')|^2 \exp[-2\pi i\mathbf{h}'[C]\mathbf{u}]$$

$\mathbf{h}'[C]$ is equal to $[C^{-1}]\mathbf{h}'$, and therefore

$$P_r(\mathbf{u}_r) = \frac{1}{V}\sum_{\mathbf{h}'}|F(\mathbf{h}')|^2 \exp[-2\pi i[C^{-1}]\mathbf{h}'\mathbf{u}]$$

$P(\mathbf{u})$ and $P_r(\mathbf{u}_r)$ must now be superimposed and $P(\mathbf{u}) \times P_r(\mathbf{u}_r)$ calculated for every position $\mathbf{u}$ within U and then the integral must be taken to obtain $R(\alpha, \beta, \gamma)$:

$$R(\alpha, \beta, \gamma) = \frac{1}{V^2}\sum_\mathbf{h}\sum_{\mathbf{h}'}|F(\mathbf{h})|^2|F(\mathbf{h}')|^2$$

$$\times \int_U \exp[-2\pi i(\mathbf{h} + [C^{-1}]\mathbf{h}')\mathbf{u}]\, d\mathbf{u} \tag{10.2}$$

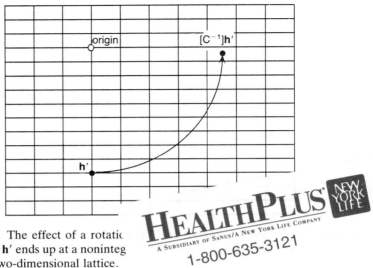

Figure 10.1. The effect of a rotatic
lattice point **h**' ends up at a noninteg
here for a two-dimensional lattice.

A problem arises here: for the ca
be sampled at positions $[C^{-1}]\mathbf{h}'$ in
because, in general, $[C^{-1}]\mathbf{h}'$ is at i
(Figure 10.1). This problem can be :
namely that an enormous number o.
multiplication is required for each i
difficult as it looks like, because of tl

$$\int_U \exp[-2\pi i(\mathbf{h} +$$

It limits the summation over **h**' to only   ....ver of **h**'. This can
be understood in the following way. Suppose a crystalline lattice has a
very special structure: it contains in each unit cell a body with the shape
and the volume of U. The center of U is at the origin of the unit cell. The
electron density inside U is flat $[\rho(\mathbf{x}) = \rho]$, and outside U the unit cell is
empty: $\rho(\mathbf{x}) = 0$ (Figure 10.2). The structure factor of this special structure
at reciprocal lattice position $-(\mathbf{h} + [C^{-1}]\mathbf{h}')$ is

$$\mathbf{F}[-(\mathbf{h} + [C^{-1}]\mathbf{h}')] = V \int_V \rho(x) \exp[-2\pi i(\mathbf{h} + [C^{-1}]\mathbf{h}')\mathbf{x}] \, d\mathbf{x}$$

Because of the special electron density distribution

$$\mathbf{F}[-(\mathbf{h} + [C^{-1}]\mathbf{h}')] = V\rho\,(x) \int_U \exp[-2\pi i(\mathbf{h} + [C^{-1}]\mathbf{h}')\mathbf{x}] \, d\mathbf{x} \quad (10.3)$$

If the Fourier transform of the body with the shape and volume of U and
unit electron density is **G**, then the value of the transform for the body

with uniform electron density ρ at reciprocal lattice position
$-(\mathbf{h} + [C^{-1}]\mathbf{h}')$ is

$$U \times \rho \times \mathbf{G}[-(\mathbf{h} + [C^{-1}]\mathbf{h}')] \qquad (10.4)$$

Comparing Eqs. (10.3) and (10.4) gives

$$\int_U \exp[-2\pi i(\mathbf{h} + [C^{-1}]\mathbf{h}')\mathbf{x}]\,d\mathbf{x} = \frac{U}{V} \times \mathbf{G}[-(\mathbf{h} + [C^{-1}]\mathbf{h}')] \quad (10.5)$$

The rotation function can thus be written as

$$R(\alpha, \beta, \gamma) = \frac{U}{V^3}\sum_{\mathbf{h}}\sum_{\mathbf{h}'}|F(\mathbf{h})|^2|F(\mathbf{h}')|^2 \times \mathbf{G}[-(\mathbf{h} + [C^{-1}]\mathbf{h}')] \quad (10.6)$$

The properties of $\mathbf{G}[-(\mathbf{h} + [C^{-1}]\mathbf{h}')]$ allow us to solve the two problems
mentioned above. Usually U is assumed to be spherical and the transform
of a sphere at the origin of a unit cell is

$$G = \frac{3(\sin 2\pi x - 2\pi x \cos 2\pi x)}{(2\pi x)^3}$$

x is in our case equal to $(\mathbf{h} + [C^{-1}]\mathbf{h}') \cdot \mathbf{r}$. The graphic representation of
the function is shown in Figure 10.3. $\mathbf{G}$ has its maximum value for $[C^{-1}]\mathbf{h}'$
$= -\mathbf{h}$ and falls off very rapidly for values of $[C^{-1}]\mathbf{h}'$ differing from $-\mathbf{h}$.
Therefore the summation in Eq. (10.2) can be performed for every $\mathbf{h}$ with
only a limited number of $\mathbf{h}'$ terms, namely only those for which $[C^{-1}]\mathbf{h}'$ is
close to $-\mathbf{h}$. This solves the second problem.

The fall off of G can be illustrated with an example. Let the cell

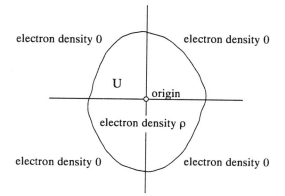

Figure 10.2. The integral in Eq. (10.2) is developed by using a special structure
that has a flat electron density inside the three-dimensional body $U[\rho(\mathbf{x}) = \rho]$,
and no electron density outside $U[\rho(\mathbf{x}) = 0]$. The center of U is in the origin of
the unit cell.

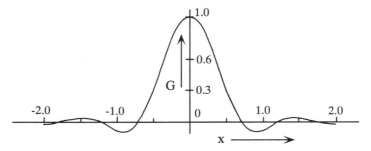

Figure 10.3. The function $G = [3(\sin 2\pi x - 2\pi x \cos 2\pi x)]/(2\pi x)^3$ is plotted as a function of x. Note the rapid fading away for increasing x.

dimension be $80\,\text{Å}$ and the radius of the sphere $r = 20\,\text{Å}$, then we obtain the following values for G:

Distance from $-\mathbf{h}$ in Reciprocal Lattice Units	x	G
1	0.25	0.78
2	0.50	0.30
3	0.75	-0.029

To solve the first problem, $|F([C^{-1}]\mathbf{h}')|^2$ is calculated for a number of integral lattice points around $([C^{-1}]\mathbf{h}')$ and the $|F|^2$-value at $([C^{-1}]\mathbf{h}')$ is obtained by interpolation, giving a weight $G[(\mathbf{h} + [C^{-1}]\mathbf{h}')]$ to the $|F|^2$-values at the integral lattice points around $([C^{-1}]\mathbf{h}')$.

In the application of the rotation method it is important that all strong reflections are present because the calculation of the rotation function basically depends on the rotation of a Patterson map. Another point to consider is the resolution range of the data used in the calculation of the rotation function. Low resolution data can be excluded because they are rather insensitive to rotation; moreover they are determined to an appreciable extent by the solvent region. High resolution data are more discriminating but are also more sensitive for the model. The best range is often found between 3 and $5\,\text{Å}$. Also, because of computational limitations, the integration is extended to a rather modest resolution.

Other parameters to choose are the shape and the size of the region U. For a matter of convenience the region is assumed to be spherical. Its radius can be chosen equal to, or somewhat less than the diameter of the molecule. In the calculation of the rotation function, the shorter intermolecular vectors confuse the situation. This can be improved if in the calculation of the rotation function the known molecule is put into a large artificial unit cell having no crystallographic symmetry (space group $P1$). The dimensions of the cell should be such that all cross-vectors are longer than the diameter of the molecule. Instead of working with the X-ray data from the crystal structure of the known molecule, the calculated structure factors of the artificial lattice are used. It is not always easy to find the optimal model structure and different models must be tried if the first results are unsatisfactory. For instance, the original model can be truncated by deleting side chains, doubtful parts, using one monomer if the original model was an oligomer, and using just one domain of the model molecule.

The magnitude of the rotation function is plotted in a three-dimensional space with the three angular rotations as the coordinates. Several alternatives and conventions for the directions, names, signs, and origins of the rotation angles exist. This can cause a great deal of confusion and it is extremely important to know the procedure in the available software package. The usual system works with Eulerian angles because then the symmetry of the rotation function shows up clearly. The system used by Rossmann and Blow in their original paper (Rossmann and Blow, 1962) applies first a rotation by the angle α around z of an orthogonal coordinate system, then around the new x-axis by an angle β, and finally a rotation by γ around the new z axis. However, another convention is now generally used (Machin, 1985): Rotation by the angle α around the z-axis, next a rotation by the angle β around the new y-axis, and finally a rotation by the angle γ around the new z-axis (Figure 10.4a). The sign for

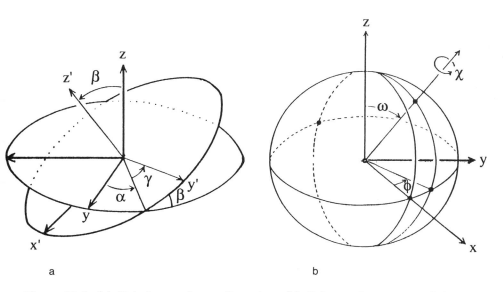

Figure 10.4. (a) Eulerian angles α, β, and γ; (b) Polar angles χ, ω, and ϕ. (Reproduced from the Proceedings of the Daresbury Study Weekend on Molecular Replacement, 15–16 February, 1985, with permission from the Daresbury Laboratory, Daresbury, Warrington, U.K.)

the rotation of the axes is positive for a clockwise rotation when looking from the origin along the positive rotation axis.

If one is searching for noncrystallographic symmetry in an asymmetric unit (self-rotation function) a zero rotation results in a high value for R, because it simply superposes the Patterson map on itself. An odd feature of R is the ridge in the section $\beta = 0$. It represents the set of equivalent zero rotations $(\alpha, 0, -\alpha)$. This stems from the fact that for $\beta = 0$ the rotations α and γ have the same effect on the rotation and, therefore, all rotations with the same $\alpha + \gamma$ are identical. The same is also true for $\beta = 180°$, where $(\alpha - \gamma)$ rotations are equivalent. Equivalent effects can also be obtained for different combinations of the three angular coordinates, which causes symmetry in the rotation function. It depends on symmetry in the Patterson functions that are rotated with respect to each other and on the choice of the system of variables chosen for the rotation. Because of the symmetry in the rotation function it need to be calculated only for its asymmetric unit. Methods for deriving the asymmetric unit in the rotation function have been given by Tollin and Rossmann (1966), Narasinga Rao et al. (1980), and Moss (1985).

When searching for noncrystallographic symmetry, it is convenient to work with spherical polar rotation (Figure 10.4b). ω and ϕ determine the position of the rotation axis and χ is the rotation around this axis. The advantage of this system derives from the fact that rotations of $\chi = 180°$ and $120°$ are very common and the search can be restricted to a fixed value for χ. In Figure 10.4b, Z is the polar axis. However, when working in a monoclinic space group it is convenient to have the unique y-axis as the polar axis.

From Eq. (10.1) it is clear that the strong reflections will dominate the calculation of R. This is true to such an extent that it suffices to incorporate only a fraction of all reflections in the calculation, for instance, 10% with the highest intensities (Tollin and Rossmann, 1966). To obtain an impression of the quality of the rotation function it is advisable to give the ratio of the highest to the next highest peak in the rotation map.

An, in principle, simpler way than the Rossmann and Blow method to solve the rotation problem was proposed by Huber and his colleagues (Huber, 1985). In their method the Patterson map is also rotated and the rotated map is superimposed on the original map. However, now the operation is performed, not in reciprocal, but in direct space. A number of high peaks (a few hundred to a few thousand) in the Patterson map are selected for a rough rotational search, which is done in steps of 10°. These peaks lie within a sphere around the origin where most of the self-Patterson peaks are located. However, the innermost region of this sphere, close to the high origin peak of the Patterson map, is neglected. As fit criterion the product of the map and its rotated version at corresponding grid points is used, as in the Rossmann and Blow procedure. After a highest or a few high peaks are found in the product function, the search can be continued in finer steps around these peaks.

10.2.1. The Locked Rotation Function

If the cross-rotation function is applied with a model molecule to be oriented in an unknown crystal structure, several solutions will be found if the crystal structure has crystallographic symmetry, but also because of noncrystallographic symmetry operators. If the latter do exist and are known from the self-rotation function, the solutions of the cross-rotation function are not independent but related through the noncrystallographic symmetry. This knowledge can be used as a constraint in the calculation of a "locked" rotation function, which is the average of n independent rotation functions and, consequently, has an improved peak-to-noise ratio (Tong and Rossmann, 1990; Hiremath et al., 1990). By the same token the self-rotation function can be improved if an assumed point group symmetry is imposed on the unknown molecule or combination of molecules.

10.2.1.1. The Locked Self-Rotation Function

For a locked self-rotation function an assumed point group in a standard orientation is rotated into the unknown unit cell by matrix $[E]$. Within this point group are n symmetry elements $[I_i]$ with $i = 1, \ldots, n$. Their application leaves the point group unchanged. A position vector $\mathbf{U}_1$ in the point group is moved to $\mathbf{U}_i$ by the application of the symmetry element $[I_i]$:

$$\mathbf{U}_i = [I_i] \times \mathbf{U}_1 \quad \text{with} \quad i = 1, \ldots, n$$

By application of $[E]$ the vector $\mathbf{U}_1$ in the point group is moved to $\mathbf{X}_1$ in the crystal:

$$\mathbf{X}_1 = [E] \times \mathbf{U}_1$$
$$\mathbf{X}_i = [E] \times \mathbf{U}_i$$

For the point group as well as for the crystal, an orthogonal lattice is defined. The relationship between each $\mathbf{X}_i$ and $\mathbf{X}_1$ is then.

$$\mathbf{X}_i = [E] \times [I_i] \times \mathbf{U}_1 = [E] \times [\mathbf{I}_i] \times [\mathbf{E}^{-1}] \times \mathbf{X}_1$$

From the self-rotation function we know that

$$\mathbf{X}_i = [\rho_i] \times \mathbf{X}_1$$
$$[\rho_i] = [E] \times [I_i] \times [E^{-1}] \tag{10.7}$$

In self-rotation the Patterson function is rotated and superimposed on itself. The rotation is by matrix $[C]$ in a real (not necessarily orthogonal) lattice.

$$[C] = [\alpha] \times [\rho] \times [\beta] \qquad (10.8)$$

where matrix $[\beta]$ orthogonalizes the real lattice and $[\alpha]$ deorthogonalizes it. Combining Eqs. (10.7) and (10.8):

$$[C_i] = [\alpha] \times [E] \times [I_i] \times [E^{-1}] \times [\beta] \qquad (10.9)$$

$[C_i]$ tests the ith symmetry element and this must be done for each of the n symmetry elements. Each $[C_i]$ corresponds with a self-rotation function R_i. By combining the results, the value of the locked rotation function is obtained as R_L:

$$R_L = \frac{\sum\limits_{i=1}^{n} R_i}{n} \qquad (10.10)$$

The noise of this function will be $\sqrt{n}$ smaller than for the normal self-rotation function.

10.2.1.2. The Locked Cross-Rotation Function

In the calculation of this function one model molecule is oriented in the unknown crystal structure, which contains one or more similar molecules. In case of more molecules, the cross-rotation function gives several peaks corresponding with the superposition of the model molecule on each of these separate molecules. From the self-rotation function the relative orientation of these separate molecules is usually known and can be used as a constraint in the calculation of the cross-rotation function. If $[E]$ is the matrix that relates the known model molecule with the first molecule in the unknown cell (cell with unknown molecular structure), we have

$$\mathbf{X}_1 = [E] \times \mathbf{U}$$

where $\mathbf{U}$ is a position vector in the model molecule. If $[\beta_u]$ is the orthogonalization matrix in the known cell and $[\alpha_x]$ the deorthogonalization matrix in the unknown cell

$$\mathbf{x}_1 = [\alpha_x] \times [E] \times [\beta_u] \times \mathbf{u} \qquad (10.11)$$

with $\mathbf{x}$ and $\mathbf{u}$ fractional coordinates in the unknown and known cell, respectively. $[I_i]$, with $i = 1, \ldots, n$, is a matrix that moves position vector $\mathbf{X}_1$ in the unknown structure to $\mathbf{X}_i$ in an orthogonal coordinate system; $\mathbf{X}_1$ and $\mathbf{X}_i$ are related by the noncrystallographic symmetry. In fractional coordinates

$$\mathbf{x}_i = [\alpha_x] \times [I_i] \times [\beta_x] \times \mathbf{x}_1 \qquad (10.12)$$

Combining Eqs. (10.11) and (10.12), it follows that

$$\mathbf{x}_i = [\alpha_x] \times [I_i] \times [\beta_x] \times [\alpha_x] \times [E] \times [\beta_u] \times \mathbf{u}$$

or

$$\mathbf{x}_i = [\alpha_x] \times [I_i] \times [E] \times [\beta_u] \times \mathbf{u}$$

The cross-rotation function relates $\mathbf{x}_i$ to $\mathbf{u}$ by means of the matrix $[C_i]$.

$$[C_i] = [\alpha_x] \times [I_i] \times [E] \times [\beta_u]$$

The locked cross-rotation function is now calculated as the average of n cross-rotation functions, each calculated with a different $[C_i]$.

$$R_L = \frac{\sum\limits_{i=1}^{n} R_i}{n} \tag{10.13}$$

Because n rotation functions instead of 1 must be calculated, the calculation time would be n times longer. However, it can be shown that the plot of the locked cross-rotation function has an n times higher symmetry and, therefore, the time of calculation for a normal and a locked cross-rotation function is not much different. The locked rotation function has the advantage of a better peak-to-noise ratio and the interpretation of its result is simpler because it involves the location of fewer peaks. A further advantage is that only the very strong reflections—even fewer than for the normal rotation function—need to be used, which speeds up the calculation appreciably.

10.3. The Translation Function

The rotation function is based on the rotation of a Patterson function around an axis through its origin. A translation is not incorporated. However, for the final solution of the molecular replacement method the translation required to overlap one molecule (or subunit) onto the other in real space must be determined, after it has been oriented in the correct way with the rotation function. The simplest way to do this is by trial and error. The known molecule is moved through the asymmetric unit and structure factors are calculated—$\mathbf{F}$(calc)—and compared with the observed structure factor by calculating an R-factor or the correlation coefficient as a function of the molecular position.

$$R = \frac{\sum\limits_{hkl} ||F(\text{obs})| - k|F(\text{calc})||}{\sum\limits_{hkl} |F(\text{obs})|}$$

The standard linear correlation coefficient C is

$$C = \frac{\sum_{hkl}(|F(\text{obs})|^2 - \overline{|F(\text{obs})|^2}) \times (|F(\text{calc})|^2 - \overline{|F(\text{calc})|^2})}{\left[\sum_{hkl}(|F(\text{obs})|^2 - \overline{|F(\text{obs})|^2})^2 \sum_{hkl}(|F(\text{calc})|^2 - \overline{|F(\text{calc})|^2})^2\right]^{1/2}}$$

The advantage of this correlation coefficient over the R-factor is that it is scaling insensitive; replacement of $|F(\text{obs})|^2$ by $k|F(\text{obs})|^2 +$ a constant (k is the scale factor for the intensities) gives the same value. During R-factor search calculations, one need not start calculating the $F(\text{calc})$ values from atomic coordinates every time the molecule is shifted, but instead calculate phase shifts for each set of the molecules related by crystallographic symmetry. This saves considerable computer time. The result from the rotation function can be refined by changing the rotation parameters in small steps. With increased computing power in the future, it might be possible, instead of calculating the rotation and translation function, to carry out a six-dimensional search with the three rotation angles and the three translation components as parameters. This has already been applied successfully in the structure determination of oligonucleotides and nucleic acids at low resolution (Rabinovich and Shakked, 1984). It can also be helpful to exploit packing analysis; the protein molecules in the unit cell cannot penetrate each other and this limits the possible positions of the molecules. Although not necessarily giving a unique solution, it excludes parts of the unit cell and in this way reduces the computer time (Hendrickson and Ward, 1976).

In a more straightforward method than the trial and error search, a translation function is calculated that gives the correlation between a set of cross-Patterson vectors for a model structure and the observed Patterson function. Cross-Patterson vectors in this context mean vectors in the Patterson map derived from vectors between atoms in two molecules in the model structure related by a crystallographic symmetry operation $[C]$ $+ \mathbf{d}$. In space group $P1$, in which no crystallographic symmetry exists, the origin can be chosen everywhere and this has no influence on the absolute value of the structure factor. The calculation of the translation function is then not necessary.

Here, the translation function will be presented as derived by Crowther and Blow (1967) and we shall do this for an unknown structure with crystals belonging to space group $P222$ (Figure 10.5). They have one molecule in the asymmetric unit and therefore four molecules (1–4) in the unit cell. We choose one pair of molecules, e.g., 1 and 2. Their orientation is known from the rotation function, but not their position in the unit cell. With the translation function we can determine the position of molecule 1 with respect to the symmetry related molecule 2, and subsequently for any other pair of symmetry related molecules.

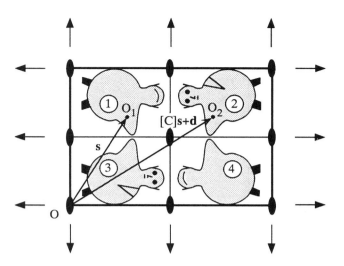

Figure 10.5. A unit cell for space group $P222$. It contains four molecules, 1–4. The origin of the unit cell is in O. Molecule 1 has its local origin in O_1 at position s, and the origin of molecule 2 is in O_2 at position $[C]s + d$, where matrix $[C]$ transfers molecule 1 to molecule 2; see also Figure 10.6.

The local origin of molecule 1 is in O_1 and of molecule 2 in O_2. The origin of the unit cell is in O. Cross-Patterson vectors between the two molecules can then be calculated with

$$P_{1,2}(\mathbf{u}) = \int_V \rho_1(\mathbf{x}) \times \rho_2(\mathbf{x} + \mathbf{u})\, d\mathbf{x} \qquad (10.14)$$

If the electron density expressed with respect to the local origin of the first molecule, the model molecule M, is ρ_M, then (Figure 10.6)

$$\rho_1(\mathbf{x}) = \rho_M(\mathbf{x} - \mathbf{s})$$

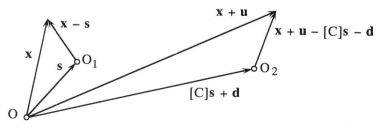

Figure 10.6. The position $(\mathbf{x})$ in molecule 1 and $(\mathbf{x} + \mathbf{u})$ in molecule 2. O_1 and O_2 are local origins.

and

$$\rho_2(\mathbf{x} + \mathbf{u}) = \rho(\mathbf{x} + \mathbf{u} - [C]\mathbf{s} - \mathbf{d})$$

for the local origin in O_2. This is equal to the electron density in the model molecule (molecule 1) at the symmetry related position $[C^{-1}](\mathbf{x} + \mathbf{u} - [C]\mathbf{s} - \mathbf{d})$ and, therefore

$$\rho_2(\mathbf{x} + \mathbf{u}) = \rho_M\{[C^{-1}](\mathbf{x} + \mathbf{u} - [C]\mathbf{s} - \mathbf{d})\}$$

Equation (10.14) becomes

$$P_{1,2}(\mathbf{u}, \mathbf{s}) = \int_V \rho_M(\mathbf{x} - \mathbf{s}) \times \rho_M\{[C^{-1}](\mathbf{x} + \mathbf{u} - [C]\mathbf{s} - \mathbf{d})\} \, d\mathbf{x}$$

If ρ_M is written as a Fourier series in terms of the structure factors $\mathbf{F}_M$, we have

$$P_{1,2}(\mathbf{u}, \mathbf{s}) = \int_V \sum_{\mathbf{h}} \mathbf{F}_M(\mathbf{h}) \exp[-2\pi i \mathbf{h} \cdot (\mathbf{x} - \mathbf{s})]$$

$$\times \sum_{\mathbf{p}} \mathbf{F}_M(\mathbf{p}) \exp[-2\pi i \mathbf{p}[C^{-1}](\mathbf{x} + \mathbf{u} - [C]\mathbf{s} - \mathbf{d})] \, d\mathbf{x}$$

$$= \sum_{\mathbf{h}} \sum_{\mathbf{p}} \mathbf{F}_M(\mathbf{h}) \times \mathbf{F}_M(\mathbf{p}) \exp[2\pi i (\mathbf{h} \cdot \mathbf{s} + \mathbf{p}[C^{-1}]([C]\mathbf{s} + \mathbf{d}))]$$

$$\times \exp[-2\pi i \mathbf{p}[C^{-1}]\mathbf{u}] \int_V \exp[-2\pi i (\mathbf{h} + \mathbf{p}[C^{-1}])\mathbf{x}] \, d\mathbf{x}$$

Because $[C]$ is a crystallographic rotation, $\mathbf{p}[C^{-1}]$ is a reciprocal lattice point and, therefore, $(\mathbf{h} + \mathbf{p}[C^{-1}])$ is an integral number and as a consequence the integral vanishes, unless $(\mathbf{h} + \mathbf{p}[C^{-1}]) = 0$ (see Figure 4.15). Then the integral is equal to V with $\mathbf{p} = -\mathbf{h}[C]$. Deleting the constant V

$$P_{1,2}(\mathbf{u}, \mathbf{s}) = \sum_{\mathbf{h}} \mathbf{F}_M(\mathbf{h}) \cdot \mathbf{F}_M(-\mathbf{h}[C]) \exp[2\pi i \mathbf{h}(\mathbf{s} - [C]\mathbf{s} - \mathbf{d})] \exp[2\pi i \mathbf{h} \cdot \mathbf{u}]$$

If the intermolecular vector $\mathbf{t}$ is between O_1 and O_2:

$$\mathbf{t} = -\mathbf{s} + [C]\mathbf{s} + \mathbf{d}$$

Because $\mathbf{F}_M(-\mathbf{h}[C]) = \mathbf{F}_M^*(\mathbf{h}[C])$ with $\mathbf{F}_M^*$ the complex conjugate of $\mathbf{F}_M$:

$$P_{1,2}(\mathbf{u}, \mathbf{t}) = \sum_{\mathbf{h}} \mathbf{F}_M(\mathbf{h}) \cdot \mathbf{F}_M^*(\mathbf{h}[C]) \exp[-2\pi i \mathbf{h} \cdot \mathbf{t}] \exp[2\pi i \mathbf{h} \cdot \mathbf{u}] \qquad (10.15)$$

This is the cross-Patterson function of the model structure in which two molecules are related by crystallographic symmetry. This should now be compared with the observed Patterson function $P(\mathbf{u})$. To this end the translation function $T(\mathbf{t})$ is calculated:

$$T(\mathbf{t}) = \int_V P_{1,2}(\mathbf{u}, \mathbf{t}) \times P(\mathbf{u}) \, d\mathbf{u} \qquad (10.16)$$

When the intermolecular vector $\mathbf{t}$ is equal to the true intermolecular vector $\mathbf{t}_0$, the function $T(\mathbf{t})$ will reach a maximum value, because then the computed Patterson $P_{1,2}(\mathbf{u}, \mathbf{t})$ fits correctly on the observed Patterson function $P(\mathbf{u})$. If $P_{1,2}(\mathbf{u}, \mathbf{t})$ in Eq. (10.16) is replaced by the right part of Eq. (10.15) and $P(\mathbf{u})$ by $\sum_{\mathbf{p}}|F_{\text{obs}}(\mathbf{p})|^2 \exp[-2\pi i\mathbf{p} \cdot \mathbf{u}] \, d\mathbf{u}$ the translation function becomes

$$T(\mathbf{t}) = \int_V \sum_{\mathbf{h}} \mathbf{F}_{\mathrm{M}}(\mathbf{h}) \cdot \mathbf{F}_{\mathrm{M}}^*(\mathbf{h}[C]) \exp[-2\pi i\mathbf{h} \cdot \mathbf{t}] \exp[2\pi i\mathbf{h} \cdot \mathbf{u}]$$

$$\times \sum_{p}|F_{\text{obs}}(\mathbf{p})|^2 \exp[-2\pi i\mathbf{p} \cdot \mathbf{u}] \, d\mathbf{u}$$

Because the integration is over $\mathbf{u}$ we can take all terms with $\mathbf{u}$ together under the integral

$$T(\mathbf{t}) = \sum_{\mathbf{h}} \mathbf{F}_{\mathrm{M}}(\mathbf{h}) \cdot \mathbf{F}_{\mathrm{M}}^*(\mathbf{h}[C]) \exp[-2\pi i\mathbf{h} \cdot \mathbf{t}]$$

$$\times \sum_{p}|F_{\text{obs}}(\mathbf{p})|^2 \int_V \exp[2\pi i(\mathbf{h} - \mathbf{p}) \cdot \mathbf{u}] \, d\mathbf{u}$$

For the same reason as before, the integral vanishes unless $\mathbf{h} - \mathbf{p} = 0$ or $\mathbf{p} = \mathbf{h}$ and, therefore, apart from the constant V

$$T(\mathbf{t}) = \sum_{\mathbf{h}}|F_{\text{obs}}(\mathbf{h})|^2 \cdot \mathbf{F}_{\mathrm{M}}(\mathbf{h}) \cdot \mathbf{F}_{\mathrm{M}}^*(\mathbf{h} \cdot [C]) \exp[-2\pi i\mathbf{h} \cdot \mathbf{t}] \quad (10.17)$$

This final form of the translation function is a Fourier summation in which the coefficients are known. Therefore, it can easily be calculated. Unwanted background in the translation function is caused by self-Patterson vectors (vectors between atoms within one molecule) and by ignoring the Patterson vectors between molecules other than those under consideration. Self-Patterson vectors can easily be eliminated from the observed Patterson map, assuming that the known and unknown molecules have the same structure and, therefore, the same self-Patterson vectors. As an example we use again crystals with $P222$ symmetry. The orientation of the four molecules in the unit cell is known from the rotation function. Therefore, self-Patterson functions for each of the molecules can be calculated with coefficients $|F_{\mathrm{M}(n)}(\mathbf{h})|^2$, where $n = 1 - 4$. The self-Patterson-corrected translation function is then for the example of Figure 10.5:

$$\mathbf{T}_1(\mathbf{t}) = \sum_{\mathbf{h}}\left\{|F_{\text{obs}}(\mathbf{h})|^2 - \sum_{n=1}^{4}|F_{\mathrm{M}(n)}(\mathbf{h})|^2\right\} \cdot \mathbf{F}_{\mathrm{M}}(\mathbf{h}) \cdot \mathbf{F}_{\mathrm{M}}^*(\mathbf{h} \cdot [C])$$

$$\times \exp[-2\pi i\mathbf{h} \cdot \mathbf{t}] \quad (10.18)$$

In addition, the intermolecular vectors for pairs of molecules that have already been solved could be subtracted.

The translation functions $T(\mathbf{t})$ and $T_1(\mathbf{t})$ are two-dimensional with the intermolecular vectors **t** perpendicular to the symmetry axis under consideration. For a complete solution of the unknown structure, the various two-dimensional translation functions must be combined. This is straightforward for the $P222$ example discussed above, but more complicated in high-symmetry space groups. This is the reason that $T_1(\mathbf{t})$ is no longer a very popular translation function. An improved translation function has been derived by Crowther and Blow (1967); it results in peaks corresponding to all possible intermolecular vectors in the unknown structure. The model structure now contains not a pair of molecules, but the same number of molecules as the unknown crystal structure has in its unit cell.

Because of the large number of intermolecular vectors, it is now more convenient to use the position vector **m** of the model molecule M as the variable. The positions and orientations of the other molecules ($j = 2 \ldots n$) in the unit cell are derived from the model molecule by the operations $[C_j]\mathbf{m} + \mathbf{d}_j$. We must now derive an expression for the calculated Patterson function.

$$\mathbf{F}_{\text{calc}}(\mathbf{h}, \mathbf{m}) = \sum_{j=1}^{n} \mathbf{F}_{\text{M}}(\mathbf{h}[C_j]) \exp[-2\pi i\mathbf{h}([C_j]\mathbf{m} + \mathbf{d}_j)]$$

where $\mathbf{F}_{\text{M}}(\mathbf{h}[C_j])$ is the contribution to the structure factor of reflection **h** by the jth molecule with respect to its local origin in the orientation defined by $[C_j]$, and $\exp[-2\pi i\mathbf{h}([C_j]\mathbf{m} + \mathbf{d}_j)]$ takes care of the fact that the origin of the molecule is at $[C_j]\mathbf{m} + \mathbf{d}_j$.

$$\mathbf{F}_{\text{calc}}(\mathbf{h}, \mathbf{m}) = \sum_{j=1}^{n} \mathbf{F}_{\text{M}}(\mathbf{h}[C_j]) \exp[-2\pi i\mathbf{h}\mathbf{d}_j] \exp[-2\pi i\mathbf{h}[C_j]\mathbf{m}]$$

Because $|\mathbf{F}_{\text{calc}}(\mathbf{h}, \mathbf{m})|^2 = \mathbf{F}_{\text{calc}}(\mathbf{h}, \mathbf{m}) \cdot \mathbf{F}^*_{\text{calc}}(\mathbf{h}, \mathbf{m})$

$$|\mathbf{F}_{\text{calc}}(\mathbf{h}, \mathbf{m})|^2 = \sum_{j=1}^{n} \sum_{k=1}^{n} \mathbf{F}_{\text{M}}(\mathbf{h}[C_j])\mathbf{F}^*_{\text{M}}(\mathbf{h}[C_k]) \times \exp[-2\pi i\mathbf{h}(\mathbf{d}_j - \mathbf{d}_k)]$$
$$\times \exp[-2\pi i\mathbf{h}([C_j] - [C_k])\mathbf{m}] = Q$$

The calculated Patterson function is then $\mathbf{P}_{\text{calc}}(\mathbf{m}, \mathbf{u}) = Q \exp[-2\pi i\mathbf{h} \cdot \mathbf{u}]$, and the new translation function

$$\mathbf{T}_2(\mathbf{m}) = \int_V P_{\text{obs}}(\mathbf{u}) \times P_{\text{calc}}(\mathbf{m}, \mathbf{u}) \, d\mathbf{u}$$

As before, this equation contains the integral

$$\int_V \exp[2\pi i(\mathbf{h} - \mathbf{p}) \cdot \mathbf{u}] \, d\mathbf{u}$$

which vanishes unless $\mathbf{h} - \mathbf{p} = 0$, and therefore

$$T_2(\mathbf{m}) = \sum_{\mathbf{h}} |\mathbf{F}_{\text{obs}}(\mathbf{h})|^2 \sum_{j=1}^{n} \sum_{k=1}^{n} \mathbf{F}_{\text{M}}(\mathbf{h}[C_j])\mathbf{F}^*_{\text{M}}(\mathbf{h}[C_k])$$
$$\times \exp[-2\pi i\mathbf{h}(\mathbf{d}_j - \mathbf{d}_k)] \times \exp[-2\pi i\mathbf{h}([C_j] - [C_k])\mathbf{m}]$$

This can be calculated as a Fourier summation if, instead of the normal index **h**, the index is taken as $\mathbf{h}([C_j] - [C_k])$.

The name $T_2(\mathbf{m})$ is confusing because it suggests a two-dimensional function, whereas, in fact, it is a three-dimensional function, since it utilizes all symmetry operators simultaneously. So far we have assumed that only one molecule is present in the asymmetric unit. Driessen et al. (1991) expanded this to asymmetric units containing more than one molecule (subunit) by associating each subunit in the asymmetric unit with an independent translation vector. An improvement of the signal-to-noise ratio can be obtained if from both the observed and the calculated Pattersons, the self-Patterson vectors are subtracted. For further improvement it is recommended that normalized structure factor amplitudes be used (Section 6.3) because this sharpens the Patterson map. Alternatively, a negative temperature factor parameter B can be applied.

In the two-step procedure, first the calculation of the rotation function and subsequently the translation function, the latter usually causes more problems than the first. For example, the search model differs too much from the unknown structure, or the highest peak in the rotation function does not correspond to the correct orientation. Several methods have been proposed to improve this situation:

- Combine the translation search with a limited systematic variation of the orientation parameters using the R-factor or the correlation coefficient as criterion.
- Refine the search model and its orientation after the rotation, but before the translation search (Patterson correlation refinement).
- Combine any existing phase information from isomorphous replacement with the translation function (phased translation function).

The first method has been described and successfully used by Fujinaga and Read (1987) using the standard linear correlation coefficient. The second method (Patterson correlation refinement) was developed by Brünger (1990). In fact Brünger introduced two techniques for increasing the success in finding the correct translation of the search model. First he calculates a normal rotation function; peaks close together are clustered to a single peak. He selects not only the highest peak in the rotation function but a number of peaks, e.g., 200, and calculates the standard linear correlation coefficient, C_{tr}, between the squares of the normalized observed $(E_{obs})^2$ and calculated $(E_{calc})^2$ structure factors, as a function of the coordinates of the center of gravity of the search model and its symmetry mates. This three-dimensional search for the optimal coordinates is done for each of the selected orientations and the orientation that gave the highest value for the correlation coefficient is then chosen for the translation search.

$$C_{tr} = \frac{\overline{|E_h(\mathrm{obs})|^2 \times |E_h(\mathrm{calc})|^2} - \overline{|E_h(\mathrm{obs})|^2} \times \overline{|E_h(\mathrm{calc})|^2}}{[\{\overline{|E_h(\mathrm{obs})|^4} - (\overline{|E_h(\mathrm{obs})|^2})^2\} \times \{\overline{|E_h(\mathrm{calc})|^4} - (\overline{|E_h(\mathrm{calc})|^2})^2\}]^{1/2}}$$

If this search is unsuccessful, the highest peaks of the rotation function are again selected, but now, before a translation search is carried out, the search model and its orientation are adjusted by minimizing $E_{\text{total}}(\mathbf{r})$ in Eq. (10.19). A single copy of this search model is put into a triclinic cell, identical in geometry to the crystal unit cell and in an orientation derived from the rotation function. The translation is then of no relevance because a change of the molecule's position with respect to the origin changes only the phases and not the magnitudes of the structure factors. The target function to be minimized in the refinement is the energy term

$$E_{\text{total}}(\mathbf{r}) = E_{\text{PC}}(\mathbf{r}) + E_{\text{emp}}(\mathbf{r}) \tag{10.19}$$

$E_{\text{emp}}(\mathbf{r})$ is an empirical energy function (Section 13.4.4). $E_{\text{PC}}(\mathbf{r})$ is a pseudoenergy term, related to the standard linear correlation coefficient, $C(\mathbf{r}, \Omega)$, which measures the correlation between the squares of the normalized observed $(E_{\text{obs}})^2$ and calculated $(E_{\text{calc}})^2$ structure factors:

$$E_{\text{PC}}(\mathbf{r}) = W_{\text{PC}}\{1 - C(\mathbf{r}, \Omega)\}$$

Ω is the rotation matrix defining the orientation.

If the correlation is at its maximum, $E_{\text{PC}}(\mathbf{r})$ has a minimum value. W_{PC} is a suitably chosen weighting factor that determines the relative weight of the empirical and the pseudoenergy term. In many applications the minimization is carried out exclusively with $E_{\text{PC}}(\mathbf{r})$.

The refinement is particularly important if the protein molecule has flexible parts, which have different relative positions in the crystal structure to be solved, compared with the search model. This was, e.g., true for the structure determination of the antigen-binding fragment of an immunoglobulin molecule (Brünger, 1991). The orientation and translation of the individual domains of the search model (a homologous antigen binding fragment) were appreciably modified in the refinement. The combination of the adjusted search model and its orientation produced an unambiguous solution for the translation search.

For the third method, the phased translation function, any bit of phase information, even from a poor heavy atom derivative, can facilitate the resolution of the translation problem. The method is based on overlapping the electron density map computed with the prior phase information, with the electron density map of one copy of the search model correctly oriented in the unit cell (Read and Schierbeek, 1988; Bentley and Houdusse, 1992). The variable is the translation vector $\mathbf{t}$, which moves the model away from its arbitrary position in the unit cell to its correct position. The criterion is the standard linear correlation coefficient Corr.(t).

$$\text{Corr.}(\mathbf{t}) = \frac{\int_V [\rho_{\text{P}}(\mathbf{x}) - \overline{\rho_{\text{P}}}] \times [\rho_{\text{M}}(\mathbf{x} - \mathbf{t}) - \overline{\rho_{\text{M}}}]\, d\mathbf{x}}{\left\{\int_V [\rho_{\text{P}}(\mathbf{x}) - \overline{\rho_{\text{P}}}]^2 d\mathbf{x} \times \int_V [\rho_{\text{M}}(\mathbf{x} - \mathbf{t}) - \overline{\rho_{\text{M}}}]^2 d\mathbf{x}\right\}^{1/2}} \tag{10.20}$$

Alternatively the symmetry operations in the unit cell can be applied to the search model and this would improve the signal somewhat. However, it has been shown that the simple "one copy of search model" technique works satisfactorily.

Equation (10.20) can be simplified because the average electron densities $\overline{\rho_P}$ and $\overline{\rho_M}$ are zero if $F(000)$ is omitted from the Fourier summation. Moreover the integral $\int_V [\rho_M(x - t)]^2 dx$ (with a single copy of the search model in the unit cell) is independent of the actual position of the model in the unit cell and is, therefore, independent of t; the integral is equal to $\int_V [\rho_M(x)]^2 dx$.

$$\rho_P(x) = \frac{1}{V} \sum_h m_P |F_0(h)| \exp[i\alpha_P] \exp[-2\pi i(h \cdot x)]$$

$$\rho_M(x) = \frac{1}{V} \sum_{h'} F_M(h') \exp[-2\pi i(h' \cdot x)]$$

$$= \frac{1}{V} \sum_{h'} F_M^*(h') \exp[2\pi i(h' \cdot x)]$$

because $F_M(-h') = F_M^*(h')$, the complex conjugate of $F_M(h')$; m_p is the figure of merit. In the integration in the nominator of Eq. (10.20) all terms cancel except if $h' = h$, and it can easily be verified that the result is

$$\int_V \rho_P(x) \times \rho_M(x - t)\, dx = \frac{1}{V} \sum_h m_P |F_0(h)| \exp[i\alpha_P] F_M^*(h) \exp[-2\pi i(h \cdot t)]$$

It can be shown in a similar way for the denominator terms that

$$\int_V \{\rho_P(x)\}^2 dx = \frac{1}{V} \sum_h \{m_P |F_0(h)|\}^2$$

and

$$\int_V \{\rho_M(x)\}^2 dx = \frac{1}{V} \sum_h \{|F_M(h)|\}^2$$

The final result for Corr.(t) is

$$\text{Corr.}(t) = \frac{\frac{1}{V} \sum_h m_P |F_0(h)| \exp[i\alpha_P] F_M^*(h) \exp[-2\pi i(h \cdot t)]}{\frac{1}{V} \left[\sum_h \{m_P |F_0(h)|\}^2 \times \sum_h \{|F_M(h)|\}^2 \right]^{1/2}} \quad (10.21)$$

Because $F_M^*(h) = |F_M(h)| \exp[-i\alpha_M]$, the correlation function can now straightforwardly be calculated as a Fourier summation with amplitudes $m_P |F_0(h)| \times |F_M(h)|$ and phase angles $(\alpha_P - \alpha_M)$, multiplied with

$$V \left[\sum_h \{m_P |F_0(h)|\}^2 \times \sum_h \{|F_M(h)|\}^2 \right]^{-1/2}.$$

The maximum of Corr.(t) should give the correct translation vector t.

The translation function can also be helpful in determining the correct space group by comparing the observed peaks in Harker sections with the peaks predicted, assuming a certain space group. If, for instance, the choise is between $P3_121$ and $P3_221$, the translation function will indicate that molecules at a position $1/3$ c higher along the c-axis are rotated with respect to the previous one by $120°$ ($P3_121$) or $240°$ ($P3_221$).

Summary

For the molecular replacement technique a known structure is required, which serves as a model for the unknown structure. Homology in the amino acid sequence is an indication of whether a model is suitable. The solutions of the rotation and translation functions are not always found in a straightforward way. It can be necessary to modify the model, for instance, by ignoring side chains and deletions/additions in the model, and to play with the resolution range of the X-ray data. With the rapid increase in the number of successful protein structure determinations, molecular replacement has become an extremely useful technique for protein phase angle determination.

Chapter 11
Direct Methods

The major problem in X-ray crystallography is to determine the phase angles of the X-ray reflections. In protein crystallography this problem is solved by the application of either isomorphous replacement or molecular replacement or multiple wavelength anomalous dispersion. In small molecule crystallography a completely different solution is applied. There, direct methods are the standard techniques for determining the phase angles of the structure factors. They use the principle that phase information is included in the intensities and this principle depends on the basic assumptions that the electron density is always positive [$F(000)$ included in the Fourier summation] and the crystal consists of discrete atoms that are sometimes even considered to be equal. Phase relations based on probability theory have been formulated and these phase relations are applied to suitably chosen clusters of reflections. Although these direct methods work perfectly well for small molecule crystals, it has thus far not been easy to extend them successfully to protein crystals (Karle, 1989). However, the field has attracted great attention and the first successful results have been published in Acta Crystallogra · **D49**, Part 1, January 1993.

A nonclassical approach in direct phase angle determination for proteins, which is mathematically very demanding, has been pioneered by Bricogne (1993). It applies the maximum entropy principle, which originated in information theory. Skilling (1988) proposed that the entropy $S(f, m)$ of an image f relative to a model m, is

$$S(f, m) = -\int f(x) \log \frac{f(x)}{m(x)} dx \qquad (11.1)$$

This is true for both $f(x)$ and $m(x)$ normalized. Equation (11.1) cannot be proven but it has been shown that it is the only one that gives correct results. In crystallography the image $f(x)$ is the normalized electron density distribution in the unit cell: $q(\mathbf{x}) = \rho(\mathbf{x})/F(000)$ with $F(000) = \int_v \rho(\mathbf{x})dv$. The formula for the entropy is

$$S(q,m) = -\int q(\mathbf{x}) \log \frac{q(\mathbf{x})}{m(\mathbf{x})} d\mathbf{x}$$

or, for discrete grid points

$$S(q,m) = -\sum_j q_j \log \frac{q_j}{m_j}$$

The m_j distribution is the prior information that exists about the electron density distribution. If no other information (no structure factors) is available $q_j = m_j$ for all j and $S(q,m)$ has a maximum value equal to zero. If besides m_j, extra information is available, $S(q, m) < 0$, because the experimental data impose restrictions on q_j and, therefore, the entropy is reduced. q_j is always ≥ 0 and $q_j \geq m_j$.

In the various maximum entropy methods $S(q,m)$ is maximized with respect to q under the restraints of the extra information. More specifically, the maximization of $S(q,m)$ should occur under the conditions that

$$(|F_{\text{obs}}(h\ k\ l)| - |F_{\text{calc}}(h\ k\ l)|)^2$$

or

$$(I_{\text{obs}}(h\ k\ l) - I_{\text{calc}}(h\ k\ l))^2$$

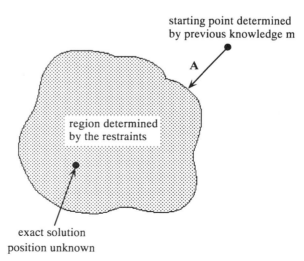

Figure 11.1. Simple schematic picture of the mathematical process in the application of the maximum entropy method.

and any other X-ray terms (for instance, related to phase information) are minimized. In Figure 11.1 the procedure is expressed in a pictorial way. Maximizing $S(q, m)$ is finding the shortest route (vector **A** in Figure 11.1) from the starting point to the region determined by the restraints. If in a next step more restraints can be added, the true solution can be approached in an interative way. This is a formidable mathematical problem and the progress in the use of the maximum entropy formalism for the phase determination of a protein depends largely on solving these problems. A *de novo* structure determination of a protein by maximum entropy alone is not yet possible. However, a combination of maximum entropy with existing information from, for instance, MIR or MAD, which by itself gives an uninterpretable map, does result in some cases in a successful solution of the protein structure. Also knowledge of the molecular envelop could be useful.

Summary

So far, direct methods have been used in protein X-ray crystallography with only limited success and they have not yet been promoted to the level of standard techniques but are still in a state of development. However, much effort is put into improving them and in the not too distant future they may become of extreme importance in solving protein crystal structures.

Chapter 12
Laue Diffraction

12.1. Introduction

When a stationary crystal is illuminated with X-rays from a continuous range of wavelengths (polychromatic or "white" radiation), a Laue diffraction pattern is produced. The very first X-ray diffraction pictures of a crystal were in fact obtained in this way by Friedrich, Knipping, and Laue in 1912. However, since then, monochromatic beams were used nearly exclusively in X-ray crystal structure determinations. This is due to the fundamental problem that a single Laue diffraction spot can contain reflections from a set of parallel planes with different d/n, where d is the interplanar distance and n is an integer. These spots are multiplets instead of singlets. This is easily explained by Bragg's law:

$$2d \sin \theta = \lambda$$

$$2 \sin \theta = \frac{\lambda}{d} = \frac{\lambda/2}{d/2} = \frac{\lambda/3}{d/3} = \text{etc.}$$

The reflection conditions are satisfied, not only for the interplanar spacing d and wavelength λ, but also for $d/2$ and wavelength $\lambda/2$ and $d/3$ and wavelength $\lambda/3$, etc. Another problem with conventional X-ray sources is that their spectral properties with anode-specific lines are not very suitable for Laue diffraction.

The availability of synchrotrons as X-ray sources has changed this situation. Their fully polychromatic beam with a smooth spectral profile, having very high intensity and very small divergence, make them excellent sources for Laue diffraction of protein crystals. Moreover the harmonics (or multiplet) problem turned out not to be as serious as previously

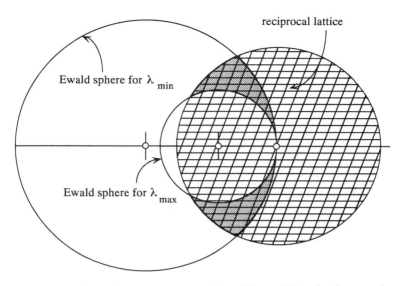

Figure 12.1. A reciprocal space representation of Laue diffraction by a stationary crystal (and thus a stationary reciprocal lattice). For the reciprocal lattice points in the shaded area the reflection conditions are satisfied, at least if not truncated by a maximum diffraction angle.

thought and not to be a limiting obstacle. The extremely high intensity of synchrotron X-ray sources, combined with their broad effective spectrum, allows X-ray diffraction pictures taken in milliseconds. This opens perspectives for time-resolved X-ray structure determinations. Major contributions to the application of the Laue method in the area of protein X-ray crystallography have been made in the Daresbury Laboratory of the Science and Engineering Research Council in the U.K.

12.2. The Accessible Region of Reciprocal Space

The range of reflections registered on a Laue photograph depends on the minimum and maximum values of the wavelength region ($\lambda_{max} - \lambda_{min}$ is called bandpass) and on the resolution limit. This is illustrated in Figure 12.1. Absorption and radiation damage increase with the wavelength and become very serious around 2 Å, which determines the useful maximum wavelength. These problems exist to a far lesser degree at shorter wavelength, but here the weaker diffraction intensity is limiting, because of its proportionality to λ^2 (see Section 4.15). The efficiency of the detector as a function of the wavelength also plays a role.

12.3. The Multiplet Problem

A Laue spot can contain the reflections from a set of planes that are "harmonics" of each other, for instance, 3 1 7; 6 2 14; 9 3 21, etc., or in general a set of reflections $nh\,nk\,nl$, where n is an integer $\geqslant 1$ and $h\,k\,l$ the first harmonic, which has 1 as the greatest common divisor of its indices. In reciprocal space such a set of reflections forms a line through the origin and the nth harmonic reflects in the same direction as $h\,k\,l$, but with a spacing $d(nh\,nk\,nl) = (1/n) \times d(h\,k\,l)$ and for a wavelength $\lambda(nh\,nk\,nl) = (1/n)\lambda(h\,k\,l)$ (Figure 12.2). The maximum multiplicity of a Laue spot is $d(h\,k\,l)/d_{min}$, where d_{min} is the resolution limit. However, due to the finite wavelength bypass the multiplicity may be lower (Figure 12.2).

For the processing of the data one must know whether a spot is a singlet or a multiplet. The intensities of the singlets can be used directly, but the multiplets must be unscrambled. Fortunately a large fraction of the observed spots will be singlets as can be shown in the following way. If the common divisor is p, then every index (h or k or l) has the chance of $1/p$ to have that divisor. For the three indices together, it is $1/(p^3)$. The

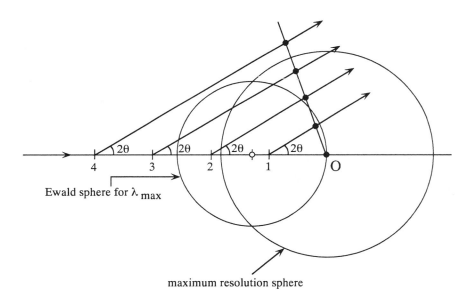

Figure 12.2. Reciprocal space construction for a doublet. In this example the first harmonic does not diffract, because it falls inside the Ewald sphere for λ_{max} with radius $1/\lambda_{max}$. The fourth and higher harmonics fall outside the resolution range. The origin of the reciprocal lattice is in O. The points 1, 2, 3, and 4 are the centers of the $\lambda(h\,k\,l)$, the $\lambda(2h\,2k\,2l)$, the $\lambda(3h\,3k\,3l)$, and the $\lambda(4h\,4k\,4l)$ spheres, respectively.

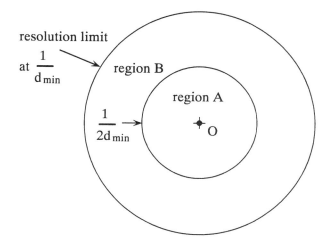

Figure 12.3. Region A in reciprocal space is within the sphere with radius $1/2d_{min}$ and region B is the shell between the two spheres. Of the reflections in region B 83% are measured as singlets, but all reflections in region A are—in principle—members of a multiplet.

probability that p is not a common divisor is $\{1 - 1/(p^3)\}$; p has one of the prime numbers 2, 3, 5, 7, . . . , and the probability that the point is the first on an harmonics line is

$$\{1 - 1/(2^3)\} \times \{1 - 1/(3^3)\} \times \{1 - 1/(5^3)\} \times \{1 - 1/(7^3)\} \times \cdots = 0.83$$

This gives the confidence that 83% of the reflections, corresponding with a spacing d, which is *smaller* than half the resolution limit (reflections in region B in Figure 12.3) are measured as singlets. However, all reflections corresponding with a spacing *larger* than half the resolution limit (reflections in region A in Figure 12.3) are measured as multiplets, unless all but one of the harmonics are excluded by the wavelength limiting Ewald spheres. Therefore, the low resolution reflections suffer most from harmonic overlaps. In addition, due to the Laue geometry, only relatively few low resolution reflections are in diffracting position (Figure 12.1).

12.4. Unscrambling of Multiplet Intensities

The intensity of a multiplet spot is the sum of the component intensities. To separate them, the fact that the components are stimulated by different wavelengths, combined with a difference in absorption characteristics for these wavelengths, is used. We shall explain this for photographic film as the detector, but for other detectors the same principle can be applied.

Suppose the intensity of a doublet is collected on a pack of two films: a front film A and a second film B. Intensity of the spot on film A:

$$I_A = I_a + I'_a$$

I_a is from one component and I'_a from the other. Intensity of the spot on film B:

$$I_B = I_b + I'_b$$

The intensities on film B are lower because of absorption in film A, but the scaling factors depend on the wavelength.

$$I_a = K \times I_b$$
$$I'_a = K' \times I'_b$$
$$I_A = K \times I_b + K' \times I'_b$$
$$\underline{K' \times I_B = K' \times I_b + K' \times I'_b}$$
$$I_A - (K' \times I_B) = (K - K') \times I_b$$

K and K' are known from the absorption characteristics of the photographic film and, therefore, I_b can be calculated as well as I'_b, I_a, and I'_a. For the unscrambling of higher order multiplets the film pack must contain at least the same number of films as the order of the multiplet, although in practice unscrambling beyond doublets is not often done.

12.5. The Spatial Overlap Problem

Although the divergence of a synchrotron beam is small and the spots on the detector are sharp, there are so many spots on a protein Laue photograph (Figure 12.4) that spatial overlap of neighboring spots is a serious problem. To reduce this problem the crystal-to-detector distance can be increased; one should, however, realize the effect of this increase on the resolution. Profile fitting also reduces the problem. Standard profiles should be derived from nonoverlapping spots in subregions of reciprocal space and applied to partially overlapping spots in the same region. Profile fitting also improves the accuracy of weak intensities, assuming that strong and weak reflections share a common profile.

12.6. Wavelength Normalization

One of the greatest problems in the evaluation of Laue diffraction data is to compensate for wavelength-dependent parameters influencing the observations. They are numerous, for instance:

1. The spectral characteristics of the white radiation at the sample.
2. Wavelength-dependent source polarization.

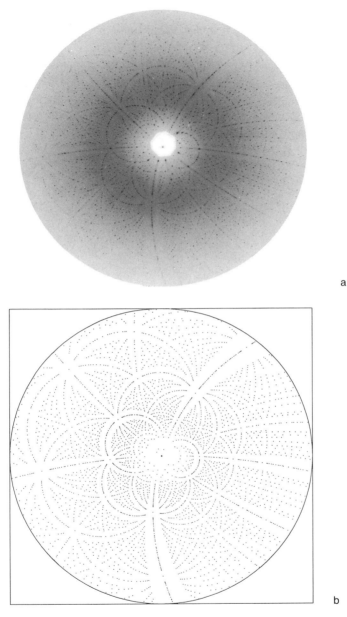

a

b

Figure 12.4. (a) A Laue diffraction picture of a crystal of the human oncogene product Ha-*ras*-p21 (molecular weight 21 kDa). The film was exposed for less than a second on the Wiggler beamline 9.5 at the SRS in Daresbury (U.K.). (b) The calculated diffraction picture for the same crystal setting. (Source: Dr. Axel J. Scheidig, Max-Planck-Institut für Medizinische Forschung, Heidelberg, Germany.)

3. Sample absorption, which is stronger for longer wavelength.
4. Wavelength-dependent detector response including absorption edges.
5. Anomalous scattering if present.
6. The crystal scattering dependence on λ^2.

All these factors are corrected for by multiplying each reflection intensity with a wavelength dependent factor $1/g(\lambda)$. This factor is determined empirically by using symmetry-related reflections, measured at different wavelengths within a single filmpack. In practice the entire wavelength region is divided into bins (slices) of, e.g., 0.05 Å and an arbitrary bin is chosen as the standard. Excluded are the regions around absorption edges of the heavier elements in the detector (Ag and Br if the detector is X-ray film) and the specimen. The combined information from the scale factors between all bins is used to determine the scale factor for each bin with respect to the standard bin. An interpolation polynomial through this set of scale factors is used to obtain $1/g(\lambda)$ for a given λ.

In the detection of structural changes the difference Laue method can profitably be used. In this method, the relative intensity changes on subsequent Laue photographs can be used for the calculation of difference Fourier maps with the amplitudes

$$\frac{F_B(\text{Laue}) - F_A(\text{Laue})}{F_A(\text{Laue})} \times F_A(\text{mono})$$

and phases from monochromatic data. $F_A(\text{mono})$ are the structure factor amplitudes of the initial structure, measured with monochromatic radiation, $F_A(\text{Laue})$ for the corresponding Laue set, and $F_B(\text{Laue})$ for the modified structure. The advantage is that wavelength- and position-dependent corrections are not required. However, the spectral properties of the X-ray beam should remain the same during the experiment and the X-ray data must be collected with the crystal in the same orientation for data sets A and B.

Summary

The advantages of the Laue method:

1. Extremely short data collection time with synchrotron radiation.
2. Consequently structural changes in the $100\,\mu\text{sec}-1\,\text{sec}$ range can be observed.
3. One or only a few exposures at different angular settings cover a substantial portion of reciprocal lattice. The higher the symmetry in the crystals, the fewer exposures are needed.
4. Very small crystals can be used in principle but the mosaicity of the crystal and background scattering may be unfavorably high.

The main problems:

1. An unbalanced coverage of reciprocal space with relatively few low order reflections.
2. The crystal must withstand short exposures to extremely intense X-ray radiation.
3. Spatial overlap.

For time-resolved structure determinations it is important that a chemical reaction in the crystal is synchronized in all unit cells.

The time needed for data collection with Laue photographs is very short and is of the order of seconds, or even shorter. In future work it might be possible to utilize the pulsed nature of the synchrotron beam and to work on a picosecond time scale.

Chapter 13
Refinement of the Model Structure

13.1. Introduction

From isomorphous replacement or molecular replacement an approximate model of the protein structure can be obtained in which the broad features of the molecular architecture are apparent. Structure factors calculated on the basis of this model are generally in rather poor agreement with the observed structure factors. The agreement index between calculated and observed structure factors is usually represented by an R-factor as defined in Eq. (13.1). Thus an R-factor of 50% is not uncommon for the starting model, whereas for a random acentric structure it would be 59% (Wilson, 1950).

$$R = \frac{\displaystyle\sum_{hkl} ||F_{\text{obs}}| - k|F_{\text{calc}}||}{\displaystyle\sum_{hkl} |F_{\text{obs}}|} \times 100\% \qquad (13.1)$$

Refinement is the process of adjusting the model to find a closer agreement between the calculated and observed structure factors. Several methods have been developed and, if applied, they lower the R-factor substantially, reaching values in the 10 to 20% range or even lower. The adjustment of the model consists of changing the positional parameters and the temperature factors for all atoms in the structure, except the hydrogen atoms. Because hydrogen atoms have one electron only, their influence on X-ray scattering is low and they are normally disregarded in the structure determination. But still the number of nonhydrogen atoms is very high. In the refinement of the papain crystal structure at 1.65 Å resolution 25,000 independent X-ray reflections had been measured. The

242

parameters to be refined were three positional parameters (x, y, and z) and one isotropic temperature factor parameter (B) for each of the 2000 nonhydrogen atoms, making a total of 8000 parameters. Therefore, the ratio of observations to parameters is only 3, and this is a poor over-

as many as possible additional
refinement process. They are in
from small molecular structures.
n determined with high precision
: data for amino acids and small
further "observation" is that the
ween protein molecules in their
ind should appear as a flat region
nt flattening"—which has already
erefore, be imposed on the map.
iection 8.4)—if it does exist and is
nakes an important contribution
:ture by imposing the equality in
y related molecules or subunits.
ormation on bond lengths, bond

- They are taken as rigid and only dihedral angles can be varied. In this case the geometry and the refinement are called *constrained*. This effectively reduces the number of parameters to be refined. In the application of this method it is difficult to move small parts of the structure to a "best fit" position because many angular motions are involved.

- If, on the other hand, the stereochemical parameters are allowed to vary around a standard value, controlled by an energy term, the refinement is called *restrained*. The atomic coordinates are the variables and the restraints are on bond lengths, bond angles, torsion angles, and van der Waals contacts. Restraints are "observations." This allows an easy movement of small parts of the structure, but it is difficult to move large parts, for instance, an entire molecule or domain.

Since protein structures are very complicated, their refinement is computationally a large size project. It is, therefore, fair to say that only through the availability of fast computers, especially vector processing machines, has the thorough and at the same time rapid refinement of protein structures become possible. It is perhaps superfluous to state that it makes sense to refine a structure only if careful attention has been paid to the determination of the cell dimensions and the measurement and correction of the X-ray intensity data. It is preferable to measure intensities of the reflections more than once, for instance, in another symmetry-related position. Low order reflections, having Bragg spacings longer than about 7 Å, are usually omitted in the refinement process

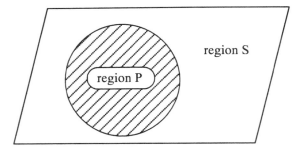

Figure 13.1. In this two-dimensional unit cell the region P represents the size and shape of a protein molecule. Region S contains the disordered solvent.

because their intensities are rather seriously affected by the diffraction of the continuous solvent. Moreover, many data collection techniques for proteins are not designed to measure the low order reflections accurately. That the diffraction by the solvent affects only the low order reflections can be understood in the following way. Suppose the unit cell in Figure 13.1 is homogeneously filled with the same electron density ρ in P and S. P has the size and shape of the protein molecule. The diffraction intensities will be zero; all structure factors are zero. For a structure in which P only is filled with homogeneous density ρ and region S is empty, the structure factors are $\mathbf{G_P}$ where $\mathbf{G_P}$ is the transform of the homogeneously filled particle P. If only region S is filled with homogeneous density ρ, and P is empty, the structure factor must be $-\mathbf{G_P}$, because the sum of the two separate structures has diffraction zero. For the diffraction by a particle of the type P, which is normally close to spherical, we can refer to Figure 10.3, where the shape of the diffraction curve by a homogeneously filled, perfect sphere is given. For such particles, with the size of a protein molecule, the diffraction fades away rapidly with increasing diffraction angle. It has an appreciable contribution to lower order reflections only, and, therefore, this is also true for the disordered solvent in the crystal. Ordered solvent molecules do contribute to the scattering up to high resolution. They are located as electron density peak positions obeying H-bond geometry, and during refinement they are usually introduced into the molecular model at a resolution better than $2.5\,\text{Å}$.

13.2. The Method of Least Squares

The refinement techniques in protein X-ray crystallography are based on the principle of least squares. An introduction to this method has been given in Section 7.14, but it will now be treated more extensively. Before we do so it must be stated that the method of least squares is a special case of a more general refinement method: "maximum likelihood." In least squares the observations have fixed values and the parameters are varied such that the calculated values approach the observations as closely as possible in the refinement. It can easily be shown that maximum likelihood gives the same result as least squares for the special case of a Gaussian distribution of the observations. However, for other probability distributions the results are different.

We shall first discuss the least-squares method for the case where the X-ray data are the only observations. Later, in the treatment of more specific refinement methods, constraints and restraints also play a role. Refinement by least squares is an iterative process. In each step (or cycle) the parameters to be refined change, or rather should change, toward their final value without reaching them right away. Usually a great many refinement cycles are carried out before the changes in the parameters become small enough. The refinement has then converged to the final parameter set. The range of convergence is the maximum distance for the atoms to move to their final position. If they are further away there is a good chance that the function to be minimized will be trapped in a local minimum that is not the true minimum. The progress of a refinement can be monitored by calculating after each cycle the crystallographic R-factor [Eq. (13.1)].

For a structure determination with data to 2.0 Å resolution the final R-factor should not be higher than 20%. In the least-squares refinement $\Sigma_{hkl}(|F_{obs}| - |F_{calc}|)^2$ is minimized. More accurately the function to be minimized is

$$Q = \sum_{hkl} w(h\ k\ l)(|F_{obs}(h\ k\ l)| - |F_{calc}(h\ k\ l)|)^2 \qquad (13.2)$$

The summation is over all crystallographically independent reflections and w is the weight given to an observation. The usual weighting factor in small molecule crystallography is $w(h\ k\ l) = 1/\sigma^2(h\ k\ l)$; σ is the standard deviation. For proteins some $(\sin\theta)/\lambda$ − dependent function is more satisfactory. It is assumed that the $|F_{obs}(h\ k\ l)|$ values are on absolute scale. The minimum of Q is found by varying the atomic parameters u_j ($j = 1\ldots n$) that determine $|F_{calc}(h\ k\ l)|$, and this is done by putting the differentials of Q with respect to all u_j equal to zero: $\partial Q/\partial u_j = 0$ or

$$\sum_{hkl} w(h\ k\ l)(|F_{obs}(h\ k\ l)| - |F_{calc}(h\ k\ l)|)\frac{\partial|F_{calc}(h\ k\ l)|}{\partial u_j} = 0 \qquad (13.3)$$

Each $|F_{obs}(h\ k\ l)|$ is a constant and each $|F_{calc}(h\ k\ l)|$ depends on the variables u_j. For the solution of these equations $|F_{calc}(h\ k\ l)|$ is expressed in a Taylor expansion:

$$|F_{calc}(h\ k\ l;\ u)| = |F_{calc}(h\ k\ l;\ u_s)| + \sum_i \varepsilon_i \left[\frac{\partial |F_{calc}(h\ k\ l;\ u)|}{\partial u_i} \right]_{u_s}$$

$$+ \left| \frac{1}{2} \sum_j \sum_i \varepsilon_j \varepsilon_i \frac{\partial^2 |F_{calc}(h\ k\ l;\ u)|}{\partial u_j \partial u_i} + \cdots \right.$$

$$\left. \right| \rightarrow \text{neglected} \qquad\qquad (13.4)$$

$|F_{calc}(h\ k\ l;\ u)|$ indicates that the $|F_{calc}|$ depend on the parameters u. The starting values of u are u_s and are changed by a small amount ε. For parameter u_i we have $\varepsilon_i = u_i - u_{i,s}$. $[\partial |F_{calc}(h\ k\ l;\ u)|/\partial u_i]_{u_s}$ means that the differential of $|F_{calc}(h\ k\ l;\ u)|$ with respect to u_i is calculated at the starting value u_s. Because the ε-values are small, higher order terms in ε can be neglected. Combination of Eqs. (13.4) and (13.3) gives the so called normal equations:

$$\sum_{hkl} w(h\ k\ l)(|F_{obs}(h\ k\ l)| - |F_{calc}(h\ k\ l;\ u_s)|) \times \left[\frac{\partial |F_{calc}(h\ k\ l;\ u)|}{\partial u_j} \right]_{u_s}$$

$$- \sum_i \varepsilon_i \sum_{hkl} w(h\ k\ l) \left[\frac{\partial |F_{calc}(h\ k\ l;\ u)|}{\partial u_i} \right]_{u_s} \times \left[\frac{\partial |F_{calc}(h\ k\ l;\ u)|}{\partial u_j} \right]_{u_s} = 0$$

With these n equations ($j = 1 \rightarrow n$), the ε-values must be found and then applied to the variables u. Because of the truncation of higher order terms in the Taylor series the final values are approached by iteration. In other words in the next cycle of refinement the process is repeated until convergence is reached. For each cycle new values of $|F_{calc}(h\ k\ l; u)|$ and its derivatives with respect to u_j must be calculated. This requires much computing power.

The principle of solving the normal equations is as follows. In abbreviated form they can be written as $\sum_i (\varepsilon_i a_{ij}) - b_j = 0$ or $\sum_i \varepsilon_i a_{ij} = b_j$.

$$\text{For} \quad j = 1: \quad a_{11}\varepsilon_1 + a_{21}\varepsilon_2 + a_{31}\varepsilon_3 + \ldots = b_1$$

$$j = 2: \quad a_{12}\varepsilon_1 + a_{22}\varepsilon_2 + a_{32}\varepsilon_3 + \ldots = b_2$$

These equations can be expressed in matrix form:

$$\begin{bmatrix} a_{11}\ a_{21}\ a_{31}\ ----\ \\ \\ a_{12}\ a_{22}\ a_{32}\ ----\ \\ ---------- \\ ---------- \end{bmatrix} \times \begin{bmatrix} \varepsilon_1 \\ \varepsilon_2 \\ \varepsilon_3 \\ - \\ - \\ - \end{bmatrix} = \begin{bmatrix} b_1 \\ b_2 \\ b_3 \\ - \\ - \\ - \end{bmatrix}$$

or $[A] \times [\varepsilon] = [b]$. $[A]$ is called the normal matrix. Since $j = 1 \ldots n$ and $i = 1 \ldots n$, it is a square matrix with n rows and columns; moreover the matrix is symmetric. Its elements are

$$\sum_{hkl} w_{(hkl)} \left[\frac{\partial |F_{calc}(h\ k\ l;\ u)|}{\partial u_i} \right]_{u_s} \times \left[\frac{\partial |F_{calc}(h\ k\ l;\ u)|}{\partial u_j} \right]_{u_s}$$

[ε] is the unknown vector and [b] the known gradient vector containing the elements

$$\sum_{hkl} w(h\ k\ l)(|F_{obs}(h\ k\ l)| - |F_{calc}(h\ k\ l;\ u_s)|) \times \left[\frac{\partial |F_{calc}(hkl;u)|}{\partial u_j}\right]_{u_s}$$

Since matrix [A] is a square matrix another matrix can be derived, [A^{-1}], which is the inverse or reciprocal of [A]. Its property is [A^{-1}] × [A] = [E], where [E] is the unit matrix:

$$[E] = \begin{bmatrix} 1 & 0 & 0 & - & - & - & - & - \\ 0 & 1 & 0 & - & - & - & - & - \\ 0 & 0 & 1 & - & - & - & - & - \\ - & - & - & - & - & - & - & - \\ - & - & - & - & - & - & - & - \end{bmatrix}$$

[A^{-1}] × [A] × [ε] = [A^{-1}] × [b] or [E] × [ε] = [A^{-1}] × [b]. Since the property of a unit matrix is [E] × [ε] = [ε], the solution of the normal equations is [ε] = [A^{-1}] × [b]. If [A] is not a very large a matrix its inverse [A^{-1}] can be calculated without too much effort and the problem of finding the parameter shifts [ε] can easily be solved. However, in protein X-ray crystallography [A] is a huge matrix. Its number of rows and columns is equal to the number of parameters to be refined and this can easily be of the order of 10,000 or more. This prohibits the calculation of [A^{-1}]. Fortunately, many elements of matrix [A] are zero or close to zero for the following reason. The elements of matrtix [A] are

$$a_{ij} = \sum_{hkl} w(h\ k\ l)\left[\frac{\partial |F_{calc}(h\ k\ l;\ u)|}{\partial u_i}\right]_{u_s} \times \left[\frac{\partial |F_{calc}(h\ k\ l;u)|}{\partial u_j}\right]_{u_s} \quad (13.5)$$

If u_i and u_j are positional parameters x or y or z of the same atom, then for an orthogonal system of axes, the derivatives are not correlated and the elements a_{ij} will have a low value. This is not true for $i = j$, when both derivatives are with respect to the same parameter for the same atom. If u_i and u_j concern different atoms, and these atoms are well resolved, small changes in a parameter of one atom do not affect the other atom and the elements a_{ij} are again small. Correlation between positional parameters and temperature factors is also neglected, although some correlation usually does exist. It follows that the diagonal elements of matrix [A] are in general larger than the off-diagonal elements and the simplification is that all off-diagonal elements are set to zero.

With a diagonal matrix (all off-diagonal elements zero) the calculation of [A^{-1}] is trivial and a set of parameter shifts [ε] can easily be calculated. However, because the diagonal matrix is not the ideal matrix and because of the neglect of higher terms in the Taylor expansion this set of shifts is not the final one and the procedure is continued as an iterative process: recalculate [A] with the new parameters, find a new set of shifts, etc. until convergence is reached. To increase the rate of convergence the conjugate gradient method is applied, which is discussed below.

If besides X-ray information, geometric or energy information is also incorporated in the refinement, the elements of matrix $[\mathbf{A}]$ are

$$a_{ij} = \sum_{hkl} w(h\ k\ l)\left[\frac{\partial|F_{\text{calc}}(hkl;\ u)|}{\partial u_i}\right]_{u_s} \times \left[\frac{\partial|F_{\text{calc}}(hkl;\ u)|}{\partial u_j}\right]_{u_s}$$

+ terms to account for the extra observations. The elements of vector matrix $[\mathbf{b}]$ also contain extra terms:

$$\sum_{hkl} w(h\ k\ l)(|F_{\text{obs}}(h\ k\ l)| - |F_{\text{calc}}(h\ k\ l;\ u_s)|) \times \left[\frac{\partial|F_{\text{calc}}(h\ k\ l;\ u)|}{\partial u_j}\right]_{u_s}$$

+ extra terms. The extra terms contribute to off-diagonal elements and these elements can no longer be set to zero. As a consequence $[\mathbf{A}^{-1}]$ is not easy to calculate and the refinement must be carried out by some numerical method, approaching the final parameter set in a cyclic way. The most popular numerical method in protein X-ray crystallography is the conjugate gradient technique.

The method depends on matrix $[\mathbf{A}]$ to be symmetric. One starts with an initial estimate of the parameter shifts $[\varepsilon_0]$, which can be taken as zero if no other choice is available. Next a residual vector matrix $[\mathbf{r}_0] = [\mathbf{b}] - [\mathbf{A}] \times [\varepsilon_0]$ is calculated. A second new vector matrix required is the search direction vector $[\mathbf{z}]$ along which the function Q [Eq. (13.2)] is minimized. Choose the first $[\mathbf{z}]$, that is $[\mathbf{z}_0]$, equal to $[\mathbf{r}_0]$. In a number of iterative steps $n = 0, 1, 2, \ldots$, the vectors $[\varepsilon_{n+1}]$, $[\mathbf{r}_{n+1}]$, and $[\mathbf{z}_{n+1}]$ are calculated with the following recipe:

$$[\varepsilon_{n+1}] = [\varepsilon_n] + \alpha_n[\mathbf{z}_n] \quad \text{with} \quad \alpha_n = \frac{[\mathbf{r}_n]\cdot[\mathbf{r}_n]}{[\mathbf{z}_n]\cdot[\mathbf{A}]\times[\mathbf{z}_n]}$$

$$[\mathbf{r}_{n+1}] = [\mathbf{r}_n] - \alpha_n[\mathbf{A}] \times [\mathbf{z}_n]$$

$$[\mathbf{z}_{n+1}] = [\mathbf{r}_{n+1}] + \beta_n[\mathbf{z}_n] \quad \text{with} \quad \beta_n = \frac{[\mathbf{r}_{n+1}]\cdot[\mathbf{r}_{n+1}]}{[\mathbf{r}_n]\cdot[\mathbf{r}_n]}$$

With α_n and β_n chosen as indicated, it can be proven that the search directions $[\mathbf{z}]$ are all conjugate to each other: $[\mathbf{z}_{n+1}]\cdot[\mathbf{A}] \times [\mathbf{z}_j] = 0$ for all $j = 0, 1, 2, \ldots, n$. This guarantees that an efficient path is followed in parameter space toward the minimum of function Q [Eq. (13.2)]. It can also be shown that the residuals $[\mathbf{r}]$ are independent of each other: $[\mathbf{r}_{n+1}]\cdot[\mathbf{r}_j] = 0$, for all $j = 0, 1, 2, \ldots, n$.

The iteration process can be further accelerated by "preconditioning." A matrix $[\mathbf{K}]$ is chosen that resembles $[\mathbf{A}]$, but that can easily be inverted to $[\mathbf{K}^{-1}]$. The expression $[\mathbf{A}] \times [\varepsilon] = [\mathbf{b}]$ is now replaced by $[\mathbf{K}^{-1}] \times [\mathbf{A}] \times [\varepsilon] = [\mathbf{K}^{-1}] \times [\mathbf{b}]$. The more $[\mathbf{K}]$ resembles $[\mathbf{A}]$, the better $[\mathbf{K}^{-1}] \times [\mathbf{A}]$ resembles the unit matrix $[\mathbf{E}]$ and the faster the convergence is. During the procedure matrix $[\mathbf{A}]$ is retained unchanged. This is a great advantage because the nonzero elements can then be stored for the matrix multiplications. After convergence has been reached [A] is recalculated and another cycle of refinement can be started. In the beginning of the refinement only the X-ray data to moderate resolution are incorporated and during the refinement process the resolution is gradually extended. Structure factors and their derivatives can be conveniently calculated with a method proposed by Agarwal (1978) that uses the fast Fourier transform algorithm (see next section).

The inverse matrix [A^{-1}] also serves another purpose. From its diagonal elements a_{jj}, the standard deviation σ of the parameter u_j at the end of the refinement can be estimated:

$$\sigma^2(u_j) = a_{jj}\left(\frac{\sum_{h=1}^{p} w_h(\Delta F_h)^2}{p-n}\right)$$

where p is the number of independent reflections, n is the number of parameters, and $(\Delta F_h) = |F_{obs}(h\ k\ l)| - |F_{calc}(h\ k\ l)|$ calculated with the present parameter value.

13.3. The Principle of the Fast Fourier Transform (FFT) Method

A very time consuming step in the refinement procedure is the calculation of all structure factors and their derivatives from the new parameter set at the end of each cycle in the refinement. To speed up these calculations fast Fourier algorithms are used. A detailed discussion of the application of the fast Fourier technique in crystallography is given by Ten Eyck (1973); see also Agarwal (1978). They enormously reduce the time needed for calculating structure factors from an electron density distribution or the other way around: the calculation of the electron density map from a series of structure factors. The electron density is sampled at grid points, usually at distances equal to one-third of the maximum resolution. The number of grid points is then

$$\frac{V}{\left(\frac{1}{3}d\right)^3} = 27\frac{V}{d^3}$$

where V is the unit cell volume and d is the maximum resolution. At this maximum resolution the number of structure factors in the volume of a reciprocal space sphere is

$$\frac{\frac{4}{3}\pi(1/d)^3}{V^*} = \frac{4}{3}\pi\frac{V}{d^3}$$

because the volume of the unit cell in reciprocal space, V^*, is equal to $1/V$ (Section 4.8).

The FFT technique requires the number of structure factors and the number of grid points to be the same. The former is usually smaller than the latter, but dummy structure factors can be added up to the number of grid points. For simplicity we shall deal with a one-dimensional case only. Let us write the Fourier inversion as

$$X(k) = \sum_{j=0}^{N-1} x(j) W_N^{jk}$$

Suppose $F(h)$ is calculated from the $\rho(x)$ map; j indicates the grid points: $x = j/N$; k is the index for the structure factors and W_N^{jk} is the exponential term: $W_N^{jk} = \exp[2\pi i(j \cdot k/N)]$. To calculate the $\rho(x)$ map from the structure factors the form of the equation remains the same, but then $W_N^{jk} = \exp[-2\pi i(j \cdot k/N)]$.

The principle of the FFT method is to change the linear series of j terms into a two-dimensional series. To do this N is written as the product of two numbers, N_1 and N_2: $N = N_1 \times N_2$. Also j and k are split up: $j = j_2 + j_1 \times N_2$ and $k = k_1 + k_2 \times N_1$. If $j_2 = 0 \ldots (N_2 - 1)$ and $j_1 = 0 \ldots (N_1 - 1)$ all the integers in the range $0 \leq j < N$ are generated once and only once. The same is true for k, if $k_1 = 0 \ldots (N_1 - 1)$ and $k_2 = 0 \ldots (N_2 - 1)$.

$$x(j) = x(j_2, j_1) = x(j_2 + j_1 N_2)$$

and

$$X(k_1, k_2) = \sum_{j_2=0}^{N_2-1} \sum_{j_1=0}^{N_1-1} x(j_2, j_1) \times W_N^{jk}$$

$$W_N^{jk} = W_N^{(j_2+j_1 N_2)(k_1+k_2 N_1)}$$

$$= W_N^{j_1 k_1 N_2} \times W_N^{j_2 k_1} \times W_N^{j_2 k_2 N_1} \times W_N^{j_1 k_2 N}$$

$$W_N^{j_1 k_2 N} = W_N^N = \exp\left[2\pi i \frac{N}{N}\right] = \cos 2\pi + i \sin 2\pi = 1$$

$$W_N^{N_2} = \exp\left[2\pi i \frac{N_2}{N}\right] = \exp\left[2\pi i \frac{1}{N_1}\right] = W_{N_1}^1$$

$$W_N^{jk} = W_{N_1}^{j_1 k_1} \times W_N^{j_2 k_1} \times W_{N_2}^{j_2 k_2}$$

$$X(k_1, k_2) = \sum_{j_1=0}^{N_1-1} W_{N_1}^{j_1 k_1} \times \sum_{j_2=0}^{N_2-1} x(j_2, j_1) \times W_N^{j_2 k_1} \times W_{N_2}^{j_2 k_2}$$

Grouping the terms depending on j_1 together:

$$X(k_1, k_2) = \sum_{j_2=0}^{N_2-1} W_N^{j_2 k_1} \times W_N^{j_2 k_2} \times \sum_{j_1=0}^{N_1-1} x(j_2, j_1) \times W_{N_1}^{j_1 k_1}$$

$\sum_{j_1=0}^{N_1-1} x(j_2, j_1) \times W_{N_1}^{j_1 k_1}$ is a Fourier transform of length N_1 and must be done for each j_2, so N_2 times. The outer summation over j_2 is a Fourier transform of length N_2. To calculate all $X(k)$ it must be done N_1 times.

The time needed for evaluating a Fourier summation is proportional to the number of terms (N) and the number of grid points (N). Therefore, the time needed for calculating a normal Fourier transform of length N would be proportional to N^2 and with FFT:

$$N_2 \times N_1^2 + N_1 \times N_2^2 = N \times (N_1 + N_2)$$

Suppose $N = 2500$ and $N_1 = N_2 = 50$, then we must compare $N^2 = (2500)^2 = 625 \times 10^4$ with $2500 \times 100 = 25 \times 10^4$, an appreciable reduction in time.

13.4. Specific Refinement Methods

13.4.1. The Agarwal Method (Agarwal, 1978, 1985)

We shall first discuss a method that uses a minimum of geometric information in the refinement of the positions and thermal parameters of a rough set of atoms by least squares. The atomic positions can be taken from the model based, for instance, on a multiple isomorphous replacement (MIR) map. If the electron density map is not interpretable in terms of amino acids, one can even start with a set of dummy atoms, which should obey the following conditions:

1. The dummy atoms must be distributed over those regions of the electron density map where protein atoms can be expected.
2. The distance between pairs of atoms is of the order of atomic distances.
3. Atoms have never more than three close neighbors.
4. The number of electrons for the dummy atoms should roughly match the local electron density.

The function minimized is

$$Q = \sum_{hkl} w(h\,k\,l)\{|F_{obs}(h\,k\,l)| - k \times |F_{calc}(h\,k\,l)|\}^2$$

k is the scale factor between observed and calculated structure factors. It is calculated with

$$k = \frac{\sum_{hkl}|F_{obs}(h\,k\,l)| \times |F_{calc}(h\,k\,l)|}{\sum_{hkl}\{|F_{calc}(h\,k\,l)|\}^2}$$

k should be calculated at the beginning of each cycle.

To give more weight to the inner reflections—which are stronger on the average—at the beginning of the refinement, w $(h\ k\ l)$ is chosen as

$$\left(\frac{1}{d}\right)^n = \left(\frac{2\sin\theta(h\ k\ l)}{\lambda}\right)^n$$

with n ranging from -1 in the initial stages of the refinement to 0 in the later refinement cycles. The program does not constrain or restrain bond lengths and angles in any way. This can easily lead to a chemically unrealistic structure and, therefore, the structure should be regularized at intervals by some model fitting program. The resolution is gradually increased during the refinement.[1] It is advised to calculate a difference electron density map before extending the resolution. This is to avoid gross errors in the interpretation of the electron density map. This checking of the electron density at frequent intervals requires much time and is, therefore, a disadvantage of the method.

13.4.2. Rigid Body Refinement

Sussman and co-workers developed a *co*nstraint/*re*straint *le*ast-*s*quares refinement program, CORELS (Sussman, 1985). In this program a rigid geometry is assigned to parts of the structure and the parameters of these constrained parts are refined rather than individual atomic parameters. Optionally specified dihedral angles within a group can also be refined, which is then no longer completely rigid. It is possible to regard an entire molecule as a rigid entity and to refine its position and orientation in the unit cell. This is often done as a first step in a refinement procedure, for instance, after the molecular replacement procedure has given starting values for the position and orientation of the molecule. With CORELS the molecule can then be more properly positioned. The rigid entity can also be of smaller size, for instance, a folding unit consisting of β-strands and α-helices, or a prosthetic group, or, in nucleic acid structures, a nucleotide. The method increases the data/parameter ratio appreciably and is, therefore, applicable if only moderate resolution data are available.

Because CORELS is based on the conventional method of structure factor calculation and, therefore, is slow, rigid body refinement is performed much faster with a number of other rigid body refinement programs in which fast Fourier transform techniques are employed, for instance, Brünger's XPLOR package or Tronrud's TNT program. However, the principle is the same. In pure crystallographic refinement without adding stereochemical information, the quantity to be minimized is

$$Q = \sum_{hkl} w(h\ k\ l)\{|F_{obs}(h\ k\ l)| - |F_{calc}(h\ k\ l)|\}^2$$

---

[1] An increase in resolution means going to a higher resolution, that is incorporating more reflections corresponding to smaller plane spacings d.

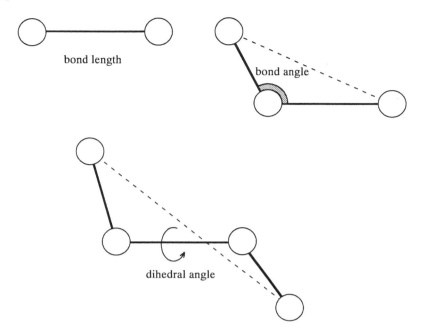

Figure 13.2. In the CORELS refinement method all restraints are introduced as distances: a bond length as the distance between nearest neighbors, a bond angle as the distance between next nearest neighbors, and a dihedral angle as the distance between a first and a fourth atom.

In the CORELS program the constrained entities contribute as such to the calculation of the $|F_{calc}(h\ k\ l)|$ values. Restraints modify the least-squares criterion to the minimization of

$$Q = \sum_{hkl} w(h\ k\ l)\{|F_{obs}(h\ k\ l)| - |F_{calc}(h\ k\ l)|\}^2$$
$$+ w_D\sum_d w_d\{D_{obs}(d) - D_{calc}(d)\}^2$$
$$+ w_T\sum_i w_x\sum_x \{X_T(i,\ \mathbf{x}) - X(i,\ \mathbf{x})\}^2$$

$D_{obs}(d)$ is the standard distance, corresponding to bond lengths, but also to angles and van der Waals distances, because in CORELS all restraints are introduced as distances: a bond length as the distance between nearest neighbors, a bond angle as the distance between next nearest neighbors, and a dihedral angle as the distance between a first and a fourth atom (Figure 13.2). $D_{calc}(d)$ is the distance calculated from the current model. $w_d = 1/\sigma_d$ where σ_d is the standard deviation for distances of type d bonds as observed in small molecule structures. The third term restrains the coordinate vectors $\mathbf{x}$ ($= x, y, z$) of a model atom to a corresponding target position. For crystallographic refinement the third term is omitted by putting $w_T = 0$. It plays a role in model building for which $w(h\ k\ l) = 0$. By choosing the weighting factors $w(h\ k\ l)$ and w_D properly, a relative weight can be given to the X-ray and the stereochemical restraints in the refinement process. The quantity Q is minimized with respect to all positional coordinates and thermal parameters in the usual way with the least-squares method.

13.4.3. Stereochemically Restrained Least-Squares Refinement

Stereochemical restraints are fully incorporated in this program and frequent regularization—as, for instance, in the Agarwal program—is not required, because the program itself takes care of it. However, the occasional calculation of an electron density map, a difference electron density map, or OMIT map (Section 8.2) is useful for manually correcting major imperfections in the model. The Konnert–Hendrickson program, PROLSQ (Hendrickson, 1985), has found wide application in the accurate structure determination of protein molecules, but now a more efficient and flexible program (TNT), written by Tronrud et al. (1987) using the fast Fourier transform algorithm, is mainly used for stereochemically restrained least-squares refinement.

The function to be minimized consists of a crystallographic term (a) and several stereochemical terms (b–f):

$$Q = \sum_{hkl} w(h\ k\ l)\{|F_{\text{obs}}(h\ k\ l)| - |F_{\text{calc}}(h\ k\ l)|\}^2 \tag{a}$$

$$+ \sum_{\text{dist.} j} w_D(j)(d_j^{\text{ideal}} - d_j^{\text{model}})^2 \tag{b}$$

$$+ \sum_{\substack{\text{planes coplanar} \\ k \quad \text{atoms } i}} w_P(i,\ k)(\mathbf{m}_k \cdot \mathbf{r}_{i,k} - d_k)^2 \tag{c}$$

$$+ \sum_{\substack{\text{chiral} \\ \text{centers } l}} w_C(l)(V_l^{\text{ideal}} - V_l^{\text{model}})^2 \tag{d}$$

$$+ \sum_{\substack{\text{nonbonded} \\ \text{contacts } m}} w_N(m)(d_m^{\text{min}} - d_m^{\text{model}})^4 \tag{e}$$

$$+ \sum_{\substack{\text{torsion} \\ \text{angles } t}} w_T(t)(X_t^{\text{ideal}} - X_t^{\text{model}})^2 \tag{f}$$

(a) is the usual X-ray restraint. All other terms are stereochemical restraints.

(b) restrains the distance between atoms, defining bond lengths, bond angles, or dihedral angles.

(c) imposes the planarity of aromatic rings. The same applies to the

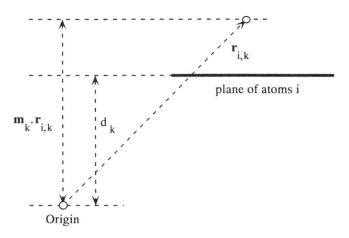

Origin

Figure 13.3. Planarity restraining in the Konnert–Hendrickson refinement method is on the deviation of the atoms from the least-squares plane of the group. d_k is the distance from the origin to the current least-squares plane. For an atom at position $\mathbf{r}_{i,k}$, the distance from the least-squares plane is expressed by $\mathbf{m}_k \cdot \mathbf{r}_{i,k} - d_k$. Here $\mathbf{m}_k$ is the unit vector normal to the plane.

guanidyl part of arginine and to peptide planes. The actual restraining is on the deviation of the atoms from the least-squares plane of the group (see Figure 13.3). d_k are the parameters of the current least-square plane. For an atom at position $\mathbf{r}_{i,k}$ the distance from the least-squares plane is expressed by $\mathbf{m}_k \cdot \mathbf{r}_{i,k} - d_k$. Here $\mathbf{m}_k$ is the unit vector normal to the plane and d_k is the distance from the origin to the plane.

(d) restrains the configuration to the correct enantiomer. A protein structure has many chiral centers: at the C_α atoms (except for glycine) and at the Cβ of threonine and isoleucine. Chirality can be expressed by a chiral volume, which is calculated as the scalar triple product of the vectors from a central atom O to three attached atoms 1, 2, and 3; $\{(O \rightarrow 1). [(O \rightarrow 2) \times (O \rightarrow 3)]\}$ or shorter: $\{\mathbf{1} \cdot [\mathbf{2} \times \mathbf{3}]\}$. This is the scalar product of vector $\mathbf{1}$ with a new vector $\mathbf{4}$, which is the vector product of vector $\mathbf{2}$ and vector $\mathbf{3}$ (Figure 13.4). The new vector $\mathbf{4}$ is perpendicular to both vectors $\mathbf{2}$ and $\mathbf{3}$; its length equals the surface area of the parallelogram formed by $\mathbf{2}$ and $\mathbf{3}$; multiplied by $\mathbf{1}$, a scalar results that equals six times the volume of the pyramid that has O as top and triangle 1, 2, 3 as its base. For the enantiomeric configuration two vectors are interchanged and because $\{\mathbf{1} \cdot [\mathbf{2} \times \mathbf{3}]\} = - \{\mathbf{3} \cdot [\mathbf{2} \times \mathbf{1}]\} = - \{\mathbf{1} \cdot [\mathbf{3} \times \mathbf{2}]\} = - \{\mathbf{2} \cdot [\mathbf{1} \times \mathbf{3}]\}$, the triple product will have the opposite sign.

(e) introduces restraints for nonbonded or van der Waals contacts. They prevent the close approach of atoms not connected by a chemical bond and are stop signs for those atoms. As such they play an important

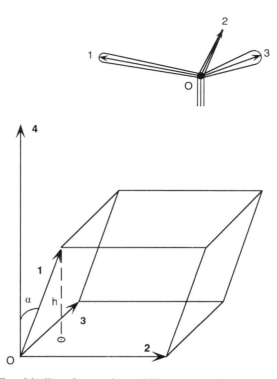

Figure 13.4. The chirality of an amino acid is expressed as a chiral volume, which is calculated as the scalar triple product of the vectors from a central atom O to three attached atoms 1, 2, and 3:$\{1 \cdot [2 \times 3]\}$. Vector 4 is the vector product of 2 and 3. The area of the parallelogram formed by vectors 2 and 3 is $|2 \times 3|$. The volume of the parallelepid formed by vectors 1, 2, and 3 is $V = h \cdot |2 \times 3| = h \cdot |4|$, where h is the altitude; h is parallel to 4 and equals $|1| \cdot |\cos \alpha|$ (because $0 < \alpha < 180°$, $\cos \alpha$ may be negative and, therefore, the absolute value of $\cos \alpha$ is taken). $V = |1| \cdot |4| \cdot |\cos \alpha| = |1 \cdot 4| = |1 \cdot [2 \times 3]|$. The volume of the pyramid with O as the top and triangle 1, 2, and 3 as the base is $\frac{1}{3} \cdot h \cdot \frac{1}{2}|2 \times 3| = \frac{1}{6} \cdot V$.

role in protein structures. Only the repulsive term of the van der Waals potential is taken into acount:

$$E_{\text{repulsive}} = A \times r^{-12}$$

For contacts between C, N, O, and S atoms, and for d-values near and shorter than the equilibrium distance $d^{\min}$, the repulsive term can be approximated by

$$E(d) - E(d^{\min}) = \frac{1}{\sigma^4}(d - d^{\min})^4$$

and the function to be minimized becomes

$$\sum_{\substack{\text{nonbonded} \\ \text{contacts } m}} w_N(m)(d_m^{\text{min}} - d_m^{\text{model}})^4$$

(f) restrains torsion angles. Although a free rotation is in principle possible around single bonds, there are certain restrictions imposed by nonbonded repulsion. For instance the rotations around the $C_\alpha \rightarrow N$ and the $C_\alpha \rightarrow C = O$ bond in the peptide main chain are limited to certain combinations. Also in aliphatic side chains the staggered conformation is more stable than the eclipsed one.

All weighting factors w can be chosen with some freedom, although the normal choice is $w = 1/\sigma^2$, except for w_N, which is taken as $1/\sigma^4$; σ is the standard deviation of the expected distribution. Besides the restraints (a)–(f) several others can be added. For instance, it can be expected that the B-parameters of the temperature factors of neighboring atoms are related because large temperature movements of an atom will cause its neighbors to move also over more than average distances. On the other hand, rigid parts restrict the movement of their neighbors. This correlation can be introduced by restraining the B-value of an atom to those of its neighbors.

In structural papers the statistics of the refinement results are usually given in table form, for instance, as in Table 13.1.

Table 13.1. The Resulting Statistics of TNT Refinement of the Bifunctional Enzyme Phosphoribosylanthranilate Isomerase: Indoleglycerolphosphate Synthase at 2.0 Å Resolution[a]

Resolution range (Å)	15–2.0
Number of observed data	44,611
Number of atoms	4,353
R-factor (%)	17.3
Bond length (Å)[b]	0.010
Bond angle (deg.)[b]	3.2
Trigonal planarity (Å)[b]	0.008
Nontrigonal planarity (Å)[b]	0.017
Number of bad contacts	129
Bad contacts (Å)[c]	0.094

[a] From Wilmanns et al. (1992).
[b] rms deviation from standard geometry values, as determined with the TNT program package.
[c] rms difference of the observed distances between all atoms, flagged as "bad contacts," and the theoretical minimum distances, provided by the TNT program package.

13.4.4. Energy Refinement (EREF)

In the Konnert–Hendrickson refinement the least squares function

$$\sum_h w(h)(|F_{\text{obs}}(h)| - |F_{\text{calc}}(h)|)^2$$

is minimized simultaneously with a number of geometric terms related to bond lengths, angles, etc. In another refinement method—proposed by Jack and Levitt (1978)—the X-ray term is minimized together with a potential energy function including terms for bond stretching, bond angle bending, torsion potentials, and van der Waals interactions. Electrostatic interactions are usually ignored, because they act over rather long distances and are not sensitive to small changes in atomic position. Moreover the calculations are performed assuming the molecule to be in a vacuum and the electrostatic energy would be extremely high, unless artificial dielectric constants are introduced. The function to be minimized is

$$Q = (1 - w_X) \times E + w_X \times \sum_h w(h\ k\ l)(|F_{\text{obs}}(h\ k\ l)| - |F_{\text{calc}}(h\ k\ l)|)^2$$

E is the energy term and w_X controls the relative contribution of the energy and the X-ray term. Its choice, between $w_X = 0$ (pure energy minimization) and $w_X = 1$ (pure X-ray minimization) is rather arbitrary and depends on experience; however, a more objective way for determining w_X has been presented by Brünger (1993) by optimizing the free R-factor (Section 15.2). For the potential energy of a bond the harmonic approximation is used:

$$E_{\text{bond}} = \tfrac{1}{2}K_{\text{bond}}(b - b_0)^2$$

with b_0 the minimum energy distance and b the actual distance between the atoms. K_{bond} and b_0 can be derived from the vibration spectra of small molecules. The same assumption is made for the bond angles:

$$E_{\text{bond angle}} = \tfrac{1}{2}K_\tau(\tau - \tau_0)^2$$

The torsion energy around a bond is expressed as

$$E_{\text{torsion}} = \tfrac{1}{2}K_\xi(\xi - \xi_0)^2$$

The energy for a dihedral angle is

$$E_{\text{dihedral}} = K_\theta\{1 + \cos(m\theta + \delta)\}$$

(see Figure 13.5). θ is the rotation angle and δ a phase angle determining the zero point of rotation. m is the rotation frequency (3 for the C—C bond in ethane). This is a very simple presentation of the dihedral energy and it is only approximately true for bonds that have a large group on either side. For the van der Waals interaction energy both the attractive

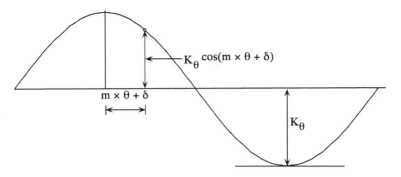

Figure 13.5. The energy for a dihedral angle. θ is the rotation angle and δ a phase angle determining the zero point of rotation. m is the rotation frequency (for instance 3 for the C—C bond in ethane).

term ($B \times r^{-6}$) and the repulsive term ($A \times r^{-12}$) are taken into account:

$$E_{\text{van der Waals}} = A \times r^{-12} + B \times r^{-6}$$

Although EREF is somewhat less popular than the Konnert–Hendrickson refinement method, it can play a useful role in minimizing the energy of a system before refining it with the molecular dynamics technique, which will be discussed in the next section.

13.4.5. Molecular Dynamics or Simulated Annealing

The refinement procedures described so far are based on the least-squares method. The function to be minimized follows a downhill path toward its minimum value and if the starting model is not too different from the real structure the refinement easily converges to the correct solution. However, if the distance between the atoms in the model and in the real structure is rather large, the refinement may be trapped in a local minimum instead of reaching the global or true minimum. To avoid this situation a refinement technique is required that allows uphill as well as downhill search directions to overcome barriers in the Q-function. This technique is supplied by molecular dynamics and was introduced by Brünger et al. (1987). In molecular dynamics the dynamic behavior of a system of particles is simulated. This simulation yields an ensemble of structures that is energetically allowed for a given temperature and pressure: the energy distribution of the structures in the ensemble follows Boltzmann's law, which states that the number of structures with a potential energy ε_{pot} is proportional to $\exp[-\varepsilon_{\text{pot}}/kT]$; k is Boltzmann's constant and T is the absolute temperature. The potential energy depends on the relative positions of the atoms and is calculated on the basis of known potential energy functions, which are always only approximately accurate. The potential energy terms are similar to those in EREF (Section 13.4.4). However, in the molecular dynamics refinement an electrostatic term is added. It is calculated as

$$\sum \frac{q_i \times q_j}{4\pi\varepsilon_0\varepsilon_r r_{ij}}$$

ε_0 is the permittivity constant: $4\pi\varepsilon_0 = 1.11264 \times 10^{-10} C^2 N^{-1} m^{-2}$. ε_r is the local dielectric constant, which is given an estimated value between 1 and 80, depending on the position of the atoms i and j with interatomic distance r_{ij} or, alternatively, instead of $\varepsilon_r > 1$ the electric charges can be reduced.

A molecular dynamics calculation on a molecule starts with assigning to the atoms velocities derived from a Maxwellian distribution at an appropriate temperature. At time $t = 0$ the atoms are in a starting configuration that has a potential energy E_{pot} for the entire molecule. On each atom i at position $\mathbf{r}_i$, a force is acting that is the derivative of the potential energy: force $(i) = -\partial E_{pot}/\partial \mathbf{r}_i$. With the equation from Newtonian mechanics, force $(i) = m_i(d^2\mathbf{r}_i/dt^2)$, the acceleration $d^2\mathbf{r}_i/dt^2$ for atom i with mass m_i can be calculated and then applied. After a short time step Δt, in the femtosecond range (1 fsec = 10^{-15} sec), the process is repeated with the atoms in the new positions. If the number of steps is sufficient (10^3–10^4), the minimum of E_{pot} is reached and information about the dynamic behavior of the atoms in the molecule is obtained. If the temperature of the system is raised to a higher value, more atoms have a higher speed and a higher kinetic energy and can overcome higher energy barriers. The basic idea of molecular dynamics as a superior refinement technique is to raise the temperature sufficiently high for the atoms to overcome energy barriers and then to cool slowly to approach the energy minimum. The method is called simulated annealing (SA) in comparison with, for instance, removing internal strain from glass by heating it first and then slowly cooling it down. In an alternative method the temperature is kept constant but all potential energy terms are scaled by an overall scale factor c, with $0 \leqslant c \leqslant 1$. This is based on Boltzmann's law. An increase in T with constant ε_{pot} has the same effect as diminishing ε_{pot} at constant T.

A typical example of a high energy barrier occurs in the flipping of a peptide plane. It is impossible for the other refinement techniques to overcome this barrier, but not so for simulated annealing. In the application of MD (or SA) to crystallographic refinement, the calculated structure factors of the system are restrained to the observed structure factors as target values, by adding the crystallographic discrepancy term

$$E_x = k_x \times \sum_{hkl}[|F_{obs}(h\ k\ l)| - k|F_{calc}(h\ k\ l)|]^2 \qquad (13.5)$$

as a pseudoenergy term to the potential energy E_{pot} of the system. k_x is a weighting factor and k is the scale factor between $|F_{obs}(h\ k\ l)|$ and $|F_{calc}(h\ k\ l)|$ with $|F_{calc}(h\ k\ l)|$ calculated for the present model.

The total energy, $E_x + E_{pot}$, is minimized during the refinement. In principle $\mathbf{F}_{calc}$ must be calculated after each time step Δt. The same is true for the derivatives of $|F_{calc}|$ with respect to atomic parameters. These derivatives are required for calculating the "force." However, the atomic parameters change only very little during Δt and, therefore, it is sufficient to calculate $\mathbf{F}_{calc}$ and its derivatives only after a preset change in the coordinates has been reached, e.g., 1/10 of the resolution. MD refinement is usually preceded by energy refinement (EREF) with or without X-ray restraints, to reduce possibly high energies in the system.

13.4.5.1. Advantage of MD Refinement

An advantage of MD refinement is the large radius of convergence, which can be several Å units long. In other words, MD draws groups of atoms, originally several Ås away from their final position, corresponding with the potential energy minimum, toward those final positions without any manual intervention. Large errors in the starting model can be corrected. This speeds up the refinement appreciably. The method is very demanding in computer time but with modern high speed computers this is not a problem.

13.4.5.2. The Time-Averaging MD Technique

In MD refinement the dynamic system of moving atoms is restrained by the X-ray data of a static model including isotropic temperature factors. This is, in principle, not correct because in fact the atomic movements are not necessarily isotropic, but can just as well be anisotropic and anharmonic. It is possible to improve the MD refinement technique by calculating, instead of Eq. (13.5), another pseudoenergy term (Gros et al., 1990).

$$E_x = k_x \times \sum_{hkl}[|F_{obs}(h\ k\ l)| - k\ |\{F_{calc}(h\ k\ l)\}_{average}|]^2$$

$\{\mathbf{F}_{calc}(h\ k\ l)\}_{average}$ is not the structure factor of a single model (based on the atomic coordinates x, y, z and the temperature factor parameter B), but the ensemble average of calculated structure factors without temperature factor:

$$\{\mathbf{F}_{calc}(h\ k\ l)\}_{average} = \frac{\displaystyle\int_{t=0}^{t'} P_t \mathbf{F}_{calc}^t(h\ k\ l)\, dt}{\displaystyle\int_{t=0}^{t'} P_t\, dt}$$

t' is the total trajectory time (for instance, 1.000 time steps). t is any time in the trajectory.

P_t is the weight given to the structure factor $\mathbf{F}^t_{\text{calc}}$ $(h\ k\ l)$, calculated for the model at time t. P_t is chosen as $\exp[-(t' - t)/\tau_x]$. The effect of this choice is that an exponentially decreasing weight is given to "older" structures (small t) with a relaxation time τ_x, which regulates the contribution from an "old" structure: the larger τ_x, the more it contributes.

$$\int_{t=0}^{t'} P_t\, dt = \tau_x \left\{ 1 - \exp\left[-\frac{t'}{\tau_x} \right] \right\} \approx \tau_x$$

$$\{\mathbf{F}_{\text{calc}}(h\ k\ l)\}_{\text{average}} = \frac{1}{\tau_x} \int_{t=0}^{t'} \exp\left[-\frac{t' - t}{\tau_x} \right] \mathbf{F}^t_{\text{calc}}(h\ k\ l)\, dt$$

The structure factor $\mathbf{F}^t_{\text{calc}}(h\ k\ l)$ of an individual structure at time t in the trajectory depends on positional parameters only. No individual thermal parameters are assigned to the atoms but instead their movement is now represented by their spatial distribution during the complete trajectory. This is not necessarily isotropic but can also be anisotropic and anharmonic.

In the execution of the method $\{\mathbf{F}_{\text{calc}}(h\ k\ l)\}_{\text{average}}$ at time $t = 0$ is taken equal to the classical $\mathbf{F}_{\text{calc}}(h\ k\ l)$, including the temperature factor parameter B. In the course of the process these B-parameters are gradually lowered to $1\,\text{Å}^2$ and the relaxation time τ increased from 0 to, for instance, $10\,\text{psec}$ ($1\,\text{psec} = 10^{-12}\,\text{sec}$). In this way a gradual change from classical to time-averaging MD is accomplished. There is no need to calculate $\mathbf{F}_{\text{calc}}(h\ k\ l)$ of the structure after each time step Δt. It is sufficient to do it for an ensemble of, for instance, 100 structures. The derivatives of $|F_{\text{calc}}|$, as obtained by a fast Fourier technique according to Agarwal (1978), must be recalculated more often because of the small but rapidly changing fluctuations in the atomic positions. It should be remarked that each individual structural model, that is a model calculated after a time step Δt, is a bad representation of the actual structure: the atoms are not in their equilibrium position and no real B-parameters are incorporated. It is the complete collection of the individual models that approaches the ideal one. Therefore, time-averaging MD is not a refinement technique in the pure sense, but a sampling technique that provides us with an excellent model of the structure, including a more complete description of the atomic fluctuations around the equilibrium positions, as the conventional X-ray structure does.

With this time-averaging MD technique remarkably low R-factors—near 10%—can be reached. It will be clear that even more computer time is needed than for the molecular dynamics technique without time averaging, and still more if solvent molecules would be included in the refinement.

Although the convergence range is large for MD refinement and manual intervention is less frequently required than with the previous refinement techniques, nevertheless the electron density map should be checked occasionally for large errors, such as side chains placed in the density of solvent molecules that are not included in the refinement.

Summary

From a first model of a protein structure, for instance, obtained with isomorphous replacement, important biological information can already be derived. However, for more reliable information and finer details, the structure must be refined. The poor overdetermination limits the refinement, in general, to the positional parameters and an isotropic, but not anisotropic, temperature factor for each atom. Existing stereochemical information from small molecules adds additional "observations" and changes the observation/parameter ratio favorably. The refinement methods use the least-squares formalism for approaching the final solution, often after a great many cycles in which the fast Fourier transform method is essential.

Molecular dynamics or simulated annealing is a more recent refinement technique, which has rapidly gained popularity. It combines, in the function to be minimized, energy terms with the difference between calculated and observed structure factor amplitudes. It has the advantage of a large radius of convergence.

Chapter 14
The Combination of Phase Information

14.1. Introduction

In the multiple isomorphous replacement method the phase information from the various heavy atom derivatives and from anomalous scattering is combined by multiplying the individual phase probability curves. If the electron density map, which results from isomorphous replacement, can be fully interpreted, the crystallographer immediately starts with model refinement and the isomorphous phase information is left behind. However, if the electron density map is inadequate for complete interpretation, map improvement (= phase refinement) should precede model refinement. Solvent flattening and the inclusion of molecular averaging are examples of map improvement techniques (Chapter 8). Another way to improve the existing model is by combining the isomorphous replacement phase information with phase information from the known part of the structure. It is clear that a general and convenient way of combining phase information from these various sources would be most useful. Such a method has been proposed by Hendrickson and Lattman (1970) and has been based on previous studies by Rossmann and Blow (1961). Hendrickson and Lattman propose an exponential form for each individual probability curve of the following type:

$$P_s(\alpha) = N_s \exp[K_s + A_s \cos\alpha + B_s \sin\alpha + C_s \cos 2\alpha + D_s \sin 2\alpha]$$

$P_s(\alpha)$ is the probability for phase angle α derived from source s. K_s and the coefficients A_s, B_s, C_s, and D_s contain, e.g., structure factor amplitudes but not the protein phase angles α. The multiplication of the available $P_s(\alpha)$ functions to the overall probability function $P(\alpha)$ is now simplified to an addition of all K_s and of the coefficients A_s–D_s in the exponential term.

$$P(\alpha) = \prod_s P_s(\alpha) = N' \exp\left[\sum_s K_s + \left(\sum_s A_s\right) \cos \alpha + \left(\sum_s B_s\right) \sin \alpha \right.$$
$$\left. + \left(\sum_s C_s\right) \cos 2\alpha + \left(\sum_s D_s\right) \sin 2\alpha \right]$$

or, combining N' and $\exp[\Sigma_s K_s]$:

$$P(\alpha) = N \exp[A \cos \alpha + B \sin \alpha + C \cos 2\alpha + D \sin 2\alpha] \quad (14.1)$$

The value of N is not important. Moreover it disappears if the "best" Fourier map is calculated with Eq. (7.38):

$$\mathbf{F}_{hkl}(\text{best}) = \frac{\displaystyle\int_\alpha P_{hkl}(\alpha)\mathbf{F}_{hkl}(\alpha)\, d\alpha}{\displaystyle\int_\alpha P_{hkl}(\alpha)\, d\alpha}$$

We shall now derive the form of the coefficients A_s–D_s for

- isomorphous replacement
- anomalous scattering
- partial structures
- solvent flattening
- molecular averaging

14.2. Phase Information from Isomorphous Replacement

In Section 7.15 the probability function $[P(\alpha)]_j$ for one reflection and derivative j in the isomorphous replacement has been presented as

$$[P(\alpha)]_j = N \exp\left[-\frac{\varepsilon_j^2(\alpha)}{2E_j^2}\right]$$

$\varepsilon_j(\alpha)$ is the "lack of closure error" for the structure factor amplitude $|F_{PH}(\text{calc})|$ of derivative j.

$$\varepsilon_j(\alpha) = \{|F_{PH}(\text{obs})|_j - k_j|F_{PH}(\text{calc})|_j\}$$

The derivation of a suitable form of the phase probability curve is easier if the error is redefined as an error in the derivative intensity instead of the structure factor amplitude. Assuming that $|F_{PH}(\text{calc})|^2$ and $|F_{PH}(\text{obs})|^2$ are on the same scale, we have

$$\varepsilon_j'(\alpha_P) = |F_{PH,j}(\text{calc})|^2 - |F_{PH,j}(\text{obs})|^2$$

$$|F_{PH,j}(\text{calc})|^2 = |\mathbf{F}_P + \mathbf{F}_{H,j}|^2$$
$$= |F_P|^2 + |F_{H,j}|^2 + 2|F_P| \times |F_{H,j}| \times \cos(\alpha_{H,j} - \alpha_P)$$

(see Figure 7.16b)

$$\varepsilon_j'(\alpha_P) = |F_P|^2 + |F_{H,j}|^2 - |F_{PH,j}(\text{obs})|^2$$
$$+ 2|F_P| \times |F_{H,j}| \times \cos(\alpha_{H,j} - \alpha_P)$$

A Gaussian distribution for $\varepsilon_j'(\alpha_P)$ is assumed:

$$[P_{\text{iso}}(\alpha_P)]_j = N_j \exp\left[-\frac{\{\varepsilon_j'(\alpha_P)\}^2}{2(E_j')^2} \right] \tag{14.2}$$

N_j is a normalizing factor and E_j' is the estimated standard deviation of the errors in the derivative intensity.

$$\{\varepsilon_j'(\alpha_P)\}^2 = (|F_P|^2 + |F_{H,j}|^2 - |F_{PH,j}(\text{obs})|^2)^2$$
$$+ 4 \times (|F_P|^2 + |F_{H,j}|^2 - |F_{PH,j}(\text{obs})|^2)$$
$$\times |F_P| \times |F_{H,j}| \times \cos(\alpha_{H,j} - \alpha_P)$$
$$+ 4 \times |F_P|^2 + |F_{H,j}|^2 \times \cos^2(\alpha_{H,j} - \alpha_P)$$

We want to separate functions with α only from the rest. This can be done by writing for

$$\cos^2(\alpha_{H,j} - \alpha_P) \to \tfrac{1}{2}\{1 + \cos 2(\alpha_{H,j} - \alpha_P)\}$$
$$\cos(\alpha_{H,j} - \alpha_P) \to \cos \alpha_{H,j} \cos \alpha_P + \sin \alpha_{H,j} \sin \alpha_P$$

With the separation of $\mathbf{F}_{H,j}$ into its components (Figure 14.1), this results in

$$\{\varepsilon_j'(\alpha_P)\}^2 = (|F_P|^2 + |F_{H,j}|^2 - |F_{PH,j}(\text{obs})|^2)^2 + 2 \times |F_P|^2 \times |F_{H,j}|^2$$
$$+ 4 \times (|F_P|^2 + |F_{H,j}|^2 - |F_{PH,j}(\text{obs})|^2) \times |F_P| \times A_{H,j} \times \cos \alpha_P$$
$$+ 4 \times (|F_P|^2 + |F_{H,j}|^2 - |F_{PH,j}(\text{obs})|^2) \times |F_P| \times B_{H,j} \times \sin \alpha_P$$
$$+ 2 \times |F_P|^2 \times (A_{H,j}^2 - B_{H,j}^2) \cos 2\alpha_P$$
$$+ 4 \times |F_P|^2 \times A_{H,j} \times B_{H,j} \times \sin 2\alpha_P$$

Comparison of this equation with Eqs. (14.1) and (14.2) gives

$$A_{\text{iso},j} = -\frac{2(|F_P|^2 + |F_{H,j}|^2 - |F_{PH,j}(\text{obs})|^2) \times |F_P|}{(E_j')^2} \times A_{H,j}$$

$$B_{\text{iso},j} = -\frac{2(|F_P|^2 + |F_{H,j}|^2 - |F_{PH,j}(\text{obs})|^2) \times |F_P|}{(E_j')^2} \times B_{H,j}$$

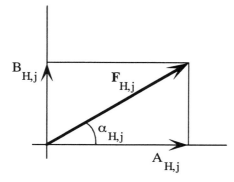

Figure 14.1. The separation of $\mathbf{F}_{H,j}$ into its components: $A_{H,j} = |F_{H,j}|\cos\alpha_{H,j}$ and $B_{H,j} = |F_{H,j}|\sin\alpha_{H,j}$.

$$C_{\text{iso},j} = -\frac{|F_P|^2}{(E'_j)^2} \times (A_{H,j}^2 - B_{H,j}^2)$$

$$D_{\text{iso},j} = -\frac{2|F_P|^2}{(E'_j)^2} \times A_{H,j} \times B_{H,j}$$

14.3. Phase Information from Anomalous Scattering

The improvement of protein phase angles by incorporating information from anomalous scattering has already been discussed in Section 9.3.

$$P_{\text{ano}}(\alpha_P) = N' \exp\left[-\frac{\varepsilon_{\text{ano}}^2(\alpha_P)}{2(E')^2}\right]$$

[see Eq. (9.2)] with $\varepsilon_{\text{ano}}(\alpha_P) = \Delta PH(\text{obs}) - \Delta PH(\text{calc})$ and

$$\Delta PH(\text{obs}) = |F_{PH}(+)| - |F_{PH}(-)|$$

$$\Delta PH(\text{calc}) = -\frac{2 \times |F_P| \times |F_H|}{k \times |F_{PH}|} \sin(\alpha_H - \alpha_P)$$

(Section 9.3)

$$\varepsilon_{\text{ano}}(\alpha_P) = |F_{PH}(+)| - |F_{PH}(-)| + \frac{2|F_P| \times |F_H|}{k \times |F_{PH}|} \sin(\alpha_H - \alpha_P)$$

$$= \underline{\qquad \Delta \qquad} + \kappa \sin(\alpha_H - \alpha_P)$$

with

$$\Delta = |F_{PH}(+)| - |F_{PH}(-)| \quad \text{and} \quad \kappa = \frac{2|F_P| \times |F_H|}{k \times |F_{PH}|}$$

$$\varepsilon_{\text{ano}}^2(\alpha_P) = \Delta^2 + 2 \times \Delta \times \kappa \sin(\alpha_H - \alpha_P) + \kappa^2 \sin^2(\alpha_H - \alpha_P)$$

As before, terms with α_P only, should be separated.

$$\sin(\alpha_H - \alpha_P) = \sin\alpha_H \cos\alpha_P - \cos\alpha_H \sin\alpha_P$$

$$\sin^2(\alpha_H - \alpha_P) = \tfrac{1}{2}\{1 - \cos 2(\alpha_H - \alpha_P)\}$$

$$= \tfrac{1}{2} - \tfrac{1}{2}\cos 2\alpha_H \cos 2\alpha_P - \tfrac{1}{2}\sin 2\alpha_H \sin 2\alpha_P$$

$$\varepsilon_{ano}^2(\alpha_P) = \Delta^2 + \tfrac{1}{2}\kappa^2 + (2 \times \Delta \times \kappa \sin\alpha_H)\cos\alpha_P$$

$$- 2 \times \Delta \times \kappa \cos\alpha_H \sin\alpha_P$$

$$- \tfrac{1}{2} \times \kappa^2 \cos 2\alpha_H \cos 2\alpha_P$$

$$- \tfrac{1}{2} \times \kappa^2 \sin 2\alpha_H \sin 2\alpha_P$$

$$-\frac{\varepsilon_{ano}^2(\alpha_P)}{2(E')^2} = -\frac{\Delta^2 + \tfrac{1}{2}\kappa^2}{2(E')^2} \qquad (= K_{ano})$$

$$-\frac{\Delta \times \kappa \sin\alpha_H}{(E')^2}\cos\alpha_P \qquad (= A_{ano}\cos\alpha_P)$$

$$+\frac{\Delta \times \kappa \cos\alpha_H}{(E')^2}\sin\alpha_P \qquad (= B_{ano}\sin\alpha_P)$$

$$+\frac{\kappa^2 \cos 2\alpha_H}{4(E')^2}\cos 2\alpha_P \qquad (= C_{ano}\cos 2\alpha_P)$$

$$+\frac{\kappa^2 \sin 2\alpha_H}{4(E')^2}\sin 2\alpha_P \qquad (= D_{ano}\sin 2\alpha_P)$$

14.4. Phase Information from Partial Structure Data, Solvent Flattening, and Molecular Averaging

For partial structure information as well as for solvent flattening and molecular averaging, we encountered the same form of the phase probability function:

$$P_{SF}(\alpha_P) = P_{average}(\alpha) = N \exp[X' \cos(\alpha_P - \alpha_{calc})]$$

[see Eq. (8.10)]

$$P_{partial}(\alpha_P) = N \exp[X \cos(\alpha_P - \alpha_{partial})]$$

see Eq. (8.9) in which $1/2\pi I_0(X)$ is now replaced by the normalizing constant N.

The exponential term for phase combination is simply

$$\underbrace{X \cos\alpha_{partial}}_{= A_{partial}} \cos\alpha_P + \underbrace{X \sin\alpha_{partial}}_{= B_{partial}} \sin\alpha_P$$

or

$$\underset{= A_{SF}}{\underbrace{X' \cos \alpha_{SF}} \cos \alpha_P} + \underset{= B_{SF}}{\underbrace{X' \sin \alpha_{SF}} \sin \alpha_P}$$

or

$$\underset{= A_{average}}{\underbrace{X' \cos \alpha_{average}} \cos \alpha_P} + \underset{= B_{average}}{\underbrace{X' \sin \alpha_{average}} \sin \alpha_P}$$

Summary

The major advantage of the Hendrickson and Lattman formalism is that one need not calculate phase probability distributions afresh every time some new information is added to the protein phases. The new information can easily be combined with previous information by simple addition to the coefficients A, B, C, and D in the general phase probability distribution $P(\alpha) = N \exp[A \cos \alpha + B \sin \alpha + C \cos 2\alpha + D \sin 2\alpha]$.

Chapter 15
Checking for Gross Errors and Estimating the Accuracy of the Structural Model

15.1. Introduction

After the molecular model of the protein structure has been refined, it may still contain errors that have creeped into the model during the interpretation of the electron density map, particularly of the regions where the electron density is weak. Some of the errors are obvious and should cause immediate suspicion, for instance, the presence of left-handed helices can almost always be ruled out. Most of the available modeling programs allow regularization of geometry, but do not guarantee overall good quality of the final model. A very qualitative impression of the accuracy of the structural model can be obtained by inspection of the electron density map:

- the connectivity of the main chain and the side chains
- the bulging out of the carbonyl oxygen atoms from the main chain
- the interpretation of the side chain electron density.

15.2. R-Factors

A more quantitative impression of the accuracy of the structure is obtained from the various residual indices (see Appendix 2). The common crystallographic R-factor is

$$R = \frac{\sum_{hkl} ||F_{obs}| - k|F_{calc}||}{\sum_{hkl} |F_{obs}|}$$

where k is a scale factor.

For acentric model structures with the atoms randomly distributed in the unit cell, $R = 0.59$. For structures refined to high resolution, for instance, 1.6 Å, the *R*-factor should not be much higher than 0.16. This *R*-factor is an overall number and does not indicate major local errors. More useful in this respect is $R_{\text{real space}}$ (Jones et al., 1991). It is obtained in the following way: The final electron density map is plotted on a grid G_1 and a calculated map on an identical grid G_2. This calculated map is obtained by a Gaussian distribution of electron density around the average position for each atom in the model, with the same temperature factor for all atoms. The two density sets are scaled together. Now the electron densities of separate residues, or groups of atoms in a residue, are selected on both grids and built on a grid $G_3(\text{obs})$ and a grid $G_3(\text{calc})$, respectively. For nonzero elements in the two G_3 grids R is calculated as

$$R_{\text{real space}} = \frac{\sum |\rho_{\text{obs}} - \rho_{\text{calc}}|}{\sum |\rho_{\text{obs}} + \rho_{\text{calc}}|}$$

It is plotted as a function of the residues along the polypeptide chain (Figure 15.1). The fitting of the main chain alone can be obtained by incorporating just the N, C(α), C(β), C, and O atoms in the calculation. The fitting of the side chains in the density can be checked by taking only the side chain atoms.

It has been shown that the normal crystallographic *R*-factor can reach surprisingly low values in the refinement of protein structural models that

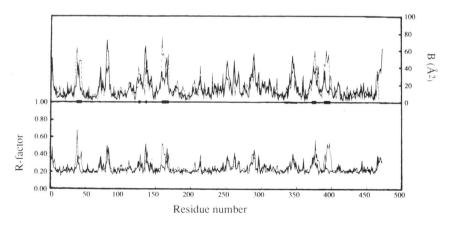

Figure 15.1. Real space *R*-factor (lower panel) and average *B*-factor (upper panel) of the *Azotobacter vinelandii* lipoamide dehydrogenase. Misplaced loops have been indicated by a thin line and after their correction by a thick line. Note the correspondence between the *R*- and the *B*-factor at the problem sites. (Source: Dr. Andrea Mattevi.)

appear later to be incorrect, for instance, because the number of model parameters is taken too high. Brünger (1992, 1993) suggested improving this situation with the introduction of a free R-factor, which is unbiased by the refinement process. In this method one divides the reflections into a "test set (T)" of unique reflections and a "working set (W)." The test set is a random selection of 10% of the observed reflections. The refinement is carried out with the working set only, and the free R-factor is calculated with the test set of reflections only:

$$R_T^{\text{free}} = \frac{\sum\limits_{hkl \subset T} ||F_{\text{obs}}| - k|F_{\text{calc}}||}{\sum\limits_{hkl \subset T} |F_{\text{obs}}|}$$

where $hkl \subset T$ means all reflections belonging to test set T. Brünger could show that a high correlation exists between the free R-factor and the accuracy of the atomic model phases.

15.3. The Ramachandran Plot

The stereochemistry of the main chain folding can be investigated with a Ramachandran plot in which the dihedral angles Φ and Ψ for each residue are plotted in a square matrix (Figure 15.2). It is customary to have the conformation of the fully extended chain in the corners of the square. Short contacts between atoms of adjacent residues prevent Φ and Ψ from taking on all possible angles between $-180°$ and $+180°$. They are clustered in regions in the Ramachandran matrix, with boundaries depending on the choice of the permitted van der Waals distances and tetrahedral angles. Usually a conservative and a more relaxed boundary are given, as in Figure 15.2. For highly refined structures nearly all the Φ/Ψ values do lie within the allowed regions. Due to the lack of a side chain, glycyl residues can adopt a larger range of Φ and Ψ angles. The electron density for nonglycine residues lying outside the allowed region should be carefully checked.

15.4. Stereochemistry Check

Unusual ω angles (Figure 15.3) and eclipsed dihedral angles in side chains should cause suspicion. Another feature to observe is whether the structure shows more than a few unsatisfied H-bonds. If it does, this would be energetically extremely unfavorable. Attention should also be given to residues or parts of residues with conspicuously high B-values as well as to unpaired charged residues in the interior of the molecule and to abnormally close van der Waals contacts. This checking of the stereo-

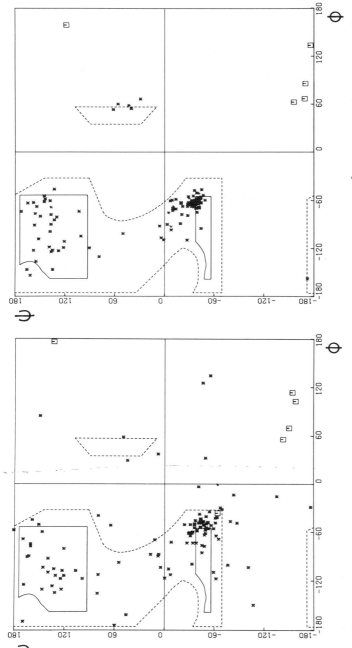

Figure 15.2. Ramachandran plot of the polypeptide chain conformation in phospholipase A_2 at 1.7 Å resolution. Glycine is denoted by open squares, all other residues by asterisks. Continuous lines enclose regions in which the tetrahedral angle (N, C_α, C) = 110° and broken lines enclose regions with the angle (N, C_α, C) = 115°. The left figure is for the structural model before the refinement and the right one after the refinement. The convention for the sense of the Φ and Ψ angle rotation is the following: the angles are positive for a right-handed rotation: when looking along any bond from N to C_α and from C_α to C, the far end rotates clockwise relative to the near end, as is indicated by the arrows in Figure 15.3.

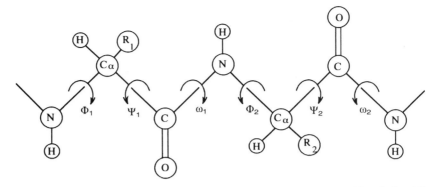

Figure 15.3. A schematic picture of a fully stretched polypeptide chain. The rotations around the C_α—NH bonds are given by the angle Φ and around the C_α—C=O bonds by the angle Ψ. The peptide planes are usually flat with $\omega = 180°$.

chemistry has been elegantly treated by Thornton and her colleagues (Morris et al., 1992). The stereochemical parameters are bond lengths and angles, dihedral angles, Φ and Ψ angles, noncovalent interactions, etc. They can be easily calculated from the atomic coordinates. Thornton et al. compare the stereochemistry of the protein to be checked, with a standard set of stereochemical parameters derived from well-resolved protein structures and from small-molecule structures. Unless strong restraints on the parameters have been used in the refinement, deviations from the standard stereochemical parameters can easily be detected and thus are an indication for possible errors in the structure. A suite of programs, PROCHECK, is available for the checking procedure; it provides output in the form of several different plots (Laskowski et al., 1993).

15.5. The 3D–1D Profile Method

An interesting method for checking the quality of a protein molecular model has been developed by Eisenberg and co-workers (Bowie et al., 1991; Lüthy et al., 1992; Wilmanns and Eisenberg, 1993). In this method, a so-called 3D profile is compared with the amino acid sequence of the protein. The 3D profile is obtained in the following way. Each residue in the chain is assigned to one of six classes of side chain environment. These classes are determined by two parameters (see Figure 15.4): (1) the area of the residue that is buried and (2) the fraction of side chain area that is covered by polar atoms (O and N). In addition to the six classes of side chain environment, three classes of local secondary structure are distinguished: α-helix, β-sheet, and others. Together there are $6 \times 3 = 18$

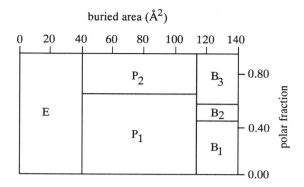

Figure 15.4. The six side chain environment categories in the Eisenberg profile method. A residue was assigned to category E (exposed) if less than 40 Å^2 of the side chain was buried. For a buried area between 40 and 114 Å^2, the residue was placed in environment category P$_1$(polar) if the polar fraction was smaller than 0.67, and in P$_2$ if the polar fraction was 0.67 or larger, where the polar fraction is the fraction of the side chain area covered by polar atoms. For buried side chains, side chains with a buried area of more than 114 Å^2, three classes were distinguished: B$_1$ with a polar fraction smaller than 0.45, B$_2$ with a polar fraction between 0.45 and 0.58, and B$_3$ with a polar fraction of 0.58 and larger.

residue number	residue type	class	3D–1D score
....	....	....	....
46	T	Eα	-0.17
47	D	E	0.22
48	Y	P1	-1.31
49	L	B1	1.10
....	....	....	....

$$+ \underline{}$$

S = total score

Figure 15.5. This figure lists four residues of an arbitrary polypeptide chain. In column 3 the class to which each residue belongs is given and in column 4 the 3D–1D score that is derived from the standard matrix. The total score S is obtained as the sum over all residues of the 3D–1D scores.

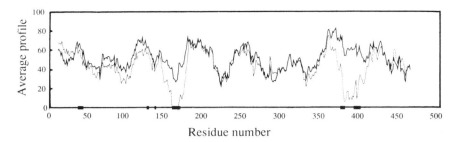

Figure 15.6. Plot of the average 3D–1D score of the first subunit in *Azotobacter vinelandii* lipoamide dehydrogenase before (thin line) and after (thick line) corrections to the model versus residue number (profile score). Because a 21 residue sliding window was used, the scores for the first and last 10 residues have no meaning and were omitted. A score below 0.20 indicates a bad part of the model. Note the improvement in the model after application of the corrections. (Source: Dr. Andrea Mattevi.)

classes. On the basis of a number of well-refined three-dimensional structures a standard matrix has been constructed giving the 3D–1D score for every type of amino acid residue in each of the 18 classes. For each residue in the polypeptide chain, the 3D–1D score is read from the matrix. The overall 3D score S for the compatibility of the model with the sequence is the sum of the 3D–1D scores for all residues in the chain (Figure 15.5). A high score is found for a correct structure, a low one for an incorrect structure. Since S depends on the length of the polypeptide chain, it should be compared for proteins with the same length. Besides the overall 3D–1D score S, a profile score for each position in the polypeptide chain can be determined to locate improperly built segments in the 3D model. This score is calculated as the average of the 3D–1D scores for 21 residues in a window with the particular residue in the center of that window (Figure 15.6).

The advantage of the profile method is that it is completely independent of any assumption introduced into the model construction, because it depends exclusively on the compatibility of the model with its own amino acid sequence.

15.6. Quantitative Estimation of the Coordinate Error in the Final Model

The indicators so far mentioned do not give a value for the error in the atomic coordinates of the molecular model. An estimation of the average value of this error, $\overline{|\Delta r|}$, can be obtained by methods proposed by, Luzzati (1952) and Read (1986, 1990b). Luzzati has derived a relationship between the average error $\overline{|\Delta r|}$ in the atomic coordinates and the difference between $|F_{obs}|$ and $|F_{calc}|$, as expressed in the crystallographic reliability factor R. The R-factor is plotted as a function of $(\sin \theta)/\lambda$ and this curve is compared with a family of calculated lines, which are functions of $\overline{|\Delta r|} \times (\sin \theta)/\lambda$. The members of the family are calculated for different values of $\overline{|\Delta r|}$ and from the line that is closest to the experimental curve, $\overline{|\Delta r|}$ for the crystal structure is derived. The assumption is that the difference between $|F_{obs}|$ and $|F_{calc}|$ is due exclusively to errors in the positional coordinates of the atoms. The mathematics of the Luzzati method is rather complicated and we shall not go into any details. For an example see Figure 15.7. In the method proposed by Read (1986), which is based on previous work by Luzzati and others, for instance Srinivasan and Ramachandran (1965), the coordinate error $\overline{|\Delta r|}$ is also obtained in a graphic way; the difference is that now a single plot is sufficient, the σ_A plot, based on Eq. (15.1):

$$\ln \sigma_A = \frac{1}{2} \ln \left(\frac{\sum_P}{\sum_N} \right) - \pi^3 (\overline{|\Delta r|})^2 \left(\frac{\sin \theta}{\lambda} \right)^2 \tag{15.1}$$

σ_A is defined as

$$\sigma_A = D \left(\frac{\sum_P}{\sum_N} \right)^{1/2}$$

where $\sum_N = \sum_{j=1}^{N} f_j^2$. The summation is over all N atoms in the structure for $\sum_N$ and over all atoms in the partially known structure for $\sum_P$. $\sum_P / \sum_N$ should be 1 if the structure is completely identified. But this is never true because of rather disordered solvent atoms in the crystal. These atoms contribute appreciably to low order reflections that should, therefore, be

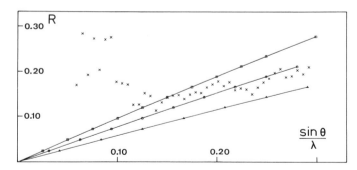

Figure 15.7. Plot of the crystallographic R-factor as a function of $(\sin \theta)/\lambda$ (crosses). Superimposed are calculated Luzzati lines for a coordinate error $\overline{|\Delta r|}$ of 0.08 Å (triangles), 0.12 Å (circles), and 0.16 Å (squares). (Reproduced with permission from Dijkstra et al. (1981).)

ignored. D is the Fourier transform of the probability distribution $p(\Delta \mathbf{r})$ of $\Delta \mathbf{r}$:

$$D(\mathbf{S}) = \int p(\Delta \mathbf{r}) \exp[2\pi i(\Delta \mathbf{r}) \cdot \mathbf{S}] \, d\Delta \mathbf{r}$$

D is in general complex but a centrosymmetric distribution for $p(\Delta \mathbf{r})$ is assumed and, therefore, D can be written as

$$D(\mathbf{S}) = \int p(\Delta \mathbf{r}) \cos[2\pi(\Delta \mathbf{r}) \cdot \mathbf{S}] \, d\Delta \mathbf{r} \qquad (15.2)$$

If $\ln \sigma_A$ is plotted vs. $\{(\sin \theta)/\lambda\}^2$ a straight line is obtained with slope $\{-\pi^3(\overline{|\Delta r|})^2\}$ and intercept of $\frac{1}{2}\ln(\Sigma_P/\Sigma_N)$ [see Eq. (15.1)]. For the derivation of Eq. (15.1) see p. 279. σ_A is obtained from an independent estimate. Different methods are available. They are discussed by Read (1986). It can, for example, be done with a method suggested by Hauptman (1982). He regarded σ_A as the square root of the correlation coefficient between the observed and calculated normalized structure factors:

$$\sigma_A = \left[\frac{\sum(|E(\text{obs})|^2 - \overline{|E(\text{obs})|^2})(|E(\text{calc})|^2 - \overline{|E(\text{calc})|^2})}{\{\sum(|E(\text{obs})|^2 - \overline{|E(\text{obs})|^2})^2 \sum(|E(\text{calc})|^2 - \overline{|E(\text{calc})|^2})^2\}^{1/2}} \right]^{1/2}$$

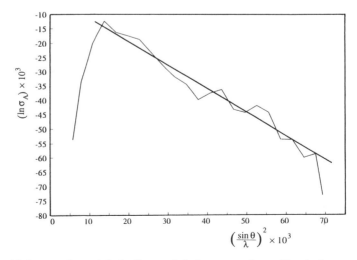

Figure 15.8. σ_A plot of haloalkane dehalogenase from *Xanthobacter autotrophicus*. The structure was determined to a resolution of 2.5 Å. (Source: Dr. K.H.G. Verschueren.)

with $\overline{|E(\text{obs})|^2} = \overline{|E(\text{calc})|^2} = 1$. It was shown by Read that this estimated value of σ_A can be refined by finding the zero of the residual function:

$$R = \sum w(\sigma_A - m|E_N||E_P^c|)$$

w is 1 for centric and 2 for noncentric reflections; m is the figure of merit. An alternative method is given by Srinivasan and Chandrasekaran (1966). They give the following expression for σ_A:

$$\sigma_A = \overline{|E(\text{obs})||E(\text{calc})|\cos[\alpha(\text{obs}) - \alpha(\text{calc})]}$$

Because D, and therefore also σ_A, is a function of resolution, σ_A must be estimated in ranges of resolution. As the example in Figure 15.8 shows, the data points at lower resolution do not fit the line. The same is true for the points at high resolution, which is probably due to measurement errors.

For well-refined structures the Luzzati method and the σ_A plot give nearly invariably estimated errors in the coordinates between 0.2 and 0.3 Å.

The Derivation of the σ_A Plot

We start with Eq. (15.2) and must first of all find $p(\Delta r)$ as a function of $|\Delta r|$. If the assumption is made that $p(\Delta r)$ is spherically symmetric (does not depend on the direction of Δr) and moreover that $|\Delta r|$ is distributed as a Gaussian function:

$$p(\Delta r) = N \exp\left[-\frac{|\Delta r|^2}{2\sigma^2}\right]$$

in which N is the normalization constant and σ the standard deviation. N can be obtained from

$$\int_0^\infty p(\Delta r)\, d(\Delta r) = 1$$

$$N \int_0^\infty \exp\left[-\frac{|\Delta r|^2}{2\sigma^2}\right] 4\pi|\Delta r|^2\, d|\Delta r| = (2\pi\sigma^2)^{3/2} \times N = 1$$

$$N = (2\pi\sigma^2)^{-3/2} \quad \text{and} \quad p(\Delta r) = (2\pi\sigma^2)^{-3/2} \exp\left[-\frac{|\Delta r|^2}{2\sigma^2}\right] \quad (15.3)$$

$$D(S) = \int p(\Delta r)\cos[2\pi(\Delta r)\cdot S]\, d\Delta r$$

$$= (2\pi\sigma^2)^{-3/2} \int \exp\left[-\frac{|\Delta r|^2}{2\sigma^2}\right]\cos[2\pi(\Delta r \cdot S)]\, d\Delta r$$

Replace $\Delta\mathbf{r}$ and $\mathbf{S}$ by their orthogonal components:

$$\Delta\mathbf{r} = \Delta\mathbf{x} + \Delta\mathbf{y} + \Delta\mathbf{z} \quad \text{and} \quad \mathbf{S} = \mathbf{h} + \mathbf{k} + \mathbf{l}$$

$$(\Delta\mathbf{r} \cdot \mathbf{S}) = h \times \Delta x + k \times \Delta y + l \times \Delta z$$

$$\cos 2\pi(\Delta\mathbf{r} \cdot \mathbf{S}) = \cos 2\pi(h \times \Delta x + k \times \Delta y + l \times \Delta z)$$
$$= \cos(2\pi h \times \Delta x) \cos(2\pi k \times \Delta y) \cos(2\pi l \times \Delta z)$$

All sin terms have vanished because of the spherical symmetry of $\Delta\mathbf{r}$.

$$\int_{\text{all } \Delta\mathbf{r}} = \int_{\Delta x=-\infty}^{+\infty} \int_{\Delta y=-\infty}^{+\infty} \int_{\Delta z=-\infty}^{+\infty} = 8 \times \int_{\Delta x=0}^{+\infty} \int_{\Delta y=0}^{+\infty} \int_{\Delta z=0}^{+\infty}$$

$$D = 8(2\pi\sigma^2)^{-3/2} \int_{\Delta x=0}^{\infty} \int_{\Delta y=0}^{\infty} \int_{\Delta z=0}^{\infty} \exp\left[-\frac{(\Delta x)^2 + (\Delta y)^2 + (\Delta z)^2}{2\sigma^2}\right]$$
$$\times \cos(2\pi h \times \Delta x) \cos(2\pi k \times \Delta y) \cos(2\pi l \times \Delta z) \, d(\Delta x) \, d(\Delta y) \, d(\Delta z)$$

Using the fact that the definite integral

$$\int_0^{\infty} \exp[-a^2 x^2] \cos bx \, dx = \frac{\sqrt{\pi}}{2a} \exp\left[-\frac{b^2}{4a^2}\right]$$

it follows that $D = \exp[-2\pi^2 |S|^2\sigma^2]$.   (15.4)

Next the relation between σ^2 and $\overline{|\Delta r|}$ must be found.

$$\overline{|\Delta r|} = \int_0^{\infty} p(|\Delta r|) \, |\Delta r| \, d|\Delta r| \qquad\qquad \text{[See Eq. (15.3)]}$$

$$= (2\pi\sigma^2)^{-3/2} \times \int_0^{\infty} 4\pi(|\Delta r|)^2 \times |\Delta r| \exp\left[-\frac{|\Delta r|^2}{2\sigma^2}\right] d|\Delta r|$$

$$= (2\pi\sigma^2)^{-3/2} \times 4\pi \int_0^{\infty} |\Delta r|^3 \exp\left[-\frac{|\Delta r|^2}{2\sigma^2}\right] d|\Delta r|$$

Splitting $|\Delta r|^3 \exp[-|\Delta r|^2/2\sigma^2]$ into $|\Delta r| \times |\Delta r|^2 \exp[-|\Delta r|^2/2\sigma^2]$ and knowing that $\int_0^{\infty} x^2 \exp[-ax^2] \, dx = \frac{1}{4}\sqrt{\pi} \times a^{-3/2}$, we obtain

$$\overline{|\Delta r|} = 2\sqrt{\frac{2}{\pi}} \times \sigma \quad \text{and} \quad \sigma^2 = \frac{\pi}{8}(\overline{|\Delta r|})^2$$

From Eq. (15.4) is follows that

$$D = \exp\left[-\frac{1}{4}\pi^3 |S|^2(\overline{|\Delta r|})^2\right] = \exp\left[-\pi^3\left(\frac{\sin\theta}{\lambda}\right)^2 (\overline{|\Delta r|})^2\right]$$

$$\sigma_A = D\left(\frac{\sum_P}{\sum_N}\right)^{1/2} \quad \text{and} \quad \ln\sigma_A = \frac{1}{2}\ln\left(\frac{\sum_P}{\sum_N}\right) - \pi^3(\overline{|\Delta r|})^2\left(\frac{\sin\theta}{\lambda}\right)^2$$

In a later paper Read (1990b) showed that his (and Luzzati's) assumption of a Gaussian $\Delta \mathbf{r}$ distribution, equal for all atoms, is in general not allowed. As a consequence, the Luzzati plot and the σ_A plot can, in principle, be used only for comparative, rather than absolute measures of the coordinate errors. However, from the comparison of independently determined structures it seems that, somewhat surprisingly, the σ_A plot gives reasonable results.

Summary

In the literature a number of protein structures have been presented that afterward turned out to be entirely or partly wrong. Apparently the density map was incorrectly interpreted. It is not quaranteed that interpretation errors will be removed in the refinement process and the best way to follow is to apply the methods presented in this chapter to check the accuracy of the model. If any suspicion is raised against part of the model, it should be carefully checked for alternative conformations. The Luzzati method and the σ_A plot give an estimate of the coordinate error. Because of underlying assumptions, which are not always true, they can, in principle, be used only for comparative, rather than absolute measures of the coordinate errors. However, from the comparison of independently determined structures it seems that the σ_A plot gives reasonable results. It is clear that a better method for the estimation of errors in a protein structure is needed, but as long as that is not available the best one can do is to use the σ_A plot.

Appendix 1
A Compilation of Equations for Calculating Electron Density Maps

Straightforward Electron Density Map

$$\rho(x\ y\ z) = \frac{1}{V}\sum_{hkl}|F(h\ k\ l)|\ \exp[-2\pi i(hx + ky + lz) + i\alpha\ (h\ k\ l)]$$

$$= \frac{1}{V}\sum_{hkl}|F(h\ k\ l)|\ \cos[2\pi(hx + ky + lz) - \alpha(h\ k\ l)]$$

The $|F(h\ k\ l)|$s are the structure factor amplitudes of the reflections $(h\ k\ l)$.

Difference Electron Density Map

$$\Delta\rho\ (x\ y\ z) = \frac{1}{V}\sum_{hkl}\Delta|F(h\ k\ l)|_{iso}\ \exp[-2\pi i(hx + ky + lz) + i\alpha_P(h\ k\ l)]$$

$$= \frac{1}{V}\sum_{hkl}\Delta|F(h\ k\ l)|_{iso}\ \cos[2\pi(hx + ky + lz) - \alpha_P(h\ k\ l)]$$

$\Delta|F(h\ k\ l)|_{iso}$ is the difference between the structure factor amplitudes for the protein and some isomorphous derivative of that protein. The phase angles $\alpha_P(h\ k\ l)$ are those of the native protein. The map shows the electron density, which is extra (or which is missing) in the derivative at half the actual height.

A $2F_{obs} - F_{calc}$ Map

$$\rho(x\ y\ z) = \frac{1}{V}\sum_{hkl}(2|F_{obs}| - |F_{calc}|)\ \exp[-2\pi i(hx + ky + lz) + i\alpha_{calc}]$$

This map can be regarded as the sum of the electron density of a model and of a difference electron density map at double height. It shows, besides the electron density of the model, the difference between the actual structure and the model at normal height. The phase angles are those calculated for the model.

A Residual, or Double Difference, Electron Density Map

$$\Delta\rho(x\ y\ z) = \frac{1}{V}\sum_{hkl}\{|F_{obs}| - |\mathbf{F}_{native} + \mathbf{F}_{attached}|\}$$
$$\times \exp[-2\pi i(hx + ky + lz) + i\alpha_{calc}]$$

$|F_{obs}|$ is the structure factor amplitude for the derivative. $\mathbf{F}_{attached}$ is the structure factor contribution by those attached atoms or groups of atoms for which the parameters are already known. The phase angles α_{calc} are for the native protein and the attached heavy atoms. This is a useful Fourier summation for the detection of extra attached atoms or groups of atoms.

An OMIT Map

$$\Delta\rho(x\ y\ z) = \frac{1}{V}\sum_{hkl}(|F_{obs}| - |F_{calc}|)\ \exp[-2\pi i(hx + ky + lz) + i\alpha_{calc}]$$

F_{calc} is the structure factor of a partial model, that is a model from which a fragment has been deleted. The phase angles α_{calc} are for the model with fragment deleted. It is a difference Fourier summation that is often used if part of the electron density map cannot be interpreted satisfactorily. This part is then deleted in the model and does not contribute to the phase angle calculation. The map should show the density corresponding to the fragment, at half the height. Alternatively one can calculate

$$\rho(x\ y\ z) = \frac{1}{V}\sum_{hkl}|F_{obs}|\ \exp[-2\pi i(hx + ky + lz) + i\alpha_{calc}]$$

This map should show the entire model with the deleted fragment at half height. Or with coefficients $2|F_{obs}| - |F_{calc}|$, which also shows the entire model but the deleted fragment at full height.

An OMIT Map with Sim Weighting

$$\Delta\rho(x\ y\ z) = \frac{1}{V}\sum_{hkl}m(|F_{obs}| - |F_{calc}|)\ \exp[-2\pi i(hx + ky + lz) + i\alpha_{calc}]$$

$m = I_1(X)/I_0(X)$ for noncentric reflections and $m = \tanh(X/2)$ for centric reflections, where

$$X = \frac{2|F_{obs}| \times |F_K|}{\sum\limits_1^n f_i^2}$$

I_0 are I_1 are modified Bessel functions of order zero and one, respectively, $|F_{obs}|$ is the observed structure factor amplitude, and $|F_K|$ is the amplitude for the known part of the structure. The f_is are the atomic scattering factors for the n missing atoms. It is assumed that the partial structure is error-free. In practice this will not be true and then X must be taken as

$$X = \frac{2\sigma_A|E_{obs}| \times |E_K|}{1 - \sigma_A^2}$$

$|E|$ is the normalized structure factor amplitude. σ_A is defined in Section 15.6.

A Weighted Electron Density Map Calculated with Phase Angles α_{calc} from the Partial Structure

$$\rho(x\ y\ z) = \frac{1}{V}\sum_{hkl}(2m|F_{obs}| - |F_{calc}|)\exp[-2\pi i(hx + ky + lz) + i\alpha_{calc}]$$

for noncentric reflections and

$$\rho(x\ y\ z) = \frac{1}{V}\sum_{hkl}m|F_{obs}|\exp[-2\pi i(hx + ky + lz) + i\alpha_{calc}]$$

for centric reflections. This map is an improvement over the $(2F_{obs} - F_{calc})$ map because it applies Sim weighting to the observed structure factor amplitudes (see above). Possible missing parts in the structure will show up more clearly in the electron density map than without Sim weighting. Sim assumed the partial structure to be error-free, but in practice this is never true. The effect of these errors is taken care of by defining X differently:

$$X = \frac{2\sigma_A|E_{obs}| \times |E_K|}{1 - \sigma_A^2}$$

and by weighting down $|F_{calc}|$:

$$\rho(x\ y\ z) = \frac{1}{V}\sum_{hkl}(2m|F_{obs}| - D|F_{calc}|)\exp[-2\pi i(hx + ky + lz) + i\alpha_{calc}]$$

with $D = \sigma_A(\Sigma_P/\Sigma_N)^{-1/2}$ (Section 15.6). $|E|$ is the normalized structure factor amplitude.

Appendix 2
A Compilation of Reliability Indices

Common Crystallographic R-Factor for Indicating the Correctness of a Model Structure

$$R = \frac{\sum\limits_{hkl} ||F_{\text{obs}}| - k|F_{\text{calc}}||}{\sum\limits_{hkl} |F_{\text{obs}}|}$$

The Free R-Factor

$$R_T^{\text{free}} = \frac{\sum\limits_{hkl \subset T} ||F_{\text{obs}}| - k|F_{\text{calc}}||}{\sum\limits_{hkl \subset T} |F_{\text{obs}}|}$$

where $hkl \subset T$ means all reflections belonging to test set T of unique reflections. The refinement is carried out with the remaining reflections, the working set W. The advantage of using this R-factor over the regular crystallographic R-factor is that it is unbiased by the refinement process.

R-Factor for Comparing the Intensity of Symmetry-Related Reflections

$$R_{\text{sym}}(I) = \frac{\sum\limits_{hkl}\sum\limits_{i} |I_i(h\ k\ l) - \overline{I(h\ k\ l)}|}{\sum\limits_{hkl}\sum\limits_{i} I_i(h\ k\ l)}$$

for n independent reflections and i observations of a given reflection. $\overline{I(h\ k\ l)}$ is the average intensity of the i observations.

R-Factor for Comparing the Structure Factor Amplitude for Symmetry-Related Reflections

$$R_{\text{sym}}(F) = \frac{\sum_{hkl}\sum_{i}||F_i(h\ k\ l)| - |\overline{F(h\ k\ l)}||}{\sum_{hkl}\sum_{i}|F_i(h\ k\ l)|}$$

for i observations each of n independent reflections. $|\overline{F(h\ k\ l)}|$ is the average value for the structure factor amplitude of the i observations of a given reflection.

R-Factor for the Comparison of N Data Sets after Merging

On $|F_{hkl}|$:

$$R_{\text{merge}} = \frac{\sum_{hkl}\sum_{j=1}^{N}||F_{hkl}| - |F_{hkl}(j)||}{\sum_{hkl}N \times |F_{hkl}|}$$

$|F_{hkl}|$ is the final value of the structure factor amplitude.

On I_{hkl}:

$$R_{\text{merge}} = \frac{\sum_{hkl}\sum_{j=1}^{N}|I_{hkl} - I_{hkl}(j)|}{\sum_{hkl}N \times I_{hkl}}$$

Real Space R-Factor

$$R_{\text{real space}} = \frac{\sum|\rho_{\text{obs}} - \rho_{\text{calc}}|}{\sum|\rho_{\text{obs}} + \rho_{\text{calc}}|}$$

The function is calculated per residue for either all atoms, or the main chain atoms only, or the side chain atoms. The summation is over all grid points for which ρ_{calc} has a nonzero value for a particular residue. The function shows how good the fit is between the model and the electron density map.

R_{Cullis}

$$R_{\text{Cullis}} = \frac{\sum\limits_{hkl} ||F_{\text{PH}} \pm F_{\text{P}}| - F_{\text{H}}(\text{calc})|}{\sum\limits_{hkl} |F_{\text{PH}} \pm F_{\text{P}}|}$$

for centric reflections only. F_{P}, F_{PH}, and F_{H} include their sign (+ or −): $F_{\text{PH}} + F_{\text{P}}$ if the signs of F_{PH} and F_{P} are opposite and $F_{\text{PH}} - F_{\text{P}}$ if they are equal.

R_{Kraut}

$$R_{\text{Kraut}} = \frac{\sum\limits_{hkl} ||F_{\text{PH}}| - |\mathbf{F}_{\text{P}} + \mathbf{F}_{\text{H}}(\text{calc})||}{\sum\limits_{hkl} |F_{\text{PH}}|}$$

This R-factor is used in isomorphous replacement methods to check the heavy atom refinement.

$R_{\text{anomalous}}$

$$R_{\text{anomalous}} = \left[\frac{\sum\limits_{hkl} (|\Delta F_{\text{obs}}^{\pm}| - |\Delta F_{\text{calc}}^{\pm}|)^2}{\sum\limits_{hkl} (\Delta F_{\text{obs}}^{\pm})^2} \right]^{1/2}$$

where $\Delta F^{\pm}$ is the structure factor amplitude difference between Friedel pairs.

Derivative R-Factor

$$R_{\text{deriv}} = \frac{\sum\limits_{hkl} ||F_{\text{deriv}}(h\ k\ l)| - |F_{\text{native}}(h\ k\ l)||}{\sum\limits_{hkl} |F_{\text{native}}|}$$

This R-factor is used for checking the quality of an isomorphous derivative.

Standard Linear Correlation Coefficient between Observed and Calculated Structure Factors

$$C = \frac{\sum_h (|F_h(\text{obs})| - \overline{|F_h(\text{obs})|}) \times (|F_h(\text{calc})| - \overline{|F_h(\text{calc})|})}{\left[\sum_h (|F_h(\text{obs})| - \overline{|F_h(\text{obs})|})^2 \times \sum_h (|F_h(\text{calc})| - \overline{|F_h(\text{calc})|})^2\right]^{1/2}}$$

The same but in a different form:

$$C = \frac{\overline{|F_h(\text{obs})| \times |F_h(\text{calc})|} - \overline{|F_h(\text{obs})|} \times \overline{|F_h(\text{calc})|}}{[\{\overline{|F_h(\text{obs})|^2} - (\overline{|F_h(\text{obs})|})^2\} \times \{\overline{|F_h(\text{calc})|^2} - (\overline{|F_h(\text{calc})|})^2\}^{1/2}]}$$

The Quality of the Heavy Atom Contribution

This is expressed as the *phasing power*, which is the ratio of the root mean square value of the calculated heavy atom scattering factor amplitude to the root mean square lack of closure error:

$$\left[\frac{\sum_n |F_{\text{H}}|^2}{\sum_n |E|^2}\right]^{1/2} \quad \text{with} \quad \sum_n |E|^2 = \sum_n \{|F_{\text{PH}}|(\text{obs}) - |F_{\text{PH}}|(\text{calc})\}^2$$

n is the number of observed scattering amplitudes for the derivative. $|F_{\text{H}}|$ is the calculated scattering amplitude of the heavy atom structure. The phasing power is given as a function of the resolution and indicates to what resolution this heavy atom derivative contributes to the protein phase determination. An alternative expression for the phasing power is $\Sigma_n |F_{\text{H}}|/\Sigma_n |E|$.

Figure of Merit

The figure of merit for a given reflection $(h\,k\,l)$ is defined as

$$m = \frac{|F(h\ k\ l)_{\text{best}}|}{|F(h\ k\ l)|}$$

where

$$F(h\ k\ l)_{\text{best}} = \frac{\sum_\alpha P(\alpha)\mathbf{F}_{hkl}(\alpha)}{\sum_\alpha P(\alpha)}$$

It can be shown that the figure of merit is the weighted mean of the cosine of the deviation of the phase angle from α_{best}.

Appendix 3
The Variation in the Intensity of X-ray Radiation

When the anode of an X-ray tube is bombarded by electrons their deceleration causes the emission of photons. One electron impact gives rise to a photon with a certain amount of energy. There is no relation between the photons, either in time or in energy. Therefore, the number of emitted photons with the same energy, if measured during a time t, is not a fixed number (Figure App. 3.1). If that number is measured n times (where n is very large) with an average value of N_0, the probability of measuring N photons is

$$P(N) = \frac{1}{N!} N_0^N \exp[-N_0] \text{ (Poisson distribution)} \quad \text{(App. 3.1)}$$

For sufficiently large N_0 ($N_0 \geq 9$) this distribution can be replaced by the Gauss distribution:

$$P(N) = \frac{1}{\sqrt{2\pi N_0}} \exp\left[-\frac{(N - N_0)^2}{2N_0}\right] \quad \text{(App. 3.2)}$$

The general form of the Gauss distribution is

$$f(x) = \frac{1}{\sigma\sqrt{2\pi}} \exp\left[-\frac{(x - \bar{x})^2}{2\sigma^2}\right] \quad \text{(App. 3.3)}$$

The spread of the curve is usually expressed in the variance of x, which is defined as

$$\sigma^2 = \int\limits_{x=-\infty}^{+\infty} (x - \bar{x})^2 f(x)\, dx \quad \text{(App. 3.4)}$$

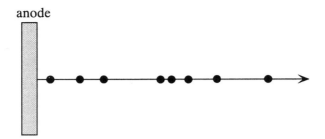

Figure App. 3.1. Photons with the same energy leaving the anode as a function of time.

By comparing Eqs. (App. 3.2) and (App. 3.3) it is found that the standard deviation σ for the X-ray photon emission is $\sqrt{N_0}$.

In practice the number of photons is usually measured only once and the value of N found in that single measurement is taken as the best value with a standard deviation $\sigma = \sqrt{N}$. This is also true for synchrotron radiation, because we do not have perfect control over the physical state of the charged particles.

References

Agarwal, R.C. Acta Crystallogr. (1978) **A34**, 791–809.

Agarwal, R.C. Methods Enzymol. (1985) **115B**, 112–117.

Arndt, U.W. and Wonacott, A.J., eds. *The Rotation Method in Crystallography*. North-Holland, Amsterdam, 1977.

Bentley, G.A. and Houdusse, A. Acta Crystallogr. (1992) **A48**, 312–322.

Blow, D.M. and Crick, F.H.C. Acta Crystallogr. (1959) **12**, 794–802.

Bowie, J.U., Lüthy, R., and Eisenberg D. Science (1991) **253**, 164–170.

Bricogne, G. Acta Crystallogr. (1974) **A30**, 395–405.

Bricogne, G. Acta Crystallogr. (1976) **A32**, 832–847.

Bricogne, G. Acta Crystallogr. (1993) **D49**, 37–60.

Brünger, A.T. Acta Crystallogr. (1990) **A46**, 46–57.

Brünger, A.T. Acta Crystallogr. (1991) **A47**, 195–204.

Brünger, A.T. Nature (London) (1992) **355**, 472–475.

Brünger, A.T. Acta Crystallogr. (1993) **D49**, 24–36.

Brünger, A.T. Kuriyan, J., and Karplus, M. Science (1987) **235**, 458–460.

Carter, C.W. Methods: Companion to Methods Enzymol. (1990) **1**, 12–24.

Chayen, N.E., Shaw Stewart, P.D., Maeder, D.L., and Blow, D.M. J. Appl. Crystallogr. (1990) **23**, 297–302.

Chayen, N.E., Shaw Stewart, P.D., and Blow, D.M. J. Crystal Growth (1992) **122**, 176–180.

Crick, F.H.C. and Magdoff, B.S. Acta Crystallogr. (1956) **9**, 901–908.

Crowther, R.A. Acta Crystallogr. (1969) **B25**, 2571–2580.

Crowther, R.A. in: *The Molecular Replacement Method*, pp. 173–178; Rossmann, M.G., ed. Gordon & Breach, New York, 1972.

Crowther, R.A. and Blow, D.M. Acta Crystallogr. (1967) **23**, 544–548.

Dijkstra, B.W. et al. J. Mol. Biol. (1981) **147**, 97–123.

Dodson, E. and Vijayan, M. Acta Crystallogr. (1971) **B27**, 2402–2411.

Driessen, H.P.C., Bax, B., Slingsby, C., Lindley, P.F., Mahadevan, D., Moss, D.S., and Tickle, I.J. Acta Crystallogr. (1991) **B47**, 987–997.

Ducruix, A. and Giegé, R. *Crystallization of Nucleic Acids and Proteins, a Practical Approach*. IRL Press, Oxford, 1992.

Fujinaga, M. and Read, R.J. J. Appl. Crystallogr. (1987) **20**, 517–521.

Gros, P., van Gunsteren, W.F., and Hol, W.G.J. Science (1990) **249**, 1149–1153.

Guss, J.M., Merritt, E.A., Phizackerley, R.P., Hedman, B., Murata, M., Hodgson, K.O., and Freeman, H.C. Science (1988) **241**, 806–811.

Hahn, T. ed., *International Tables for Crystallography*, Vol. A. D. Reidel, Dordrecht, 1993.

Harker, D. Acta Crystallogr. (1956) **9**, 1–9.

Hauptman, H. Acta Crystallogr. (1982) **A38**, 289–294.

Helliwell, J.R. *Macromolecular Crystallography with Synchrotron Radiation*. Cambridge University Press, Cambridge, 1992.

Hendrickson, W.A. and Lattman, E.E. Acta Crystallogr. (1970) **B26**, 136–143.

Hendrickson, W.A. and Ward, K.B. Acta Crystallogr. (1976) **A32**, 778–780.

Hendrickson, W.A. Methods Enzymol. (1985) **115B**, 252–270.

Hendrickson, W.A., Love, W.E., and Murray, G.C. J. Mol. Biol. (1968) **33**, 829–842.

Hendrickson, W.A., Smith, J.L., Phizackerley, R.P., and Merritt, E.A. Proteins (1988) **4**, 77–88.

Hendrickson, W.A., Horton, J.R., and LeMaster, D.M. EMBO J. (1990) **5**, 1665–1672.

Hiremath, C.N., Munshi, S.K., and Murthy, M.R.N. Acta Crystallogr. (1990) **B46**, 562–567.

Huber, R. in: *Molecular Replacement. Proceedings of the Daresbury Study Weekend*, 15–16 February, pp. 58–61; Machin, P.A., ed. SERC Daresbury Laboratory, Warrington, 1985.

Jack, A. and Levitt, M. Acta Crystallogr. (1978) **A34**, 931–935.

James, R.W. *The Optical Principles of the Diffraction of X-Rays*, Chapter 4. London, Bell, 1965.

Johnson, J.E. Acta Crystallogr. (1978) **B34**, 576–577.

Jones, T.A., Zou, J.-Y., and Cowan, S.W. Acta Crystallogr. (1991) **A47**, 110–119.

Karle, J. Int. J. Quant. Chem. Symp. (1980) **7**, 357–367.

Karle, J. Acta Crystallogr. (1989) **A45**, 765–781.

Kartha, G. and Parthasarathy, R. Acta Crystallogr. (1965) **18**, 749–753.

Krishna Murthy, H.M., Hendrickson, W.A., Orme-Johnson, W.H., Merritt, E.A., and Phizackerley, R.P. J. Biol. Chem. (1988) **263**, 18430–18436.

Laskowski, R.A., MacArthur, M.W., Moss, D.S., and Thornton, J.M. J. Appl. Crystallogr. (1993) **26**, 283–291.

Leahy, D.J., Hendrickson, W.A., Aukhil, I., and Erickson, H.P. Science (1992) **258**, 987–991.

Leslie, A.G.W. Acta Crystallogr. (1987) **A43**, 134–136.

Lüthy, R., Bowie, J.U., and Eisenberg, D. Nature (London) (1992) **356**, 83–85.

Luzzati, V. Acta Crystallogr. (1952) **5**, 802–810.

Machin, P.A. ed., *Molecular Replacement. Proceedings of the Daresbury Study Weekend*, 15–16 February. SERC Daresbury Laboratory, Warrington, 1985.

Main, P. Acta Crystallogr. (1967) **23**, 50–54.

Matthews, B.W. Acta Crystallogr. (1966) **20**, 230–239.

Matthews, B.W. J. Mol. Biol. (1968) **33**, 491–497.

Matthews, B.W. and Czerwinski, E.W. Acta Crystallogr. (1975) **A31**, 480–487.

McKenna, R., Di Xia, Willingmann, P., Ilag, L.L., Krishnaswamy, S., Rossmann, M.G., Olson, N.H., Baker, T.S., and Incardona, N.L. Nature (London) (1992) **355**, 137–143.

McPherson, A., Jr. Methods Biochem. Anal. (1976) **23**, 249–345.

McPherson, A., Jr. J. Crystal Growth (1992) **122**, 161–167.

Michel, H. *Crystallization of Membrane Proteins*. CRC Press, London, 1990.

Morris, A.L., MacArthur, M.W., Hutchinson, E.G., and Thornton, J.M. Proteins (1992) **12**, 345–364.

Moss, D.S. Acta Crystallogr. (1985) **A41**, 470–475.

Nagai, K., Oubridge, C., Jessen, T.-H., Li, J., and Evans, P.R. Nature (London) (1990) **348**, 515–520.

Nagai, K., Evans, P.R., Li, J., and Oubridge, Ch. *Proceedings of the CCP4 Study Weekend*, January, pp. 141–149. Daresbury, 1991.

Narasinga Rao, S., Jyh-Hwang Jih, and Hartsuck, J.A. Acta Crystallogr. (1980) **A36**, 878–884.

Rabinovich, D. and Shakked, Z. Acta Crystallogr. (1984) **A40**, 195–200.

Rayment, I. Acta Crystallogr. (1983) **A39**, 102–116.

Read, R.J. Acta Crystallogr. (1986) **A42**, 140–149.

Read, R.J. Crystallographic Computing School, Bischenberg, 1990a.

Read, R.J. Acta Crystallogr. (1990b) **A46**, 900–912.

Read, R.J. and Schierbeek, A.J. J. Appl. Crystallogr. (1988) **21**, 490–495.

Rosenbaum, G., Holmes, K.G., and Witz, J. Nature (London) (1971) **230**, 434–437.

Rossmann, M.G. Acta Crystallogr. (1960) **13**, 221–226.

Rossmann, M.G. Acta Crystallogr. (1990) **A46**, 73–82.

Rossmann, M.G. and Blow, D.M. Acta Crystallogr. (1961) **14**, 641–647.

Rossmann, M.G. and Blow, D.M. Acta Crystallogr. (1962) **15**, 24–31.

Rossmann, M.G. and Blow, D.M. Acta Crystallogr. (1963) **16**, 39–45.

Rossmann, M.G., McKenna, R., Liang Tong, Di Xia, Jin-Bi Dai, Hao Wu, Hok-Kin Choi, and Lynch, R.E. J. Appl. Crystallogr. (1992) **25**, 166–180.

Sim, G.A. Acta Crystallogr. (1959) **12**, 813–815.

Sim, G.A. Acta Crystallogr. (1960) **13**, 511–512.

Skilling, J. in: *Maximun Entropy and Bayesian Methods*, pp. 45–52. Skilling, J., ed. Kluwer Academic Publishers, Dordrecht, 1988.

Srinivasan, R. Acta Crystallogr. (1966) **20**, 143–144.

Srinivasan, R. and Chandrasekaran, R. Indian J. Pure Appl. Phys. (1966) **4**, 178–186.

Srinivasan, R. and Ramachandran, G.N. Acta Crystallogr. (1965) **19**, 1008–1014.

Stewart, J.M. and Karle, J. Acta Crystallogr. (1976) **A32**, 1005–1007.

Strijtveen, B. and Kellogg, R.M. Tetrahedron (1987) **43**(21), 5045.

Sussman, J.L. Methods Enzymol. (1985) **115B**, 271–303.

Templeton, D.H. and Templeton, L.K. Acta Crystallogr. (1991) **A47**, 414–420.

Ten Eyck, L.F. Acta Crystallogr. (1973) **A29**, 183–191.

Tollin, P. and Rossmann, M.G. Acta Crystallogr. (1966) **21**, 872–876.

Tollin, P., Main, P., and Rossmann, M.G. Acta Crystallogr. (1966) **20**, 404–407.

Tong, L. and Rossmann, M.G. Acta Crystallogr. (1990) **A46**, 783–792.

Tronrud, D.E., Ten Eyck, L.F., and Matthews, B.W. Acta Crystallogr. (1987) **A43**, 489–501.

Tucker, A.D., Baty, D., Parker, M.W., Pattus, F., Lazdunski, C., and Tsernoglou, D. Protein Eng. (1989) **2**, 399–405.

Wang, B.-C. Methods Enzymol. (1985) **115**, 90–112.

Wilmanns, M. and Eisenberg, D. Proc. Natl. Acad. Sci. U.S.A. (1993) **90**, 1379–1383.

Wilmanns, M., Priestle, J.P., Niermann, T., and Jansonius, J.N. J. Mol. Biol. (1992) **223**, 477–507.

Wilson, A.J.C. Acta Crystallogr. (1950) **3**, 397–398.

Index